Correspondence

Correspondence

INGEBORG BACHMANN AND PAUL CELAN

*With the correspondences between Paul Celan and Max Frisch
and between Ingeborg Bachmann and Gisèle Celan-Lestrange*

EDITED WITH COMMENTARIES BY BERTRAND BADIOU, HANS HÖLLER,
ANDREA STOLL AND BARBARA WIEDEMANN

TRANSLATED BY WIELAND HOBAN

LONDON NEW YORK CALCUTTA

This publication was supported by a grant from the Goethe-Institut India

Seagull Books 2010

Lass uns die Worte finden. Ingeborg Bachmann – Paul Celan. Briefwechsel.
Including the letters between Paul Celan and Max Frisch and the letters between Ingeborg
Bachmann and Gisèle Celan-Lestrange. Edited and commentaries in the German by
Bertrand Badiou, Hans Höller, Andrea Stoll, Barbara Wiedemann

© Suhrkamp Verlag, Frankfurt am Main, 2008

First published in English by Seagull Books, 2010
English language translation © Wieland Hoban 2010

ISBN-13   978 1 9064 9 744 6

British Library Cataloguing-in-Publication Data
A catalogue record for this book is available
from the British Library

Typeset by Seagull Books, Calcutta, India
Printed at Leelabati Printers, Calcutta, India

CONTENTS

Sources

The originals are located in the manuscripts section of the Austrian National Library in Vienna (Ingeborg Bachmann estate: letters from Paul Celan and Gisèle Celan-Lestrange, drafts and unsent letters by Bachmann), the German Literature Archive in Marbach (Celan estate: letters from Bachmann and Frisch, drafts, copies and unsent letters by Celan, dedicated book copies in the estate library), the Max Frisch Archive at the ETH Zurich (letters from Celan, drafts by Frisch), the estate of Gisèle Celan-Lestrange (Eric Celan, Paris: letters and dedicated book copies from Bachmann) and the Bachmann private estate (estate library, etchings by Gisèle Celan-Lestrange).

Editors

The text of the letters and the notes are based on a complete critical appraisal of the material. Archival work was carried out by Hans Höller for the Bachmann estate, Barbara Wiedemann and Bertrand Badiou for the Celan estate and Bertrand Badiou for the estate of Gisèle Celan-Lestrange. Missing information about the documents in the Frisch estate was provided by Walter Obschlager. Bachmann's letters were transcribed and annotated primarily by Andrea Stoll and Hans Höller, and Celan's letters by Barbara Wiedemann and Bertrand Badiou.

Letter text

The following documents sent between Ingeborg Bachmann and Paul Celan were taken up into the correspondence: all accessible letters, postcards and telegrams, unsent letters and drafts of letters, as well as dedications in books, offprints and manuscripts of the correspondents and in other books sent as gifts. Poems are only included where they were sent not as supplements, but on their own, i.e. as 'letters' in their own right. Drafts for letters later sent were taken up where they could be considered independent letters on account of significant deviations and clear differences of date; important variations in other drafts are mentioned in the notes. Printed supplements were not reproduced, but enclosed letters (including those of other authors) or copies thereof made by the correspondents were included. The same approach was used for the additional correspondences between Max Frisch and Paul Celan, and between Gisèle Celan-Lestrange and Ingeborg Bachmann.

The text appears in the version intended by the authors, i.e. without corrections or crossings-out. Crossed-out passages that are considered important for an understanding of the letters, especially when thematicized by the authors themselves, are supplied in the notes.

Incorrect letter dates have not been corrected; deviations between them and the dates given in the letter headings are discussed in the respective commentaries, however. The dating of undated documents is also discussed there.

Texts by third parties and notes made on the documents by the recipient appear in italics.

Notes

The notes on each letter are preceded by a description of the document: archival signatures for the document with supplements, manner of sending, usually the envelope with the address, as well as the place and date of the postmark. Parts of letters, envelopes or supplements classified by the editors are marked as such.

The notes have been made as brief as possible; they concentrate on factual information.

The biographical information stems in part from the works listed in the bibliography. References to letters from published correspondences include their

dates, which are vital for an understanding of their content and make them identifiable. This also applies to Celan's correspondence with Nani and Klaus Demus,
published in 2009 (Joachim Seng ed.). Literal quotations from published correspondences are attributed precisely. All information from unpublished material is
indicated according to source.

Information about persons mentioned several times is collected in a main
note; here the emphasis is on the correspondents' interest in the person and/or
relationship with them. References to these notes have not been added; in the
index of names, the letters with the corresponding notes are marked with bold
type. Persons often referred to by their first names are also included in the index.

All bibliographical information on poems written by the correspondents can
be found in the index; page numbers for commentaries or notes on the respective
poems in the cited editions have not been added, but should be considered implicit in some cases. Quotations from theoretical or fictional prose are attributed
precisely.

Contemporaneous traces of the letters and other contact (telephone, conversations with third parties) between Celan and Bachmann or between Celan and
Frisch in Celan's diaries and pocket calendars (which sometimes have the character of a diary or list correspondences) and the diaries kept for Celan by Gisèle
Celan-Lestrange have been documented as comprehensively as possible using the
originals; this work was based on a complete transcription by Bertrand Badiou.

No diaries written by Bachmann were available. Transcriptions of passages
from Bachmann's letters to her family and dedications in books from the estate
library were made available by Isolde Moser.

The editors have generally refrained from pointing out connections between
directly consecutive letters, or from making any negative comments, for example
in the case of presents that were not preserved or could not identified, or books
from the estate libraries that do not contain any reading traces and/or dedications.

The editors have consciously refrained from documenting parallels between
the letter texts and works by the correspondents not contained or mentioned in

the correspondence, unless they are directly quoted or alluded to in letters; hence both anachronisms and an unacceptable blurring of biography and fiction could be avoided. In addition, the necessary brevity of the notes would not have permitted anything more comprehensive; this applies especially in the case of Bachmann's novel *Malina*.

Timeline and indexes of cited works

The notes are augmented by the following: a timeline focusing on the time covered by the correspondence and the personal encounters during that time; separate indexes of cited works (with bibliographical information) for Bachmann and Celan, supplemented by a list of poems by Celan that have been preserved in a bundle of papers in the Bachmann estate but not mentioned in the letters or notes, as well as books relating to Bachmann in the Celan estate library; an index of names (with dates of birth and death where available); and finally a bibliography of the sources used for biographical matters.

Acknowledgements

We would like to thank the manuscripts section of the Austrian National Library for making the sources available to us and for all friendly support, the manuscripts section and library of the German Literature Archive in Marbach, the Max Frisch Archive at the ETH Zurich, Isolde and Christian Moser, as well as Heinz Bachmann and Eric Celan.

The following people were always willing to help: Eva Irblich at the Austrian National Library in Vienna, Ulrich von Bülow, Heidrun Fink, Hildegard Dieke, Thomas Kemma and Nikolai Reidel at the German Literature Archive in Marbach, Walter Obschlager at the Max Frisch Archive in Zurich, Adelheit Iguchi and her team at the Tübingen University library, as well as Anna-Elisabeth Bruckhaus, Annette Gauch and Mechthild Kellermann.

We are grateful for all manner of help to Magdalena Abele, Ute Bruckinger, Isac Chiva, Uwe Eckardt (Wuppertal City Archive), Guy Flandre, Alessandro De

Francesco, Sonia Garelli, François Giannini (Paul Celan Society, Paris), Peter Goessens (Bochum University), Lilith Jdanko-Frenkel, Barbara Klein (Kosmos-Theater Vienna), Annemarie Klinger, Marianne Korn (Schauspielhaus Zurich), Andrea Krauss (Zurich University), Hanne Lenz, Herta-Luise Ott (Grenoble University), Christiana Naumann (Deutsche Verlagsanstalt), Ute Oelmann (George Archive, Stuttgart), Halina Pichit (Zurich City Archive), Robert Pichl (Vienna University), Evelyne Polt Heinzl (Literaturhaus Vienna), Britta Rupp-Eisenreich, Frank Schmitter (Monacensia Literature Archive, Munich), Klaus Schiller (Salzburg Univesity), Wolfgang Schopf (Frankfurt University Archive), Mihal Seidmann, Joachim Seng (Freies Deutsches Hochstift) Hans-Ulrich Wagner (Hans Bredow Institute, Hamburg), Alexis Wolf, Benedikt Wolf and Thomas Wolf, as well as the patient and skilful coachman Wolfgang Kaussen (Suhrkamp Verlag), without whom this four-horse carriage would never have reached its goal.

LIST OF SCRIBAL ABBREVIATIONS
(unless otherwise indicated, page numbers
are included in the notes)

ACO	Austrian Censorship Office [*Österreichische Zensurstelle*] (censorship authority in occupied Austria until 1953).
ALA	Austrian Literature Archive in the Austrian National Library.
ALCO	Allied Censorship Office [*Alliierte Zensurstelle*] (censorship authority in occupied Austria during 1952/53).
BC	Bonn office for the Celan Edition: catalogue of Paul Celan's library (Paris and Moisville, compiled in 1972–74 (Paris) and 1987 (Moisville) by Dietlind Meinecke, Stefan Reichert and others, transcribed with corrections, additions and critical notes on the current locations of the books by Bertrand Badiou (unpublished + VOL. NO. + current number).
CAE	Paul Celan, *Die Gedichte. Kommentierte Gesamtausgabe in einem Band*, Barbara Wiedemann ed. and annot. (Frankfurt: Suhrkamp, 2003).
CaI	Ingeborg Bachmann, *Wir müssen wahre Sätze finden*, conversations and interviews, Christine Koschel and Inge von Weidenbaum eds (Munich and Zurich: Piper, 1983).
DPC	Diaries of Paul Celan (GLA).
ENS	École normale supérieure (45, Rue d'Ulm, Paris).
FAZ	*Frankfurter Allgemeine Zeitung*.

GA	Barbara Wiedemann, *Die Goll-Affäre. Dokumente zu einer 'Infamie'* (Frankfurt: Suhrkamp, 2000).
GBF	Gottfried and Brigitte Bermann Fischer, *Briefwechsel mit Autoren*, Reiner Stach ed., in collaboration with Karin Schlapp; Bernhard Zeller introd. (Frankfurt: Fischer, 1990).
GCL	Gisèle Celan-Lestrange.
GCLE	Gisèle Celan-Lestrange estate.
GLA	German Literature Archive, Marbach
GN	Paul Celan, *Die Gedichte aus dem Nachlass*, Bertrand Badiou, Jean-Claude Rambach and Barbara Wiedemann eds (Frankfurt: Suhrkamp, 1997).
GW	Paul Celan, *Gesammelte Werke in fünf Bänden*, Beda Allemann and Stefan Reichert eds, in collaboration with Rolf Bücher (Frankfurt: Suhrkamp, 1983) (+ VOL. NO.).
HKA	Paul Celan, *Historisch-kritische Ausgabe*, Bonn office for the Celan Edition ed. (Frankfurt: Suhrkamp, 1990ff.) (+ VOL. NO.).
HWL	Hans Weigel letters estate (Vienna Library of Vienna Town Hall; IB's letters 1948–53: ZPH 847).
IB	Ingeborg Bachmann.
IBE	Ingeborg Bachmann estate (Austrian National Library, Vienna).
IBPE	Ingeborg Bachmann private estate, Carinthia.
IBW	Ingeborg Bachmann, *Werke*, Christine Koschel, Inge von Weidenbaum and Clemens Münster eds (Munich and Zurich: Piper, 1978) (+ VOL. NO.).
LIB	Library of Ingeborg Bachmann
LPC	Estate library of Paul Celan (German Literature Archive, Marbach).
MAN/ANL	Manuscripts section of the Austrian National Library.
MF	Max Frisch.

MFA	Max Frisch Archive, Zurich.
MFL	Max Frisch, *Jetzt ist Sehenszeit. Briefe, Notate, Dokumente 1943–1963*, Julian Schütt ed. and afterword (Frankfurt: Suhrkamp, 1998).
MSS	Paul Celan, '*Mikrolithen sinds, Steinchen'. Die Prosa aus dem Nachlass*, Barbara Wiedemann and Bertrand Badiou eds (Frankfurt: Suhrkamp, 2005).
NDR	Norddeutscher Rundfunk.
NWDR	Nordwestdeutscher Rundfunk.
NZZ	*Neue Zürcher Zeitung*.
PC	Paul Celan.
PC/B.O.	Massimo Pizzingrilli, ' "Votre aide qui est / m'est si précieuse". Paul Celan's Mitarbeit an der Zeitschrift *Botteghe Oscure* und sein Briefwechsel mit Margherite Caetani', in *Celan-Jahrbuch 9* (*2003– 2005*), pp. 7–26.
PCE	Paul Celan estate (GLA).
PCE-Paris	Paul Celan estate (Paris, Eric Celan).
PC/GCL	Paul Celan–Gisèle Celan-Lestrange, *Briefwechsel*, with a selection of letters from Paul Celan to his son Eric, Eugen Helmlé and Barbara Wiedemann trans., Bertrand Badiou ed., in collaboration with Eric Celan (Frankfurt: Suhrkamp, 2001). Unless otherwise indicated, this abbreviation is followed by the letter numbers for VOL. 1, which apply to both the French edition (*Correspondance* [*1951–1979*] [*Paris: Editions du Seuil, 2001*]) and the German edition; references to VOL. 2 are, in the case of deviating note numbers in the two editions, marked 'Fr.' or 'Ger.'.
PCPC	Pocket calendars belonging to PC (GLA).
PCPC/GCL	Pocket calendars belonging to PC, written by GCL (GLA).
PC/HHL	Paul Celan–Hanne and Hermann Lenz, *Briefwechsel*, Barbara

	Wiedemann ed., in co-operation with Hanne Lenz (Frankfurt: Suhrkamp, 2001).
PC/Sachs	Paul Celan–Nelly Sachs, *Briefwechsel*, Barbara Wiedemann ed. (Frankfurt: Suhrkamp, 1993).
SDR	Süddeutscher Rundfunk, Stuttgart.
SZ	*Süddeutsche Zeitung.*
TA	Ingeborg Bachmann, *'Todesarten'-Projekt. Kritische Ausgabe*, directed by Robert Pichl, Monika Albrecht and Dirk Göttsche (Munich and Zurich: Piper, 1995) (+ VOL. NO.).
TCA/M	Paul Celan, *Der Meridian. Endfassung–Entwürfe–Materialien*, Bernhard Böschenstein and Heino Schmull eds (= *Tübinger Ausgabe* [Frankfurt: Suhrkamp, 1999]).

Abbreviations and transcription markings

ass.	assigned
corr.	corrected
cpy	copy (ts.)
hw.	handwritten
ms.	manuscript
ts.	typescript
tw.	typewritten
w/	with
(!)	Indicates corrections in quotations.
[ ]	Editors' additions.
[xxx]	Illegible word, part of word or letters.

INGEBORG BACHMANN—PAUL CELAN
CORRESPONDENCE

1

Paul Celan to Ingeborg Bachmann, poem and dedication in a book of Matisse paintings, Vienna, 24 (?) June 1948

'In Ägypten'
Für Ingeborg

Du sollst zum Aug der Fremden sagen: Sei das Wasser!
Du sollst, die du im Wasser weißt, im Aug der Fremden suchen.
Du sollst sie rufen aus dem Wasser: Ruth! Noemi! Mirjam!
Du sollst sie schmücken mit dem Wolkenhaar der Fremden.
Du sollst zu Ruth, zu Mirjam und Noemi sagen:
Seht, ich schlaf bei ihr!
Du sollst die Fremde neben dir am schönsten schmücken,
Du sollst sie schmücken mit dem Schmerz um Ruth, um Mirjam und Noemi.

Du sollst zur Fremden sagen:
Sieh, ich schlief bei diesen!

'In Egypt'
For Ingeborg

Thou shalt say to the strange woman's eye: be the water!
Thou shalt seek in the stranger's eye those whom thou knowest to be in the water.
Thou shalt call them from the water: Ruth! Noemi! Miriam!
Thou shalt adorn them when thou liest with the stranger.
Thou shalt adorn them with the cloud-hair of the stranger.
Thou shalt say to Ruth, to Miriam and Noemi:
Behold, I sleep next to her!

Thou shalt adorn the stranger next to thee most beautifully of all.
Thou shalt adorn her with the pain over Ruth, over Miriam and Noemi.

Thou shalt say to the stranger:
Behold, I slept next to these!

Vienna, 23 May 1948.

To the meticulous one,
     22 years after her birthday,
          From the unmeticulous one

NOTES

MAN/ANL ser. n. 25.202 c, p. 15: hw. poem (= *HKA 2–3.2 208 H⁵**; *see Figure 11*); *LIB*: hw. dedication in Peintures 1939–46, Introduction d'André Lejard (*Paris, 1946*).

'*In Ägypten*': Further documents concerning this in IBE: ts. (written above it: 'Souvenir of France') with dedication: 'For Ingeborg Bachmann, Vienna 1948' (*MAN/ANL ser. n. 25.202 c, p. 16, = HKA H⁴*); cpy w/'Paul Celan' written in top right corner (*ser. n. 25.202 a, p. 6, = HKA H¹ᵇ*).

23 May 1948: This copy was made only a few days after IB's first encounter with PC. She wrote the following messages to her parents (separately) in Vienna: 'yesterday restless visits to Dr Löcker, Ilse Aichinger, Edgar Jené (surreal painter) where it was very pleasant and I observed the well-known poet Paul Celan a little—many, many people' and 'today something else happened. The surrealist poet Paul Celan, whom I had just met two nights earlier with Weigel, and who is very fascinating, has, splendidly enough, fallen in love with me, which adds a little spice to my dreary work. Unfortunately he has to go to Paris in a month. My room is a poppy field at the moment, as he inundates me with this flower' (17 and 20 May 1948, IBPE). On her 22nd birthday she wrote: 'Two magnificent volumes of modern Fr. painting from Paul Celan with the last works of Matisse and Cézanne, a volume of Chesterton (a famous English writer), flowers, cigarettes, a poem [*presumably* "In Ägypten" (In Egypt)], which is meant to belong to me, a picture [*see Figure 2*], which I can show you in the holidays. (He is leaving for Paris tomorrow.) So I went out for a very festive evening with him yesterday, on the eve of my birthday, for dinner and a little wine' (25 June 1948, IBPE). See NO. 53.

From the unmeticulous one: The phrase used for 'meticulous', *peinlich genau*, literally means 'painfully (or embarrassingly) precise'; conversely, 'unmeticulous' is *peinlich ungenau*, or 'painfully (or embarrassingly) *im*precise'. This final word is taken up again in NO. 6. [Trans.]

2
Ingeborg Bachmann to Paul Celan, Vienna, Christmas 1948, not sent

Christmas 1948.

Dear, dear Paul!

Yesterday and today I thought a great deal about you—or about us, if you will. I am not writing to you because I want you to write again, but because it gives me pleasure and because I want to. I had also planned to meet you somewhere in Paris very soon, but then my stupid vain sense of duty kept me here and I did not leave. What does that mean anyway—'somewhere in Paris'? I don't know anything, but I do think it would have been lovely somehow!

Three months ago, someone suddenly gave me your book of poems as a gift. I didn't know it had come out. That was so . . . the ground was so light and buoyant beneath me, and my hand was trembling a little, just a very little bit. Then there was nothing for a long time again. A few weeks ago, people were saying in Vienna that the Jenés had gone to Paris. So I went along with them again.

I still do not know what last spring meant.—You know me, I always want to know everything very precisely.—It was lovely—and so were the poems, and the poem we made together.

Today you are dear to me and so present. That is what I want to tell you at all costs—I often neglected to do so during that time.

I can come for a few days as soon as I have time. And would you want to see me?—One hour, or two.

Much, much love!

Yours

Ingeborg

NOTES

MAN/ANL folder 10, p. 3: hw. letter.

write again: No traces were found of any correspondence during the first six months after PC's departure from Vienna.

book of poems: From Paris, PC halted the delivery of *Der Sand aus den Urnen* ([The Sand from the Urns]; published in late September), primarily because of its many printing errors. Only a small part of the poems date from PC's Vienna days. IB's copy (NO. 18 of 500, LIB) contains, in addition to recitation aids in unknown handwriting, pencil notes made by IB: p. 52, to the left of the poem title 'Deukalion und Pyrrha' [Deucalion and Pyrrha], a large hook; and on p. 53, the words 'der Mensch mit der Nelke'[the man with the carnation] in the final line have been replaced by the version in *Mohn und Gedächtnis* ([Poppies and Memory] new title: 'Spät und Tief' [Late and Deep]), 'ein Mensch aus dem Grabe' [a man from the grave]. Concerning the supplement, see NO. 42n.

Jenés: PC encountered the painter Edgar Jené and his wife Erica Lillegg in the context of Viennese post-war surrealism. PC's essay 'Edgar Jené. Der Traum vom Traume' [The Dream of a Dream] (LIB: copy 496 of 700) was published in August 1948 in a volume with reproductions of paintings by Jené; Jené helped finance *Der Sand aus den Urnen* and contributed two lithographs. This, as well as the careless supervision of the printing by Lillegg after PC's move, led to bad blood between them.

the poem we made together: Neither the IBE nor the PCE contain any reliable material indicating a joint poem.

3

Paul Celan to Ingeborg Bachmann, Paris, 26 January 1949

31, rue des Ecoles
Paris, 26.1.1949.

Ingeborg,

try for a moment to forget that I was silent for so long and so insistently—I had a great deal of sorrow, more than my brother could take from me, my good brother, whose house I am sure you have not forgotten. Write to me as if you were writing to <u>him</u>, to him who always thinks of you and who locked in your medallion the leaf that you have now lost.

Do not keep me, do not keep <u>him</u> waiting!

I embrace you

Paul

NOTES

MAN/ANL folder 2, pp. 1–2: hw. Airmail letter to: 'Mademoiselle Ingeb[or]g [Bachmann]/Beatrixgasse 26/<u>Vienne III</u>/Autriche'. From: 'Paul Celan, 31, rue des Ecoles/Paris 5ème/France', stamp torn off, ACO.

rue des Ecoles: Since the summer of 1948, PC had been staying in a room, rented monthly, at Hôtel d'Orléans (Hôtel Sully Saint-Germain) in the Latin Quarter.

medallion: Not found.

4

Ingeborg Bachmann to Paul Celan, Vienna, 12 April 1949

Vienna, 12 April 1949

My dear, you,

I am so glad that this letter came—and now I have kept you waiting for so long too, quite unintentionally and without a single unkind thought. You know well enough that this happens sometimes. One does not know why. Two or three times I wrote you a letter, and then left it unsent after all. But what does that really mean, when we are thinking of each other and will, perhaps, do so for a very long time yet?

I am not speaking only to your brother; today I am speaking almost entirely to you, for through your brother I am fond of you, and you must not think that I have passed over you.—Spring will be here again soon, the spring that was so peculiar and so unforgettable last year. I will certainly never walk through the city park again without knowing that it can be the whole world, or without becoming the little fish from back then.

I could sense the whole time that you were full of sorrow—let me know if receiving more letters might help!

In the autumn, some friends gave me your poems. That was a sad moment, because they came from friends and without any word from you. But every single line made up for it.

You may be glad to know that people sometimes ask after you; a while ago, I even had to give your address to some total strangers from Graz to satisfy them. And little Nani and Klaus Demus still have a look of rapture in their eyes whenever they speak about you.

Now I understand very well that it was right for you to go to Paris. What would you say if I suddenly turned up there too in the autumn? I am to receive a scholarship to America or Paris after my doctorate. I still cannot believe it. It would be too lovely.

There is not much to report about me. I have a great deal of work, my studies are approaching their end, and on the side I am writing for newspapers, the radio, etc., more than in the past. I am trying not to think of myself, to close my eyes and cross over to what is really meant. We are surely all under the greatest suspense, cannot break free and take many indirect paths. But it sometimes makes me so ill that I fear it might one day be impossible to go on.

Let me end by telling you—the leaf that you placed in my medallion is not lost, even if it has long ceased to be inside it; I think of you, and I am still listening to you.

Ingeborg.

NOTES

GLA D90.1. 2824/1: tw. letter w/hw. corrections, ACO, envelope missing. MAN/ANL, folder 10, p. 4: tw. draft (not published).

left it unsent: See NO. 2n.

your poems: *Der Sand aus den Urnen*. The friends could not be identified.

strangers from Graz: These may have included the poet and translator Max Hölzer; in April 1950, Jené and he published the almanac *Surrealistische Publikationen* [Surrealist Publications], which included poems and translations by PC.

Nani and Klaus Demus: PC met Nani Maier, IB's friend from the last year of school, and her later husband, at the end of his stay in Vienna. The poet and art historian Klaus Demus studied in Paris during 1949/50, while Maier, a Germanist, did so during 1950/51 [*see Figures 5 and 6*]. They were among PC's closest friends (see Paul Celan/Klaus and Nani Demus, *Briefwechsel* (Frankfurt: Suhrkamp, 2009).

scholarship to America or Paris: IB did not receive any of these scholarships (see NOS 10.1, 18 and 21); for her trip to Paris in the autumn of 1950, she was given a one-off payment of 300 Austrian shillings by the Municipality of Vienna (IBE).

for newspapers, the radio: The *Wiener Tageszeitung* published 'Im Himmel und auf Erden' [In Heaven and on Earth] (29 May 1949), 'Das Lächeln der Sphinx' [The Smile of the Sphinx] (25 September 1949) and 'Karawane im Jenseits' [Caravan in the Hereafter] (25 December 1949); the Vienna journal *Die Zeit* printed the poem 'Betrunkener Abend' [Drunken Evening] on 15 April 1949. No texts written for the radio station Rot-Weiss-Rot (see NO. 21) have survived.

5

Ingeborg Bachmann to Paul Celan, Vienna, late May / early June 1949 (?), aborted draft

Paul, dear Paul,

I long for you and for our fairy tale. What shall I do? You are so far away from me, and the cards you send, which satisfied me until recently, are no longer enough for me.

Yesterday I received poems of yours through Klaus Demus, poems that were new to me, including three recent ones. I can hardly bear it that they reached me by such a detour. There has to be something there for me too.

I can read them better than the others, for in them I encounter the you I have known since the end of the Beatrixgasse. You are always my concern, I ponder a great deal on it and speak to you and take your strange, dark head between my hands and want to push the stones off your chest, free your hand with the carnations and hear you sing. Nothing has happened to me to make me suddenly think more intensely of you. Everything is as usual; I have work and success, and there are somehow men around me, but it means little to me: you, beautiful things and gloomy things are spread over my fleeting days

NOTES

MAN/ANL folder 10, p. 1: tw. letter draft.

the cards you send: See NO. 2n.

three recent ones: On 26 May 1949, Demus thanked PC especially for 'Wer wie du' [Whoever, Like You] and 'Wer sein Herz' [Whoever His Heart]. The latter has been preserved as a typescript in the IBE (cpy, *MAN/ANL ser. n. 25.202 a, p. 4 = HKA 2–3.2.219H²**).

Beatrixgasse: In June 1949, IB moved from her sublet room to Beatrixgasse 26, where she was living when she met PC, in a sublet room in the apartment of her friend Elisabeth Liebel in Gottfried-Keller-Gasse 13, likewise in the 3rd district.

your hand with the carnations: Allusion to the end of PC's 'Deukalion und Pyrrha'.

6
Paul Celan to Ingeborg Bachmann, Paris, 20 June 1949

Paris, 20 June 49.

Ingeborg,

this year I am 'imprecise' and late. But perhaps it is only because I want no one except you to be there when I place poppies, a great many poppies, and memory, just as much memory, two great glowing bouquets on your birthday table. I have been looking forward to this moment for weeks.

Paul

NOTES

MAN/ANL folder 2, p. 3: *hw. airmail postcard (Marc Chagall, L'Œil vert) to*: '*Mlle Ingeborg Bachmann/~~Beatrixgasse 26~~ [crossed out and replaced in unknown handwriting by: Gottf. Kellergasse 13/10.]/Vienne III/Autriche*', *Paris, 21 June 1949, from*: '*Paul Celan, 31, rue des Ecoles, Paris 5^e*', *ACO*.

Chagall: Concerning PC's interest in the Russian-Jewish painter, see the poem 'Hüttenfenster' [Hut Window] and PC/GCL, 151.

poppies, and memory: Allusion to line 10 of 'Corona'. 'Mohn und Gedächtnis' is the title of the first cycle of *Der Sand aus den Urnen*, as well as the volume published in December 1952. Concerning 'poppies', see NO. 1n. On 24 June, IB wrote to her parents: 'A little birthday mail already trickled in today, including a magnificent arrangement of poppies from Paul Celan in Paris' (IBPE).

birthday table: IB's 23rd birthday was on 25 June 1949.

7
Ingeborg Bachmann to Paul Celan, Vienna, 24 June 1949

Vienna, 24 June 1949.

My dear,

because I was not thinking about it at all, your card truly came flying here today, on the day before—just like last year—straight into my heart; yes, it is true, I am so fond of you, I never said it back then. I felt the poppies again, deep, very deep; you performed such wonderful magic, I could never forget it.

Sometimes all I want is to go away and come to Paris, to feel you touch my hands, touch me completely with flowers, and then, once again, not know where you have come from and where you are going. To me, you are from India or some ever more remote, dark brown country; for me, you are the desert and the sea and everything that is secret. I still know nothing about you and often fear for you because of it; I cannot imagine you doing any of the things that the rest of us here do, I should have a castle for us and have you come to me, so that you can be my enchanted master in it, we will have a great many carpets inside and music, and we will invent love.

I have often reflected that 'Corona' is your most beautiful poem; it is the complete anticipation of a moment in which everything turns to marble, and remains thus forever. For me here, however, it is not becoming 'time'. I hunger for something I shall not receive, and everything is flat and stale, tired and worn out before it is even used.

I shall be in Paris in mid-August, just a few days. Do not ask me why or what for, but be there for me for one evening or two, three . . . Take me to the Seine, let us gaze into it until we become little fishes and recognize each other again.

Ingeborg.

NOTES

GLA D90.1.2824/3: *tw. letter w/hw. corrections, ACO, envelope missing. MAN/ANL folder 10, p. 5: ass. tw. draft* (*not published*).

'*Corona*'/*it is not becoming '*time*'*: See line 17 of PC's 'Corona': 'Es ist Zeit, dass es Zeit wird' [It is time that it was time]. A typescript has been preserved in the IBE (*cpy w/hw. corr., MAN/ANL folder 11, p. 2 = HKA 2–3.2., 195 H⁵*).

8

Paul Celan to Ingeborg Bachmann, Paris, 4 (?) August 1949

Ingeborg, dear,

just a few words in haste, to tell you how happy I am that you are coming.

I hope this letter arrives in time, and that you write once you are here: can I expect you? Or can I not, just as I cannot ask why or what for you are coming?

I am full of impatience and love.

Yours, Paul

Here is my telephone number:
DAN 78-41

NOTES

MAN/ANL folder 2, pp. 4–5: hw. airmail letter to: 'Mlle *Ingeborg Bachmann/Gottfried Kellergasse 13/10/ <u>Vienne III</u>/ <u>Autriche</u>', Paris, 4 August 1949, ACO.*

you are coming: IB only came to Paris in the autumn of 1950.

DAN 78–41: Telephone number of the hotel; PC did not have a telephone of his own.

9

Paul Celan to Ingeborg Bachmann, Paris, 20 August 1949

31, rue des Ecoles
Paris, 20 August 49

My dear Ingeborg,

so you are only coming in two months—why? You have not told me, nor have you told me for how long, nor told me whether you will receive your scholarship. In the meantime we can 'exchange letters', you suggest. Do you know, Ingeborg, why I have written to you so little during this last year? Not only because Paris had forced me into a terrible silence from which I could not escape; also because I did not know what you thought about those brief weeks in Vienna. What could I have concluded from those first hasty lines of yours, Ingeborg?

Perhaps I am mistaken, perhaps we are evading each other in the <u>very place</u> where we would so like to meet, maybe we are both to blame. Except that I sometimes tell myself that my silence is perhaps more understandable than yours, for the darkness that imposes it upon me is older.

You know: one must always make the big decisions alone. When I received that letter in which you asked me whether you should choose Paris or the United States, I would have liked to tell you how happy I would have been for you to

13

come. Can you understand, Ingeborg, why I did not? I told myself that if it really meant something to you (that is to say, more than something) to live in the city where I also live, you would not have asked for my advice to begin with—on the contrary.

One long year has passed now, a year in which I am sure you have experienced a great deal. But you have not told me how long ago our own May and June were before this year . . .

How far away or how close are you, Ingeborg? Tell me, so that I know whether your eyes will be closed if I kiss you now.

Paul

NOTES

MAN/ANL folder 2, pp. 6–7: hw. airmail letter to: 'M<u>lle</u> *Ingeborg Bachmann/Gottfried Kellergasse 13/10/<u>Vienne III</u>/<u>AUTRICHE</u>* , *Paris, 20 August 1949, from:* 'Paul Celan, 31, rue des Ecoles/Paris 5ème', *ACO.*

in two months [. . .] *'exchange letters'*: Is a letter missing?

hasty lines: See NO. 2n.

that letter: Is this NO. 4?

10

Ingeborg Bachmann to Paul Celan, Vienna, 24 November 1949

Vienna, 24 Nov. 1949.

Dear, dear Paul,

now it is November. My letter, which I wrote in August, is still lying here—everything is so sad. Maybe you have been waiting for it. Would you still accept it now?

I feel that I say too little, that I cannot help you. I should come, look at you, take you out, kiss you and hold you so that you will not drift away. Please believe that I shall come one day and bring you back. It frightens me a great deal to see you floating out into a great sea, but I mean to build a ship and bring you back home from your forlornness. But you must also contribute something to that, and not make it too difficult for me. Time and many other things are against us, but we must not let it destroy what we want to salvage from it.

Write to me soon, please, and tell me whether you still want to hear from me, whether you can still accept my tenderness and my love, whether anything else could help you, whether you still reach for me sometimes and darken me with that heavy dream in which I want to become light.

Try it, write to me, ask me, write everything off your chest that is burdening you!

> I am very much with you
> yours, Ingeborg

NOTES

GLA D90.1.2824/5: tw. letter w/hw. corrections; D 90.1.2824/4 (ass. supplement): letter w/tw. and hw. corrections, ACO, envelope missing.

MAN/ANL folder 10, p. 2 and pp. 6–7: tw. letter drafts w/hw. corrections for letter and supplement (not published).

10.1
Supplement

Vienna, 25 August 1949.

Dearest,

this will not be an easy letter; a year has passed without questions or answers, and with few, but very tender greetings, very small attempts to speak, that have so far yielded few results. Do you remember our first telephone conversations? How difficult that was for me; there was always something choking me, a feeling not unlike that which had carried our letters before that. I do not know whether you agree, but I shall take the liberty of presuming so.

Your silence was certainly different from mine. To me, it is self-evident that we should not be speaking about you and your motives now. They are important to me, and always will be; but if anything is to be put in the balance, it is nothing that relates to you. For me, you are you; for me, you are not 'to blame' for anything. You do not have to say anything, but the slightest word makes me happy. Things are different in my case. I am probably the simpler one of us, yet there is a greater need for me to explain myself because it is harder for you to understand.

What my silence means, first and foremost, is that I wanted to keep those weeks as they were, that all I wanted was to receive a card from you now and again to confirm that I had not been dreaming, but that everything really was the way it was. I was still fond of you, no less than before, on a level that was 'beyond the chestnuts'.

Then this last spring came, and everything became stronger, more full of yearning, and emerged from the glass cover I had placed over it. Many plans were formed; I wanted to go to Paris, to see you again, but I cannot tell you to what purpose. I do not know why I want you or what for. I am very glad about that. Normally, I know it all too well.

A great many things happened this year. I got a little further, I had a great deal of work, and I set down a first few things—with very many doubts, inhibitions and hopes.

Do you remember how you always despaired a little at my openness in some matters? I do not know which things you want to know and which not, but you can imagine that the time since you has not been devoid of relationships with other men. I fulfilled a wish you voiced back then; I have not yet told you that either.

But nothing more lasting has developed; I do not stay anywhere for long, I am more restless than ever and cannot promise anyone anything. You ask how long ago our May and our June are compared to all this?—not one day, my dear! May and June are tonight or tomorrow afternoon for me, and will still be for many years.

You write so bitterly about how strangely I acted when I had the choice between Paris and America. I understand you so well, and it still hurts me very much that it came across that way. Whatever I say in response will be wrong. Perhaps I only wanted to see if I still matter to you—not deliberately, more unconsciously. And I was not meaning to choose between you and America but, rather, something outside of us. In addition to all this, I can barely convey to you how often plans dissipate from one day to the next and take on another complexion. One day there are scholarships that are already out of the question the next, because one would have to apply by a particular deadline that one cannot meet, and then there are missing confirmations that cannot be offered. Today I have reached the point where I have two recommendations, one for a scholarship to London and the other for one to Paris, but I cannot say for sure what will become of them, and I am pursuing these matters without any specific idea, simply in the hope that one of them will work out at some point. Also, there is someone who wants to take me on a private trip to Paris. I am fairly sure it will happen eventually, as it almost did on one occasion. At the moment I myself am the obstacle, for my final examinations for the doctorate are taking longer than I would ever have thought possible.

You will conclude from all this that I am very distant from you. I can only tell you one thing, as unlikely as it seems even to me: I am very close to you.

It is a beautiful love in which I live with you, and it is only because I am afraid to say too much that I do not say it is the most beautiful.

Paul, I want to take your poor, lovely head and shake it, and make it understand that I am saying a great deal, much too much for me; for you must still know how hard it is for me to find any words. I wish you could read everything that lies between these lines of mine.

NOTES

'beyond the chestnuts': 'Only beyond the chestnuts does the world begin', the thematic line in PC's 'Drüben' [Yonder], the opening poem of *Der Sand aus den Urnen*.

a first few things: On 8 July 1949, IB told Weigel of the completion of two poems (HWL); concerning stories see NO. 4n.

two recommendations: In the draft: '[. . .] that I have two recommendations for scholarships, one from Washington, one from friends in London [. . .]'. Only the recommendation for Paris (Leo Gabriel, external lecturer at the philosophical faculty) has been preserved in the IBE (see NO. 4n.).

as it almost did: In the draft, this is followed by '[. . .] before the man was prevented by something [. . .]'.

doctorate: IB submitted her dissertation 'Die kritische Aufnahme der Existentialphilosophie Martin Heideggers' [The Critical Reception of Martin Heidegger's

Existentialist Philosophy] (Munich and Zurich: Piper, 1985) on 19 December 1949 (the viva took place on 18 March 1950, the approbation on 9 January 1950).

distant from you: In the draft, this is followed by: '[I keep thinking rather helplessly about ~~everything~~, but I should leave it be [. . .]'.

I am afraid: In the draft, this is followed by: '[. . .] of falling out of the truth that I do not say it is the most beautiful love. Perhaps it is.'

to find any words: The draft ends: 'even just to find the slightest kind word. Should I underline in red for you so that you can find them and finally understand?'

11

Ingeborg Bachmann to Paul Celan, Vienna, 10 June 1950

Vienna, 10 June 50

Dear,

in a few days Nani Maier will be travelling to Paris, and I shall ask her to discuss with you some things that are difficult for me to say in a letter.

So I simply wish to send many, many thoughts on ahead, and hope that we shall soon be looking at a body of water that borders on India, and on the dreams we once dreamt.

But if you cannot, or have already dived into the next sea, take me with the hand one keeps free for others!

I am very grateful to you,

Ingeborg.

NOTES

GLA D 90.1.2824/2: *hw. letter, ACO, envelope missing.*

to Paris: Maier collected Demus in Paris after his study year there.

12

Ingeborg Bachmann to Paul Celan, Vienna, 6 September 1950

Vienna, 6 Sept. 1950.

Dearest,

now that our friends, Nani and Klaus, have returned and I have been able to spend an evening speaking to them, I can see for the first time how many misunderstandings have come between us. Believe me, I did not—at least, not deliberately—make the mistakes that have so distanced and estranged you from me. I have been very sick in recent weeks; a nervous breakdown, with all the accompanying symptoms, crippled me and made me incapable of reacting in the right way or deciding anything. In addition, I thought—just one of our misunderstandings—that I should not write to you myself.

Forgive me if you can, yet help me to get away from here nonetheless! Perhaps you could try to send me an invitation? I could come in October, by which time I should probably have enough money to get through the first while in Paris, so that I am not too much of a burden to you.

Dear Paul, it is difficult for me to write more, because I feel that everything can only be resolved once I have the chance to see you face to face, hold your hand and tell you everything, absolutely everything.

Do not keep me waiting for your reply, however it turns out!

I embrace you and am with you in my thoughts, many thoughts!

Ingeborg.

NOTES

GLA D 90.1.2825/1: hw. letter, ACO, envelope missing.

Nani and Klaus: Maier and Demus were in Paris around 21 July 1950. They sent a card from Fécamp before that, and afterwards from Avallon, Nice and Venice.

nervous breakdown: This occurred in the first half of July, a complete 'breakdown' with 'paralytic symptoms' (to her parents, 16 July 1950). IB was treated by the Viennese psychiatrist Viktor Frankl, a friend of Weigel.

13
Paul Celan to Ingeborg Bachmann, Paris, 7 September 1950

Paris, 7 September 1950.

My dear Ingeborg,

here is the letter in which Frau Dr Rosenberg invites you to Paris: I hope it will be sufficient to acquire the French visa. Please take the necessary steps immediately, and let me know if everything takes its normal course. Do not delay, Ingeborg: if you truly want to come to Paris, it would be best to come right away. You do not need to worry about being here, not in any respect. I am glad that you are coming, and perhaps you would be here already if you had answered Nani's letter in time. Hopefully the consulate will not put off the matter of the visa—you will probably have to exert a little pressure yourself, at any rate. Klaus, who knows how things are in France, may be able to give you one or two hints.

As far as I can tell from speaking to Nani, and now also from her written accounts, you have had some grief, Ingeborg. I am sorry to hear that. But I believe that Paris can take away this grief: this grief in particular. And perhaps I can assist Paris in doing so. You see, I had to struggle for a long time before Paris accepted me properly and counted me among its own. You will not be as alone, as lonely and rejected as I was. For the first right one earns here is this: to protect one's friends from the things one had for so long to face defenceless, indeed clueless oneself.

Klaus and Nani will have told you how beautiful Paris is: I will be glad to be present when you realize it.

Give me an answer soon. I embrace you

Paul

Give my best to Klaus and Nani.

NOTES

MAN/ANL folder 2, p. 8: hw. letter, ACO, envelope missing.

Frau Dr Rosenberg: Gertrud Rosenberg, wife of Charles Rosenberg, Yvan Goll's lawyer and executor of his will. The entry visa necessary for Austrians in France had to be supported by a letter of invitation (not preserved; it was submitted with the visa application). As PC was not yet a French citizen, he could not issue the invitation.

Nani's letter: Not found.

written accounts: On 1 September 1950, Maier wrote of IB's 'drawn-out nervous breakdown' which had 'kept her in bed for almost the entire summer'.

14

Ingeborg Bachmann to Paul Celan, Vienna, after 7 September 1950

Dearest,

thank you so very much for your dear letter, the invitation, and all you are doing for me. I set everything into motion immediately—I went to the consulate, and am now waiting with longing for the visa. At the moment I do not know when I shall be able to travel, but I hope that I can leave in the first week of October.

Naturally, there is much to do before so great and decisive a trip; I am worrying a great deal about how—and how much—to fold up my tents here. In addition, I am still waiting to hear what has been decided at S. Fischer concerning my book; but I shall leave as soon as I am able, whether or not I receive word from Dr Bermann. So that I do not fall into your arms completely exhausted upon my arrival, I plan to stay with acquaintances in Innsbruck and Basel, one day or night in each—and to reach Paris well rested. It is difficult for me to write more now; let us save it all for the many days together that lie ahead.

As soon as I know more, in particular the time of departure or arrival, I shall write again.

Please extend my warmest thanks to Frau Dr de Rosenberg, even if I do not know her!

Soon completely

yours

Ingeborg.

NOTES

GLA D 90.1.2825/2: hw. letter, ACO, envelope missing.

Dr Bermann: IB attempted to interest Bermann-Fischer Verlag in *Stadt ohne Namen* [City without a Name], but abandoned the novel project in 1952. Gottfried Bermann-Fischer subsequently became more important for PC as director of S. Fischer Verlag: from 1958, he published *Sprachgitter* [Speech Grille], *Die Niemandsrose* [The No One's Rose] and *Der Meridian* [The Meridian], as well as numerous translations. PC also published in the house journal *Die Neue Rundschau*; PC had been corresponding with the publisher since 1956 (see MSS, 221).

Innsbruck: With IB's friend Lilly Sauter.

Basel: With friends and relatives of IB's friend and former companion Weigel.

15
Ingeborg Bachmann to Paul Celan, Vienna, 27 September 1950

Dearest,

I long so much for a little security that I am almost afraid I shall soon find it. You will have to be very patient with me—or have a very easy time with me. I am lost, desperate and bitter, and know that I cannot expect Paris alone to resolve all these internal difficulties, that a great deal will rather depend on me, and a great deal on our relationship.

I alternate between looking forward to what lies ahead and fearing it; the fear is still greater. Please try to be good to me and hold on to me! Sometimes, I think everything is a muddled dream and neither you nor Paris exist, only the terrible hundred-headed hydra that is poverty, which crushes me and will not let me go.

I am supposed to collect my visa on 5 October; I hope it will actually be ready by then. If the necessary money were also to arrive, I would have reason to be happy again, something I have not felt in a long time.

I embrace you, dear, and will soon let you know of my departure!

Yours

Ingeborg.

27 September 1950.

NOTES

GLA D 90.1.2825/3: *hw. letter, ACO, envelope missing.*

the necessary money: **IB** had great difficulties raising the money for the trip to Paris (see NO. 4n). She was waiting for financial support from relatives of her mother: 'Since 1 June I have had no income, as well as sick, etc. And getting a job now, at the last minute before the trip, would be impossible on account of the short time' (to O. Bachmann, 30 September 1950, **IBPE**).

16

Paul Celan to Ingeborg Bachmann, Paris, 14 October 1950 or later

Dear Ingeborg,

it is half past four and I must now go to see my student. It was our first rendezvous in Paris, my heart was beating so loudly, and you did not come.

I still have to give two lessons today; they are far away, and I will not be back before quarter to nine.

The plug contact for your iron is plugged into the lamp; but be careful, and close the door properly, so that no one in the hotel notices you are ironing. Write your letters too. Waiting for letters is difficult.

And give a little thought to what swept over me when I spoke to you.

Paul

NOTES

MAN/ANL folder 1, p. 1: *hw. note, presumably deposited in front of PC's hotel room.*

14 October 1950: The day of IB's arrival in Paris (PCPC). Another possibility would be her second stay in Paris (23 February–7 March 1951); PC was not able to meet her at the station (to Nani Demus, 23 February 1951).

student: Not identified. PC augmented his modest scholarship from the Entraide universitaire for students with refugee status primarily with private tuition in French and German, as well as through translations.

17
Paul Celan to Ingeborg Bachmann, probably Paris,
after 14 October 1950 or after 23 March 1951

Dear Inge,

I will be back around 1:45—please wait until then

Paul

NOTES

MAN/ANL folder 6, p. 9: hw. message personally deposited on a scrap of paper; on the reverse, in unknown handwriting: '~~10.30~~/ ~~[xxxx xxx]chtner~~/ à ~~[xxx]~~ 6924'.

14 October 1950–23 March 1951: See NO. 16n. The document may also date from PC's stay in Zurich between 25 and 27 November 1960; this is the context it is assigned to in the IBE. At that time, however, PC no longer addressed IB as 'Inge' in letters.

18
Ingeborg Bachmann to Paul Celan, Vienna, 4 July 1951

Dearest Paul,

Klaus is travelling to Paris tonight; I plan to give him this letter, as well as others written longer ago and more recently. Even if you do not find the time to write to me, I hope I shall soon hear from Klaus how you are faring.

Please, think hard about the matter of your poems; I do not think it would be a mistake to make something happen through Jünger and Doderer.

Above all, do not hold it against me that I have written all the most important letters with the typewriter. Typing has become such a habit—or much more—that I am scarcely able to draw words that are close to my heart with ink on paper anymore.

Today I went to the Institut Français; I learned that I might be able to come to Paris for the start of the next summer semester (February or March 1952) after all. I have become very fond of Klaus: we have often seen each other and spoken lately, and it would be lovely if the four of us never lost contact entirely.

With all my love

yours

Ingeborg.

Vienna, 4 July 1951.

NOTES

GLA D 90.1.2826/4: hw. letter; D 90.1.2826/1 (ass. supplement 1): tw. letter w/hw. corr. and additions; D 90.1.2826/3 (ass. supplement 2): part of a tw. letter w/hw. corrections; D 90.1.2826/2 (ass. supplement 2): tw. letter w/hw. corrections, envelope missing, letter and supplements provided by Klaus Demus.

Jünger: The right-wing conservative German writer Ernst Jünger had been courted repeatedly by the Nazis before and after 1933; despite initial sympathies, their attempts were unsuccessful. On Demus' initiative, PC had contacted him and asked him for help in finding a German publisher for his poems (letter from 11 June 1951; *FAZ*, 8 January 2005).

Doderer: On account of his membership in the NSDAP, the renowned Austrian novelist was only able to publish again from 1950. He supported IB in finding a publisher for *Stadt ohne Nahmen*. For PC's later view of Doderer, see the poem 'Gewieherte Tumbagebete' [Whinnied Burial Absolution Prayers].

to Paris [. . .] (*February or March 1952*): See NO. 4n and NO. 10.1n.

the four of us: Those named and Nani Maier.

18.1

Supplement

March 51.

Paul, dear,

it is Easter Monday, and I have just got out of bed for the first time after an illness that was not very severe, but very important to me; one could almost say it came wonderfully to my aid. For I no longer knew how to go about things or be satisfied here. The first mistake was to spend a week continuing my old Viennese life as if nothing had happened; then I suddenly broke it off desperately and hysterically, would not leave the house yet knew that it could not stay like that forever. And then this was compounded by something that came from without, something that was very bad, almost worse than anything before it. Then my sister came, and finally this bout of flu. Now everything is as quiet as it is after the bomb drops in the war and when the smoke clears, and one discovers that the house is no longer there and doesn't know what to say; and what is there to say?

I may already go out tomorrow and look for work. Something always turns up. The telephone has been silent all day—as if there were some secret, cheerful agreement.

I may be coming to Paris in the autumn. Nothing is final, however. But even if I have to stay here, I should not be sad. I have had so much, taken so much, that it could still see me through for a long time; but even it is not enough—one gets by with so little. When the time comes, we will not be allowed to take much luggage anyway, maybe even none at all.

I am sure you do not expect me to say anything about 'us' already today; I cannot think well right now; first, I have to get away from everything—but I fear then I will also be too far away from you.

Please write to me occasionally. To not write too vaguely, do not hesitate to tell me that the curtain in front of our window has burnt off again and people are watching us from the street—

> With all my heart
>
> yours
>
> Ingeborg

Give Nani my warm regards.

Milo Dor was very happy.

4 July: I enclose this letter,—it is one of many, but most of them have already been crumpled—so that you will know a bit more.

NOTES [*see Figure 12*]

Easter Monday: 26 March 1951.

my old Viennese life: Before her stays in Paris and London (departure from Vienna on 14 October 1949, return on 7 March 1951), IB was living in a relationship with Viennese writer and literary patron Hans Weigel.

almost worse than anything before it: IB was presumably uneasy about Weigel's roman à clef *Unvollendete Symphonie* [Unfinished Symphony] (Vienna, spring 1951), which he was completing in early 1951: the main female figure is based on IB. Immediately before returning to Vienna, she wrote him: 'Has the novel progressed far yet?!' (undated, HWL).

my sister: Isolde, married name Moser, completed a course of teacher training in Vienna and was also part of Weigel and Dor's circle of friends. After her marriage in April 1952, she lived in Kötschach (Carinthia).

after the bomb drops: IB describes the bombing of Klagenfurt in *Jugend in einer österreichischen Stadt* [Youth in an Austrian Town] (IBW 2, 90f.).

people are watching us from the street: See line 13 of PC's 'Corona'. This is followed by a passage crossed out in narrow, regular wavy lines: 'Whether or not we place our tracks together, our lives do have something exemplary, don't you think?'

Dor: PC met writer Milo Dor [*see Figure 1*], born in Budapest and grown up in Serbia, and who spent part of the war in Vienna as a 'protected prisoner' [*Schutzhäftling*], in the editorial office of *Plan*. The figure of Petre Margul in his novel *Internationale Zone* (1953) is modelled on PC during his Vienna days.

18.2

Supplement

June 1951

Dear, please, could I get your poems from Klaus or could you send them to me soon; I finally have a favourable connection with Germany now, and actually through a man who knows your work and is very interested in it. But I would have to have a manuscript by mid- or late August! (It is Heimito von Doderer of Beck-Verlag, the second oldest publishing house in Germany, after Cotta—we have been talking about you for a long time.)

NOTES

June 1951: Written by hand in the left margin; the larger upper part of the letter was cut off.

August: Originally 'June', corrected by hand.

18.3

Supplement

Vienna, 27 June 1951.

Dear, dear Paul,

in a few days Klaus is going to Paris; I want him to take the many letters I have written to you, the wrong ones and the right ones—I never had the courage to send them off. He can best tell you the most important news from here, as well as a little of the other, much more important things that one can only say with difficulty, or not at all.

I do not know if I should try.

I long for you so much, so very much, and sometimes it almost makes me ill and all I wish for is to see you again, somewhere—not some time, but soon. Yet if I try to imagine how and what you might reply, things become very dark, and the old misunderstandings that I would so like to do away with come back again.

Do you still remember that we were very happy together in spite of everything, even in our worst moments, when we were worst enemies?

Why did you never write to me? Has Frau Jené not been in Paris yet? Why do you no longer sense that I still want to come to you with my mad, confused and contradictory head, which still works against you from time to time? I am slowly beginning to understand why I resisted you so strongly, and why I may never stop doing so. I love you and I do not want to love you, it is too much and too difficult; but, above all, I love you—today I will tell you, even at the risk that you will not be able, or no longer willing, to hear it.

I absolutely cannot leave Vienna before the autumn; I have too much work, and cannot afford to give up the job I have taken. Then I shall perhaps go to Germany to have a look around, or to stay there for a while. My Paris scholarship, on the other hand, has been postponed until 1952. I cannot say yet how I will cope; what I would like most is to get through that time by spending it in America. But all these plans I am mentioning to you here are very vague; things could turn out quite differently—it could be that I have to stay here and end up achieving none of the things I hope to achieve this year.

Let me give you all my fond regards and all my love, the many kisses and embraces that you cannot accept, let me be with you for the duration of a thought . . .

Yours

Ingeborg

NOTES

the job: IB had been working for the American Occupation Authority since April. She described it as 'work from 8 a.m. until 6.30 p.m.' and that 'The office is called—News and Feature Section' (to her parents, 29 March 1951, IBPE).

Paris scholarship: see NOS 4n and 10.1n.

all my love: there is a slight play on words here. The formulaic end-of-letter phrase *alles Liebe* ('fond regards') is followed here by *alle Liebe*, meaning 'all (my) love'. [Trans.]

19

Paul Celan to Ingeborg Bachmann, Levallois-Petter, 7 July 1951

Paul Celan
c/o Dr W. Adler
14, Villa Chaptal
Levallois-Perret
(Seine)
Levallois, 7 July 1951.

My dear Inge,

a week ago Frau Jené brought me your parcel, and yesterday Klaus came with a further present from you—thank you so much for all of it! And thank you kindly for the letters: the first one Frau Jené was supposed to bring me I received some weeks ago; Frau Jené was kind enough to send it off while she was still in Vienna, as she was expecting a relatively long stay by the Saar and did not want to keep me waiting.

It is difficult to reply to these letters, Ingeborg; you know that, in fact you know it better than I do, as you can look upon the situation we are now in from a side that was decisive (not to say responsible) for its creation. By this I mean that the outlines of your own person will appear clearer to you than to me, as I—not least through your overly persistent silence—am faced with problems whose solution only produces a further problem: one of the kind that come about because one keeps feeding them with sense and significance until, finally, one stands before them as an absurdity, incapable of asking how one got there. If I were not involved—how fascinating it would be, and how fruitful, to follow these moments of reaching beyond oneself on both sides, this dialectically heightened indistinctness of our realities which have been fed with our blood nonetheless! But I am *involved*, Inge, and so I do not have an eye for what, in that carefully crossed-out, yet not completely illegible passage in one of your letters, you call the 'exemplary' quality of our relationships. And how indeed should I make an example of myself? This sort of approach has never been my concern; my eye shuts if it is ordered to be nothing more than an eye, but not *my* eye. If this were not the case, I would not write poems.

In the place where we thought we stood, thoughts work in the name of the heart—but not vice versa. The fact that precisely the opposite happened cannot undo a gesture, even if it was the only one still possible in a difficult moment. Nothing is repeatable; our time, our lifetime, halts only once, and it is terrible to know when and for how long.

It is difficult to show you, *you* of all people, what has long been part of your most personal attributes—but, tell me, would you prefer to make the world even more impenetrable than it is through a word whispered carelessly into the distance?

I would be glad if I could tell myself that you view what happened as the thing it really was: as something that cannot be retracted, but certainly recalled through faithful remembering. For that—and not only for that—you need peace, Ingeborg, peace and certainty, and I believe you will find this best if you seek it within yourself, not in others. You have been given the chance of a scholarship, Inge, so work towards this scholarship and do not try to pass the time that still lies between you and Paris by travelling to America. In any case, why America? Is it really so important to gather experience in a place where it is so often measured by success?

You have so far got more out of life than most of your contemporaries, Inge. No door has remained closed to you, and new doors are opening all the time. You have no reason to be impatient, Ingeborg, and if I could make one request, it is this—consider how readily everything is at your disposal. And now be a little more sparing with your demands.

You also have more friends, more people who do their best for you, than the rest of us. Maybe too many. Or, rather, too many who think they know which way your path leads—when they should know that their own path, the one they have already walked, by no means entitles them to gain the kind of overview that is necessary if one wishes to advise friends. I have the feeling—and this feeling has been confirmed to me by several others—that, in Vienna, it is extremely rare for someone to actually <u>be</u> what they present themselves as being. I mean to say that many of the people who call the tune in Vienna tend, in most cases, to have hidden ears and a fast mouth. Believe me, this realization embitters me no less than you, for I am attached to Vienna in spite of everything. I am telling you all this because I want to warn you of a certain success: it can only be very short-lived, and people of a heavy disposition such as yourself should know how to deal with it.

But enough of the good advice! One more thing: you know how difficult an experience lies behind them.

I have little to report. I shall be staying for about six weeks with acquaintances on the outskirts of the city, in a little house whose windows overlook three linden trees. No noisy street, no strolling students, no Americans who want to experience 'Paris by night'. . . and a typewriter. I have translated some more poems by Apollinaire, which might be published in *Merkur*.

Thank you especially for your efforts on behalf of my poems. I remember Heimito von Doderer very well—could you send me his address? Did you have a chance to see Hilde Spiel? She wrote an extremely kind review for the Munich *Neue Zeit* of the poems I published in the almanac—I would so have liked to thank her personally. Do you know if she is coming to Paris?

Dear Inge, I shall close now. I shall close with the request to write to me more often, and regularly.

All my love and best wishes!

Paul

NOTES

MAN/ANL folder 2, p. 9: *tw. letter w/hw. corrections, ACO, envelope missing.*

Levallois-Perret: Commune in the north-western suburbs of Paris. PC stayed for three months with the Bukovinan parents-in-law of his schoolfriend Sigfried Trichter.

the first one: Not found.

'exemplary' quality: See the crossed-out passage at the end of NO. 18.1n.

how difficult an experience: PC corrected his original formulation 'how difficult a decision'. Whereas 'experience' can only refer to the Jewish genocide, 'decision'— taken in the context of the literary scene in Vienna—presumably refers to his decision to leave Vienna.

'Paris by night': in English in the original. [Trans.]

Merkur: Despite the journal's prior agreement, PC's Apollinaire translations were not published there but elsewhere, between 1952 and 1959 (see MSS, 247f. and GW IV 851).

Spiel: The Austrian-Jewish publicist Hilde Spiel, married to Peter de Mendelssohn, authored what is probably the first document of PC's reception in the German-speaking world; the review of the almanac *Surrealistische Publikationen* (possibly in the *Neue Zeitung*?) has not yet been identified or found in the PCE. PC missed Spiel during his stay in London towards the end of summer 1951, but thanked her in a letter on 19 September 1951: 'That you, in the little that communicates itself to me, saw what only reveals itself to me in rare moments of uncertain hope: contours and shape—I experienced it as one of those vindications from which a door opens up onto existence' (ALA). IB met with Spiel during her stay in London on the way back from Paris in December 1950.

20

Ingeborg Bachmann to Paul Celan, Vienna, 17 July 1951

Vienna, 17 July 1951

Dear Paul,

it makes me very happy to be holding your letter in my hands, and I hope we have now started a conversation that—forgive me for assuming this in spite of every-thing—is perhaps important to both of us. What you said in response to the most intimate parts of my letters struck me like a very cool breeze, but I understand and respect you too much to let any bitterness grow inside me, and I will try to continue from the point where, from that excess of vagueness and the things 'whispered into the distance', you extracted identifiable aspects that can be spoken about.

I think I must have expressed myself somewhat unclearly if you saw fit to assume that I believe in the possibility of 'undoing' anything, and today, just like you, I am absolutely in favour of remembering faithfully. In one corner of my heart, however, I have remained a romantic person; this may be to blame for my hope—a dishonest one, even if unconsciously so—of bringing back in a beauti-fied state something I once let go for not seeming beautiful enough.

I am a little helpless in the face of your advice; I would consider your thoughts on a trip to America—which is unlikely to happen, incidentally—very important, but I do not know how much Klaus was able to tell you about the conditions involved—I do not, at any rate, have the intention of gathering experience in America; my attitude towards the country is very similar to yours, I think. All I am hoping for is an opportunity to improve my English. This was suggested to me here, and I would be helped along if my knowledge could then be of use to the 'company' by which I am employed—and an improvement in my position would also have a favourable financial effect. This is precisely where things are very difficult over here, and I am not sure which I should fear more: losing my employment—for one always has to reckon with that—or keeping it. Life in Austria has become so much harder, so much more hopeless this year that one needs a great deal of courage to find one's way in again, day after day. So what you call my successes, which you have always viewed with scepticism—and which I now see in a similar light—has become very questionable to me, so that I now ask myself what it is that people envy me for. Do not misunderstand me, I am not pitying myself and am not after pity from others—I simply want to clarify things. I do not want to hold it against myself that I make demands, perhaps excessive ones—of all the things you accuse me of, you are right about that, and also that I am impatient and dissatisfied; but I am quite sure that my restlessness does not push me towards paths on which one loses oneself. I was close to deciding against myself on a few occasions, and it is possible that I will still have to choose time and again between myself and something very clear that has always been part of me, between a person who wants to take the easy way, who seeks convenience, approval and much more, and the other, the one I truly live off and live through, and whom, ultimately, I will not—I can only say it in this banal fashion—let go for anything in the world.

Vienna is—perhaps more than any other place—a hotbed of half-measures, and one truly has to be careful not to lose one's intellectual and spiritual footing; but here, as paradoxical as it may sound, things are easier thanks to my strange profession (the word 'job' would really be more fitting), which makes it so clear to me what I have to do in the little time that is left over, how sparing I have to be, and the indiscriminate spending one can sometimes lapse into dwindles almost by itself to just a little, to what is important.

I have not heard much about Hilde Spiel lately; she was in Vienna in April, and was almost certainly still in London a few weeks ago—I learned this from a German–English magazine that had an interview with her. Her address is Mrs H. Spiel de Mendelssohn, 20, Wimbledon Close, London SW20.

Heimito von Doderer will still be in Austria for the whole of August. He is going out to the country today, but plans to come to Vienna every week and check the mail, etc. His address is: Vienna VIII., Buchfeldgasse 6.

I wish you the best for the quiet weeks in Levallois. Will you have an opportunity to see Nani and Klaus? And will you return to rue des Ecoles afterwards?

You do not write whether you have abandoned your plan to come to Austria. Poems of yours were read in the Vienna Secession recently. I have the feeling your name is becoming increasingly known here.

Please also write whether I should pass the poems of yours that Klaus gave me on to Doderer, or whether you would rather send them to him yourself.

I am staying in Vienna for the summer; perhaps I can get a week off and visit my sister in St Wolfgang. So you can always write to me in the Gottfried-Keller-Gasse—please do!

Ingeborg

NOTES

GLA D 90.1.2826/5: *tw. letter w/hw. corrections, ACO, envelope missing.*

Klaus: See NO. 18.

'company': The American Occupation Authority (see NO. 18.3n).

Life in Austria: Prices had risen by 140 per cent between 1948 and 1951; this led to nationwide strikes in the autumn of 1950.

'job': in English in the original. [Trans.]

your plan to come to Austria: This is not documented in the PCE.

Poems of yours were read in the Vienna Secession: Unclear.

St Wolfgang: IB spend the last week of August at the popular Austrian summer resort by Lake Wolfgang in the Salzkammergut.

21

Ingeborg Bachmann to Paul Celan, St Wolfgang, 30 August 1951

St Wolfgang, 30 August

Dear Paul,

hopefully you received my letter this time; for the last one, I used the address you had written on the envelope, and only later discovered the more complete one in the letter itself.

Meanwhile, I have gone to the Salzkammergut. My holiday is very short, just a week, but I am not sad for the days are so beautiful here, and in Vienna a new, better position is awaiting me that will be very demanding but more satisfactory in every respect. I will be preparing academic programmes at the radio station Rot-Weiss-Rot, and have a hand in the radio plays in the script department; that could at least amount to a professional training of sorts, and—insofar as one can even think of security—get me through the years until my return to university.

Although I do not have anything to do with the actual literary department, I wanted to ask you if I could put together a programme with the new poems of yours that Klaus gave me. I have already spoken to Dr Schönwiese (Salzburg), who would then take them over into his department. From there they would go back to the studio in Vienna and be broadcast. (I do not, however, know if I will be able to get Edith Mill as the speaker.)

Klaus visited me straight away when he came from Millstatt; I was very happy, because I have grown very fond of him; and if Nani is going to be there too, I will be less daunted by the no-man's-land that is Vienna.

The Paris scholarship will be unaffected by all these changes; I will probably find out in late September or early October whether I have been chosen.

Dear Paul, if I ask myself today what I wish for, what I truly wish for, I hesitate to answer; perhaps I have even reached the conclusion that we are not entitled to wish for anything, that we simply have a certain amount of work to take care of, that none of what we do has any effect, but that one must still pretend between eight in the morning and six in the evening that it is important to put a comma or a colon on a piece of paper.

But to return to wishes—because I am not the only one to have a certain wish: do you think you would be able to come to Austria this winter, for example at Christmas? You would not have to worry about anything as long as you were here; you should relax for once, feel like a guest and feel at home. Let all sensitivities be silent—I am speaking not only for myself, but also for Klaus, Nani and a few others who would very much like to have you here, and I am, I hope, speaking a little bit for Austria which has not yet fulfilled its responsibilities to you; and I am speaking to the poet and the person who, after all that has happened, is still left for me.

With regards and many thoughts of you!

Ingeborg

NOTES

GLA D 90.1.2826/7: *tw. letter w/hw. corrections, envelope missing.*

new, better position: IB left the American Occupation Authority and joined an editorial team in the script department of the radio station Rot-Weiss-Rot, which was also meant to develop new series of programmes (including 'Die Radiofamilie' [The Radio Family]) (see NO. 26).

Schönwiese: The director of the literature department at Rot-Weiss-Rot in Salzburg, also a poet, and editor of the journal *Das Silberboot* [The Silver Boat], had already been told about PC during the latter's time in Bucharest.

Mill: Actress at the Vienna Burgtheater and film actress.

Paris scholarship: See NO. 4n and NO. 10.1n.

a little bit: Bachmann writes 'ein "bisserl" ', using the colloquial Austrian (and South German) phrase for 'a bit'. [Trans.]

22

Paul Celan to Ingeborg Bachmann, London, 10 September 1951

10.9.51

Dear Inge, your second letter has reached me in London, where I will be staying for another two days (then my address will be the old one: 31, rue des Ecoles). I am glad to hear about your successes and thank you for making such kind efforts on behalf of the poems. I will write to you at length from Paris.

All my best!

Paul

NOTES

MAN/ANL folder 2, p. 10: hw. picture postcard (*Giacometti*: '*Three Figures Walking*'. *International Open Air Exhibition of Sculpture, Battersea Park, London, 1951*) addressed to: '*Dr. Ingeborg Bachmann/Gottfried Kellergasse 13/ Vienna III/AUSTRIA*', ACO.

Giacometti: The card is the first known document of PC's interest in the work of the Swiss sculptor; see later 'Les Dames de Venise' [The Ladies of Venice].

London: PC regularly visited his aunt Berta Antschel there, as well as other relatives who had fled there from the Nazis (see NOS 128 and 199).

23

Ingeborg Bachmann to Paul Celan, Vienna, 25 September 1951, not sent

Vienna, 25 September 1951

Dear Paul,

in the next few days I plan to send you back the ring that you gave me last year; the only obstacle is that I do not yet know whether I can simply entrust it to the postal service, or, rather, wait until someone goes to Paris. As soon as I have some information, I will let you know whether I can choose the first, simpler method.

First I must tell you that I have finally had a chance to see Nani alone; so various things were mentioned, various things that were important for me to know.

Among those things, I was less surprised by your wish to have the ring back than by the memories you associate with it. I would have understood only too well that it is important to you to keep this memento of your family, and for that reason alone I would not have hesitated for a moment to return it to you; I would certainly not have misunderstood, and would accordingly not have been offended.

But now I had to learn from Nani's hints, extremely tactful as they were, that either you or I had been tarnished by the recollection of the preconditions for this 'gift'. The suspicion you utter in your heart towards me—and presumably also towards Nani—seems so monstrous to me that now, two days after learning of this, I still have to pull myself together to formulate a single clear thought and refrain from showing the bitterness and despair threatening to close in upon me.

Paul, do you really think that I could have accepted this ring, whose history I knew—and for all your accusations, you could not claim that this history was not sacred to me—on a whim, simply because I saw it and liked it? I do not intend to justify myself to you, nor am I concerned with being right, for this is not about you and me, at least not for me—all that matters here is whether I can stand up to what this ring represents. And all I have to say to you is that my conscience in the face of the dead who wore this ring is clear. I accepted it as a gift from you, and wore it or kept it safe, always mindful of its significance.

Today I understand many things better than I did: I know that you despise me and that you harbour profound suspicion towards me, and I feel sorry for you—for I have no access to your suspicion—and will never understand it—I feel sorry for you because, in order to cope with a disappointment, you are compelled to destroy the other, the one who caused this disappointment, so thoroughly before your own eyes and those of the others.

Since then, the fact that I love you all the same has become my business. I will not, at any rate, seek as you do to deal with you, forget you or expel you from my heart in one way or another, with one accusation or another; I know today that I may never find a way of dealing with it, yet will not give up any of my pride—just as you will one day be proud to have laid your thoughts about me to rest, like thoughts about something very evil.

Please do not forget to write to me about your poems; I do not want our other arrangements to suffer on account of our personal *rencontres*.

NOTES

MAN/ANL folder 10, p. 8: tw. letter draft.
rencontres: meetings. [Trans.]

24

Ingeborg Bachmann to Paul Celan, Vienna, 4 October 1951

Dear Paul,

I spoke to Dr Schönwiese today; I selected some poems with Klaus, and plan to send them to Salzburg in the next few days. Naturally, it will still take some time before the programme is broadcast.

Wort und Wahrheit have published two poems of yours, 'Wie sich die Zeit verzweigt . . .' and 'So schlafe, und mein Aug . . .'—unfortunately the issue has not appeared yet—I only have the proofs, which I have to return. You will receive a copy as soon as it is printed.

With many warm regards

Ingeborg.

Vienna, 4 October 51.

NOTES

GLA D 90.1.2826/8: hw. letter, envelope missing.

Wort und Wahrheit: See NO. 25.

25

Paul Celan to Ingeborg Bachmann, Paris, 30 October 1951

31, rue des Ecoles

Paris, 30 October 1951

My dear Inge,

it seems that this life is a series of missed opportunities, and it is perhaps better not to puzzle over them for too long, otherwise no words would ever flow. Letters that sought to do so in the past always retreated from the frantically probing finger, returning to the realm from which they were supposed to be removed. So I am now deeply indebted to you, and that brief report from London—everything of mine, alongside your letters, presents and efforts—is fluttering about in my head. So forgive me, and let us finally speak to each other.

I would like to report a little, tell you about events—that is probably the clearest approach. In London: calm, homeliness, gardens and books, now and again a walk through the city. No encounters except for the one with Erich Fried—refreshing, invigorating through humanity and warmth. Unquestionably, a very clear, strong poetic talent. Of the other representatives of 'cultural Vienna' I only saw Hans Flesch, whom E. F. had invited on the evening I read poems at his home. I did not see Hilde Spiel, unfortunately, who was still in Austria at the time. I left a manuscript at Erich Fried's place; it seems it was passed on to Frau Spiel a few days ago. (A few lines of hers would suggest that.)

Difficult to be in Paris again: searches for a room and for people—both disappointing. Lonely times cloaked in chatter, dissolved snow landscape, private secrets whispered to the public. In short, an entertaining game with gloom—naturally, in the service of literature. Sometimes, the poem seems like a mask that only exists because the others need something from time to time to hide their sanctified, grotesque everyday faces.

But enough of these malicious words—this earth is round enough, after all, and this autumn the chestnuts in Paris have blossomed a second time.

Dear Inge, let me thank you and Klaus for the publication of the two poems in *Wort und Wahrheit**)—perhaps by this route they will reach some ear or other that is not entrenched. You will no doubt be pleased to know that the Berlin magazine *Das Lot* has now also accepted a few of my poems; they will be printed in the next issue, in February. As well, some of my things are to be translated into Swedish. Hopefully, also into German some time.

Can you tell? I act, I wander past all the houses in the area, I am running after myself . . . If only I really knew what hour has struck! But was it really in front of my door, the stone I am trying to roll away? Oh, the word only comes to me through the air and—I fear once again—in my sleep.

I do not know, Inge, whether Klaus showed you the two poems I sent him recently. Here is a new, 'latter', but hopefully not last, one. (Good God, if only you would be less sparing with your words!)

And you, Inge? Are you working? Tell me something about that, would you? And your plans? I have a guilty conscience because I advised against your planned trip abroad in my letter from Levallois—I take it all back now; my judgement was very superficial on that occasion.

Let me know everything that can be communicated, and, beyond that, perhaps occasionally one of those quieter words that come when one is alone, and can only speak into the distance. I shall then do likewise.

I send you the brightest moments of this hour!

Paul

* Mais il les [a] bien publiés <u>entre parenthèses</u>, ce cher Hansen-Löve . . .

NOTES

MAN/ANL folder 2, pp. 11–12: tw. letter w/hw. corrections; *GLA D 90.1.44* (ass. supplement): tw. poem (=*HKA 2–3, 2.258 H^{1a}*), *ACO*, envelope missing.

London: See NO. 22.

Fried: PC may have met the German-Jewish poet and translator, living in exile in London since 1938 and working as an editor at the BBC, before this. Differences of opinion concerning Israel let to an estrangement in the late 1960s. In a letter written to IB (20 November 1960), Fried still recalled the profound impression she had made upon him when they met for a joint reading at the Anglo-Austrian Society in London on 21 February 1951 (IBE).

Flesch: The Austrian writer and translator, whom IB probably first met as a friend of Spiel, had been living in exile in London since 1934; like Fried, he was working in the BBC's foreign department.

A few lines: Not found. PC had left Spiel a typescript dated to October 1950 (HKA 2–3.2, 26) still bearing the title *Der Sand aus den Urnen* but considerably extended in comparison to the published volume. According to her message from 14 October 1951 (PCE), she did not yet have it in her possession.

chestnuts . . . a second time: See line 7 of PC's 'Dunkles Aug im September' [Dark Eye in September].

Wort und Wahrheit/*Mais* [. . .] *Hansen-Löve*: The Austrian-born Danish publicist had published PC's poems 'Wie sich die Zeit verzweigt' [How Time Forks Out] and 'So schlafe, und mein Aug' [So Sleep, . . .] as an editorial staff member at the *Wiener Monatszeitschrift* (October 1951, p. 740, LPC). PC's handwritten footnote refers to the place they were assigned on the less favourable left-hand page, as filler between two socio-political articles. 'So schlafe' has been preserved as a typescript in the IBE (*cpy, MAN/ANL ser. n. 25.202 a, p. 5 = HKA 2–3.231 H³*).

Das Lot: The publication of the three poems 'Wasser und Feuer' [Water and Fire], 'Sie kämmt ihr Haar' [She Combs Her Hair] and 'Nachts, wenn das Pendel [At Night, When the Pendulum] in the Berlin journal had been arranged through Claire Goll (only in June 1952, pp. 67f., LPC).

Swedish: 'Kristall' [Crystal] was meant to appear in the culture journal *Ord & Bild* and 'Wer sein Herz' in *Vi* (not documented), both translated by the Estonian poet Ilmar Laaban, whom PC had met in Paris.

the two poems: Demus received 'Unstetes Herz' [Fickle Heart] and 'Brandung' [Surge] with the letter of 20 September 1951 (on the front and reverse of a separate sheet, D 90.1.39–40).

trip/Levallois: See NO. 19.

the brightest moments of this hour!: Added by hand.

Mais il les [a] *bien publiés <u>entre parenthèses</u>, ce cher Hansen-Löve* . . . : But he published them nicely <u>in parentheses</u>, this dear Hansen-Löve . . .

26
Ingeborg Bachmann to Paul Celan, Vienna, 10 November–16 December 1951

Vienna, 10 November 1951

Dearest Paul,

your letter made me so happy, happier than you can imagine; in fact, I wonder whether you have ever felt as close to me as you have these last few days—because, for the first time in a letter, you truly came to me. Do not misunderstand my joy, for I can certainly hear all the bitterness in your words—but I am simply glad that you were able to write to me about it.

I understand you, I can feel with you, because I simply find confirmation of what my own feeling tells me. The meaninglessness of the endeavours—can one even call them that?—around us, the culture scene, of which I myself am now a part, all this revolting bustle, the impudent conversations, the craving to please, the catchphrases about the 'new'—it is becoming more alien to me every day; I am at the very heart of it, which only makes it more eerie to observe the cosy turbulence of the others.

I do not know if you can sense that I have no one but you to strengthen my faith in the 'other', that my thoughts always search for you—not simply as the dearest person I have, but also as the one who, no less lost than I, holds the fort in which we have holed ourselves up.

First, let me reply to you: I am glad that your poems have been published; but you really must not thank me for *Wort und Wahrheit*—in fact, you should not thank me at all, ever, for in such moments I am weighed down all the more by a deeply felt, albeit indefinable, sense of guilt towards you. It would be good for you to get into contact with Hilde de Mendelssohn; I like her a great deal, and to a certain extent also value her work.—And now I shall tell you a little about what I have been doing. It will be a very banal report, and you must believe me that my outward activities do not quite represent the entirety of my thoughts and actions.

You already know that I have a position at the radio station Rot-Weiss-Rot as 'Script Writer Editor'; I sit in a room with two men and two secretaries; with these two men, I edit plays for the radio, and occasionally have a radio play of my own to write, as well as the weekly film review, and read and evaluate countless, almost always terrible manuscripts. What I come up with is not always bad; for Austria, the selection we present to our listeners is even quite daring, from Eliot to Anouilh, yet strangely enough we have actually been quite successful with it. You will perhaps hold it against me that I am 'diligent' in an alarming fashion; I have had a degree of success, and been able to find a very decent position for myself within a short time, and, although my work does not satisfy me in many ways, I enjoy it and am glad that I can work. I have resolved—but do not know if it will prove feasible—to stay here just for one year and then go to Germany, to a German station—once I have fully mastered the necessary skills. I came to this station by coincidence; previously, I would never have imagined choosing such work as a profession, but now that I see I am being given a chance—and not the worst one, if one considers how difficult it is nowadays to find a halfway decent profession—I almost want to make the most of it. Now I want to ask you what you think about it, for, as peculiar as it might seem to you, I am also thinking of 'us'.

Dear Paul, I know that you no longer love me today, that you no longer think about taking me in—and yet I cannot help still hoping, working with the hope of building a foundation for a life together with you, a foundation that could offer us a certain financial security, and that could make it possible for us to begin anew, whether over here or over there.

I can no longer make promises or declarations—nor do I want to. I am, rather, looking for some proof, whether or not you accept it; perhaps you would even consider that a false, bad proof. But I have come to believe that, as far as 'this' side of life is concerned, I can 'afford' it better; and that I must be able to afford it if I profess to love you.

Your absence makes everything easier and harder for me at the same time. I yearn for you in a painful way, yet I am sometimes glad that I do not currently have any opportunity to go to you; I still have to become more secure, I have to become more secure for you.

Do not reply—unless you feel compelled to of your own accord—to these lines of mine. But at least write to me, write to me so that I know you are there, and so that I am not so alone with these fast, fleeting days and events, with all these people and all the work.

Nani and Klaus just visited. Nani has found a room near the main customs office and is very happy about it. I know the two poems you sent Klaus; I put them in the same place as the others. Today I am copying out 'Wasser und Feuer' for Klaus so that you do not have to send it to him.

About this poem: it is completely new and surprising to me; my impression is that you have overcome an associative compulsion and opened a new door. It may be your most beautiful poem, and I have no fear that it could be a 'last' one. I am inexpressibly happy about it, and am full of hope for you in the midst of your dark days. You have often accused me of not forming any relationship with your poems. Please, I ask you to abandon this notion—and I say that not because of this poem alone, but also for the others. Sometimes I live and breathe only through them.

Accept my best wishes, and—if I may misuse some words of yours 'think that I was what I am'!

Ingeborg

Dear, I am sending you a Christmas parcel today with the same delivery; I hope it brings you a little joy. Take all my very best wishes for Christmas Eve, and try to keep in mind that I am thinking of you a great deal.

Nani and Klaus are already very eager to hear from you.

16 Dec. 1951

NOTES

GLA D 90.1.2826/10; tw. letter w/hw. corrections and additions made with different typewriter; D 90.1.2826/9 (ass. supplement): tw. letter, ACO, envelope missing.

a radio play of my own: IB's first radio play *Ein Geschäft mit Träumen* [Business with Dreams] was broadcast by Rot-Weiss-Rot on 28 February 1952.

from Eliot to Anouilh: No radio adaptations by IB have survived.

coincidence: Presumably a restructuring in the station Rot-Weiss-Rot—it was located in the same building as the American Occupation Authority which ran it.

'Wasser und Feuer' for Klaus: Demus wrote to PC on 11 November 1951 that he had seen the poem while visiting IB. IB clearly passed on the document she had been sent to Demus herself (the paper assigned to NO. 25 through the number of the ACO presumably came into the GLA from Demus' belongings).

'think that I was what I am'!: Line 23 of PC's 'Wasser und Feuer'.

26.1
Supplement

Vienna, 3 November 1951

Dear Paul,

I am so impatient to hear from you—less because I want to know if Fräulein

Wagner visited you than because the year is growing ever older and Christmas is coming closer. Whenever I meet with Nani and Klaus, we talk about your Christmas trip to Vienna but without knowing if you really want to and are able to come.

I do not know how hard I should try to persuade you to come; I certainly wish for it with all my heart, for I would have so much to tell you. I am reluctant to confide in a letter, for my letters have always brought misunderstandings to Paris. If you did not come, I would visit you at Christmas—except that I know I will only have two days off, and that is really too short for a trip to Paris.

Now on to something different: you have been invited to the spring conference of the German Gruppe 47, which will take place somewhere in West Germany. Milo Dor will write to you soon with more information. I may be coming too if it coincides with my time off, which I will be able to take around April or May. Gruppe 47 will be awarding two prizes, one of 2,000 DM and one of 1,000 DM. Aside from that it will be very important for you, as the entire German press has been invited, the literature people from the German radio stations, etc., who will immediately buy the best short stories, poems, etc.

I am quite well, aside from being constantly overworked. I hardly have time to think about what will be; all I know is that I want to and must keep this job for at least a year, that this 'professional training' is good for me. But then I want to go to Paris again, not to America and not to England—I feel very clearly now that only France has anything to offer me; and even that, if there were some possibility of living there, I would not want to live anywhere else.

NOTES

Fräulein Wagner: This is presumably the Austrian painter Hedwig Wagner, who was still studying at the Vienna Academy; Demus had acquainted her with PC's work and sent her to him.

your Christmas trip to Vienna: See NOS 20 and 21.

Gruppe 47/Dor: Possibly there had been discussions about PC in connection with the autumn conference of this most important post-war literary group, led by Hans Werner Richter, in October. No letter from Dor, who did not himself attend the conference, could be found.

'professional training': See NO. 21.

27
Ingeborg Bachmann to Paul Celan, Vienna, 26 January 1952

Vienna, 26 January 1952

My dear Paul,

it has been so long since I heard from you. I do not know if you received my letter and the parcel, or whether you will be coming to Austria. But do not take that as a reproach. I am simply worried—I really have no idea how you are, or 'where' you are.

I want to tell you one thing in particular: I can take my first holiday in April. It will only be two or three weeks, but I want to visit you and see how you are at all costs. The Hellers would put me up again. But you must know that I am coming because of you.

Write to me soon, please—it need not be a long letter. Just give me some sign of life at last!—And I would be glad if you were able to look forward just a little to my coming.

I still have a great deal of work, both rewarding and unsatisfying work, and I barely have a chance to catch my breath. The days fly past, and it is difficult to keep my awareness of lasting things awake. Nonetheless, I am still aware of them at all times, and in every hour, and one of those lasting things is you. For nothing can change the fact that a part of me is always with you, and a part of you always with me.

Ingeborg

NOTES

GLA D 90.1.2827/1: tw. letter, ACO, envelope missing.

The Hellers: **IB** stayed with the Austrian Clemens Heller, co-founder of the Maison des sciences de l'homme, and his wife, the American Mathilda Mortimer, who had a salon together, during her first Paris visit (5, rue Vaneau, Paris 6e); it was then, in early December 1950, that 'the marriage became Strindbergian' between her and PC (to Weigel, 14 November 1950, HWL).

28

Paul Celan to Ingeborg Bachmann, Paris, 16 February 1952

16.2.1952

Dear Ingeborg,

it is only because it is so difficult for me to respond to your letter that I have not replied until today. This is not my first letter to you since I began to search for an answer, but I hope this time it will finally be the letter I send.

What I have decided to say is this: let us no longer speak of things that are irretrievable, Inge—all they do is reopen the wound, they stir up anger and ill will in me, they rouse what is past—and so often these things of the past seemed to me like wrongs, as you know, as I let you feel and know. They cloak things in a darkness that one must probe for a long time to draw them out again, friendship doggedly refuses to step in and put things right—as you see, it causes the opposite of what you hope for; with a few words scattered before you by time at intervals that are not exactly small, you create elements of confusion that I must deal with as mercilessly as I dealt with you in the past.

No, let us no longer puzzle over what is irretrievable, Ingeborg. And please do not come to Paris on my account! We would only bring each other pain, you to me and I to you—and tell me, what would be the use of that?

We know enough about each other to realize that friendship is the only possibility between us. The rest is irretrievably lost.

If you write to me, I will know that this friendship means something to you. Two more questions: it seems that Dr Schönwiese no longer intends to have a programme with my poems? Milo has not written to me, so I suppose the invitation to Germany will not materialize?

As for Hilde Spiel, I received a pleasant letter from her about two months ago, that is all so far; she did not answer my letter, in which I asked if there were any prospects of finding a publisher.

I am suffering a great deal because of this business with the poems, but no one is helping me. *Tant pis.*

Let me hear from you soon, Inge. I am always glad when you write. I truly am.

Paul

I did not receive the parcel, unfortunately; it must have been lost.

NOTES

MAN/ANL folder 2, pp. 13–14: tw. airmail letter w/hw. corrections addressed to: '[hw.] Mademoiselle Ingeborg Bachmann/Gottfried Kellergasse 13/<u>Vienne III</u>/<u>Autriche</u>', Paris, 16 February 1952, from: 'Paul Celan/31, rue des Ecoles/Paris 5e', Vienna, 21 February 1952, ACO.

first letter: No draft found.

irretrievably lost: PC had probably met the visual artist Gisèle de Lestrange, descended from a wealthy aristocratic family, in early November 1951. She became his wife in late 1952.

Spiel: In her letter of 15 December 1951, she showed enthusiasm for the PC poems she had obtained through Fried (PCE, see NO. 25) and asked how she could support his work. PC's letter does indeed seem to have received no written reply.

I truly am: Added by hand.

Tant pis: Never mind.

29

Ingeborg Bachmann to Paul Celan, Vienna, 21 February 1952

21 February 1952

Dear Paul,

yesterday I received your letter of the 16th—thank you. Forgive me for asking a few questions nonetheless; you will not find them difficult to answer if you believe in the possibility of friendship between us.

So, I do not mean to confront you with new problems and burden you with taking up our relationship where we abandoned it; I will not come to Paris on your account. It is, however, possible that I may come anyway sooner or later,—my job could easily require it. And, to avoid any misunderstandings, I want to ask you whether I should let you know if I am coming, and whether or not, for example, you would come to pick me up if I did? Whether it would be unpleasant for you to see me again? Do not be cross with me for asking these things, but your letter made me very unsure, I understand you and at the same time I do not; I am always aware of how difficult everything was—your disgust and 'anger' are understandable—but what I do not understand, and I simply must say this—is this terrible irreconcilability, this 'never forgive and never forget' mentality, the frightful distrust you convey to me. When I read your letter yesterday, again and again, I was very miserable; everything seemed so meaningless and futile—my efforts, my life, my work. Do not forget that the 'elements of confusion' you attack arise because I am speaking into a void. I no longer have any way to make amends, and that is the worst thing that can happen to someone. My situation is becoming increasingly eerie. I put all my eggs in one basket and lost. What happens to me now is of little interest to me. Since returning from Paris, I am unable to live as I lived before, I have forgotten how to experiment nor do I want to anymore—I do not want anything anymore. And you need not worry that I might ever speak about it again—about what is past, I mean.

Let us talk of other things: Schönwiese will broadcast your poems—he is coming to Vienna next week, and I am sure that this 'point' will be successfully taken care of in the meetings between his studio and ours. The delay has nothing to do with you or us but is, rather, due to external difficulties. The station has just got through a major crisis, a number of things have changed—and the whole time there were so many problems of a technical nature, problems that have serious effects for a large company, that proper work was greatly neglected. What is sadder, however, is that Hilde Spiel has not responded. But do not be discouraged! You must not let it affect you.

Please, try to keep in mind that we—Nani, Klaus, I and many others—think a great deal of you, and that some day one of us will surely have some freedom and gain enough influence to change things for the better.

Ingeborg

NOTES

GLA D 90.1.2872/2 and 2827/3 (ass. supplement): *tw. letters w/hw. corrections, supplement contains hw. additions, ALCO, envelope missing.*

come to Paris/pick me up: Later, in November/December 1956, IB was in Paris for a longer stay without informing Celan.

'never forgive and never forget': Has a letter been lost?

Since returning from Paris [. . .] as I lived before: See NO. 18.1.

Schönwiese will broadcast your poems: See NO. 21.

29.1

Supplement

I separated off the last paragraph,
as your letter arrived in the meantime.

Vienna, 19 February 52.

Dear Paul

Klaus read your poems yesterday at the Art-Club. I was not able to be there, as I could not leave work at the station in time, but I met with Nani and Klaus after the reading. We sat together for a while and drank a glass of wine to your health. It was somewhat like Paris around us, and even the people looked almost like those at the Deux Magots. But all that is not so important, for the Paris atmosphere brought us your poems, or the radiance they left behind, and we wondered what you might be doing at the same time in Paris. Perhaps there was snow in Paris too, like here, and perhaps you missed Austria and also thought of us. Perhaps you threw a little snowball from your balcony and we caught it.

Apparently the room went very quiet after your poems, and people listened—as well as you could ever hope.

I have collected some recent reviews for you, but instead of enclosing them I shall bring them to you myself. In May—for it is definite now that I can come at the very start of May. Klaus also said he heard from someone that you would like to have the complete edition of Nietzsche's works. We shall try to find one; it will not be sorted out overnight, but I am quite hopeful that I will get hold of it at my regular bookshop before my departure. Is Lichtenberg not also on your wish list??

Hans Thimig read three poems at the Kosmostheater—quite superbly, I might add: 'Todesfuge' [Death Fugue], 'Wer sein Herz . . .' and 'So schlafe . . .'

Klaus withdrew the money.

NOTES

Art-Club: This association of avant-garde artists, founded in 1947, arranged exhibitions and readings, for example at the Vienna Secession (see NO. 20). Demus wrote to PC: 'I had a reading evening at the Art-Club, read your poems and mine for three quarters of an hour each. Unfortunately there were only about forty people. I managed to read your poems (almost all of the last ones, and quite a few of the earlier ones) quite well, I felt in contact with them' (5 May 1952).

Deux Magots: Café Les Deux Magots at Place St-Germain-des-Prés, popular among intellectuals.

your balcony: See Figure 6.

complete edition of Nietzsche's works/Lichtenberg: Both of PC's Nietzsche editions, the selection bought at the Akademische Buchhandlung und Antiquariat in Vienna (*Werke*, August Messer ed. [Leipzig, 1930]; bookshop stickers on both volumes) and *Briefwechsel mit Franz Overbeck*, Richard Oehler and Carl Albrecht Bernoulli eds (Leipzig, 1916), contain reading notes dating from August 1952. PC's reading of his Lichtenberg edition (*Gesammelte Werke*, Wilhelm Grenzmann ed. [Frankfurt, 1949]) is only documented from 1965.

Hans Thimig read [. . .] at the Kosmostheater: This venue, originally a cinema, was used by the American Occupation Authority to, among other things, present unknown Austrian composers and writers at 'Austrian evenings'. Asked for details by PC, Demus had responded: 'The Kosmos evening (we only learned of it through your letter) was supposedly programmed by Weigel. I could not find out which three poems were read; perhaps Inge can' (12 January 1952). The actor Hans Thimig, who was also guest director at the theatre at the time, had successfully resisted a Nazi takeover.

30
Ingeborg Bachmann to Paul Celan, Vienna, 8 April 1952

Dear Paul,

by now you will probably have received the invitation from Deutsche Verlagsanstalt Stuttgart to the conference of Gruppe 47 in Hamburg. I am very glad that it is finally happening. Milo Dor, who has just got back, told me immediately—I had discussed everything with him before his departure. I will only be able to speak to him tomorrow or the day after, however, because I have so much work again at the moment that I scarcely ever leave the station before midnight. But, for the first time in a long while, I am full of hope again. Things must change for the better now. I can also sense how your name has steadily been gaining significance here, and that it has meanwhile taken on a clear profile for many people.

Sometimes I would like to come to you, very quickly, just for a moment, and say: be patient, have a little more patience—but I know how difficult everything has already become, and how questionable, and that you have already waited and waited for a long time, for much too long. But continue to be patient, in spite of everything!

Klaus is in Greece at the moment, and will return after Easter; Nani has gone to Carinthia—yes, I should go too, at least for a few days, as my sister is getting married at Easter; but it looks, once again, as if I will not be able to get away. It was already like that at Christmas—except that I am a little gloomier this time, for I long to be out in the countryside and would like to see my parents. As well as that, the last few months have been especially strenuous. Nani says I have become 'a shadow', but it is not quite that bad; though there is some truth to it in a different sense.—I translated a play by Thomas Wolfe that was broadcast on the radio for the first time here; then I wrote a radio play of my own, which is now also to be broadcast by Radio Brussels and in Switzerland. This success made me happy, but everything is over so quickly, is pale and fleeting, and all that remains is the feeling of great exhaustion and weariness.

There is one thing you will be glad to know: I recently made the acquaintance of Hermen von Kleeborn. I find her particularly kind and humane, and we were both very happy at having an opportunity to talk about you. She has not heard from you in a long while. Could you not write to her some time?

Dear Paul, could I ask you to write soon this time? I simply must know if and when you will be travelling to Germany. If I can help you—as far as it is in my power—by taking some of the organization and travel arrangements off your hands, you must tell me. Milo Dor has the best intentions, but is slightly unreliable.

A few days ago I met with Prof. Fiechtner of *Die Furche*. The conversation turned to you, and he decided on the spot to devote a column—probably in the summer—to your poems. The poor man is truly, exceptionally courageous, and has long been trying to steer that arch-conservative journal in a new direction. He managed to run a few Benn poems in a recent issue, for example, without losing his position.

I could tell you more, but it is already very late and my eyes are falling shut— and I also want to save up a few things so that I can surprise you with them one day.

Every night I ask God to protect you.

Ingeborg

Vienna, 8 April 1952.

NOTES

GLA D 90.1.2827/4: *tw. letter w/hw. corrections, envelope missing.*

Deutsche Verlagsanstalt: PC's future publisher had contributed to the funding of the conference; no invitation could be found.

Hamburg: See NO. 32.1.

Dor: Dor was returning from a meeting in Germany with Richter, to whom he had repeated his request for PC's invitation (see NO. 26.1).

Wolfe: IB's translation of the *Mannerhouse* (1948) by the American playwright received its first broadcast as a radio play on 4 March 1952 on Rot-Weiss-Rot as *Das Herrschaftshaus*. Regarding PC's later reading of Wolfe, see CAE, 792, the notes on 'Nach dem Lichtverzicht' [After Forgoing Light].

radio play: Regarding *Ein Geschäft mit Träumen*, see NO. 26.

Kleeborn: The director of the foreign department at Amandus Edition Vienna, herself a poet, repeatedly supported PC. PC had made her acquaintance in Paris in the spring of 1949.

Prof. Fiechtner/your poems: The secondary-school teacher, composer and music journalist was in charge of the culture section of the weekly Catholic newspaper *Die österreichische Furche*, which had published IB's poems 'Ausfahrt' [Exit] and 'Abschied von England' [Farewell to England] on 17 February 1952. In the end, nothing by PC was published.

a few Benn poems: It was, in fact, only one poem ('Das Unaufhörliche' [The Incessant]), which was framed by several very conventional poems by other authors (9 February 1952). IB and PC, who knew about Benn's advocacy of the Nazis during 1933/34, viewed the separation of art and life postulated by him critically: IB attacked the dissociation cultivated by Benn (see the interview of 5 September 1965, GuI 62), and PC his concept of the artistic poem (TCA/M NO. 550).

31
Ingeborg Bachmann to Paul Celan, Vienna, 6 May 1952

6.V.52

Dear Paul,

I would have written to you earlier had I not been sick—which is why I had to ask Klaus to send you a few lines. But today I was finally able to get more precise information, so I do not wish to delay in reporting to you:

It seems the invitations from Hans Werner Richter were sent out later than I had expected, as Ilse Aichinger only received a card from him yesterday. The conference will take place from the <u>23</u>rd to the <u>25</u>th of May, in Hamburg; the precise location of the conference is still unknown. But the Nordwestdeutscher Rundfunk will provide a bus to pick up participants from Munich, Stuttgart and Frankfurt. This bus will depart from Munich on <u>Thursday the 22nd</u>, so it will reach Stuttgart, and finally Frankfurt, over the course of the day—and from there it will go directly to Hamburg. If you do not want to board it in Munich but, rather, in one of the other two cities, you should contact Deutsche Verlagsanstalt in Stuttgart and S. Fischer Verlag in Frankfurt, Falkensteinerstrasse 24, in good time, as they know precisely when the bus will be passing through on that Thursday and where it will stop off.

But I can write to you about these travel arrangements in more detail in a few days, as Hans Werner Richter is coming to Vienna.

You will receive the money to get to Munich, or to Stuttgart or Frankfurt, in good time. From there you are a guest of the Nordwestdeutscher Rundfunk and Deutsche Verlagsanstalt. It does say on the card that participants have to cover the cost of board and lodging themselves for the duration of the conference—this was never the case in the past, however, so you do not have to worry about that.

In any case, you will meet Milo Dor on the bus, and he can help you out in all organizational matters better than anyone else.

But now you really must write whether you want to come at all—and write to me, as I could still be in a very good position until mid-May to sort out everything that may have been 'messed up' from the German end.

The Zwillingers were in Vienna; I saw them twice. They have probably called you by now and passed on my greetings.

Do not be cross that this is only a factual letter. I shall now wait impatiently for a sign of life from you.

I hope for all the best in the time ahead!

Ingeborg

Hansen-Löve is coming in 15 May—to Paris. He intends to publish more poems of yours soon in *Wort und Wahrheit*.

NOTES

GLA D 90.1.2827/5: tw. letter w/hw. corrections and a hw. addition, ALCO, envelope missing.

ask Klaus: Demus had sent information on how to reach Hamburg on 5 May 1952, adding: 'If anything goes wrong, Inge can sort it out, but you would have to write immediately.'

Aichinger: The writer, one of IB's closest friends and, later, the wife of Günter Eich, had survived the Nazi era in Vienna as a 'half-Jewess'. Her novel *Die grössere*

Hoffnung [The Greater Hope] was published in 1948, the same year as PC's *Der Sand aus den Urnen*. PC had already met her among Weigel's circle of friends during his time in Vienna (see NO.1n).

Nordwestdeutscher Rundfunk: Northwest German Radio

Munich: PC did not travel to the conference on the group bus from Munich, but took the train from Paris directly to Hamburg.

Zwillingers: The Viennese poet Franz Zwillinger lived in Paris after serving in the French Foreign Legion during the war. IB first met him and his wife Ann there, possibly together with PC (to Weigel, 14 November 1950, HWL). A relationship between PC and the couple is not documented before 1959.

Wort und Wahrheit: The poems printed in Issue 7 (July 1952), pp. 498 and 506, namely 'Die Ewigkeit' [Eternity], 'Stille!' [Silence!] and 'Zähle die Mandeln' [Count the Almonds] were once again used as 'fillers'.

32

Ingeborg Bachmann to Paul Celan, Vienna, 9 May 1952, with an undated postcard to Paul Celan from Hans Werner Richter and Milo Dor

Dear Paul,

it is already terribly late, but I have to tell you quickly: Hans Werner Richter unexpectedly came to Vienna. I spoke to him immediately. Unfortunately, my silent fears were accurate; the invitation to you was never sent—not for any actual reason but because of poor organization. Richter has now written you this card, which I have taken into my possession to make sure it is really sent; it is meant more warmly than it reads, and I am truly convinced that you should go. Please write at once to Ernst Schnabel, the director of the NWDR, that Richter put you on the list of participants while he was in Vienna, so that the people in Hamburg know soon enough. Even if time is short, you should simply go straight to <u>Hamburg</u>, unless it turns out that I have to give you other directives again. For it seems that the bus from Munich to Hamburg is already overbooked. So please try to be at the Nordwestdeutscher Rundfunk in Hamburg by the evening of the 22nd or on the

23rd at the latest (Hamburg 13, Rothenbaum-Chaussee 132–34). The conference itself will only go on for two or three days, but you will still be a guest of the NWDR for a few days after that. You will definitely <u>not</u> have to cover board and lodging yourself. Nor the return journey! So now it is simply a matter of funding the trip to Hamburg: Klaus, Nani and I have now decided, as there is no more time left, to discuss with you whether to send along your Austrian fees with Hansen-Löve, who is going to Paris on the 15th or 16th of May, or to send them to you in time by some other means. But you will still have a little money in Vienna, as *Wort und Wahrheit, Die Furche* and Rot-Weiss-Rot will soon be featuring poems of yours again. One more thing: each participant will have half an hour to read unpublished material, poems or prose. I would nonetheless advise you not to use the full half hour, but only about 20 minutes. And you absolutely must read 'Todesfuge'—in spite of everything—for I think I know Gruppe 47 a little.

And please, bring all your manuscripts.

I am hopeful that everything will go well; though I cannot guarantee that your stay will have the effects we all wish for. Forgive me, I am so tired and am only trying to explain everything to you as precisely as possible. I think you can view this information as final.

Bon voyage and every success!

Ingeborg

Vienna, 9 May 1952

NOTES

GLA D 90.1.2827/6: tw. letter w/hw. corrections; *D 90.1.3160* (ass. supplement): hw. post-card (folded, no postmark) to: '*Herrn/Paul Celan/Paris 5e/31, rue des Ecoles/Hôtel d'Orléans/France*' from: '*H. W. Richter/Wien XII/Herthergasse 12/bei Milo Dor*', envelope missing.

Schnabel: IB and PC made the acquaintance of this German writer in Hamburg and Niendorf as the director of the NWDR [Northwest German Broadcasting]; he was responsible for both of the readings broadcast by the station (recording of IB on 27 May 1952, of PC on 21 and 25 May 1952). He was an important contact for IB in her capacity as an author of radio plays; he also arranged PC's first televised reading as late as 1967 (December).

poems of yours again: Only *Wort und Wahrheit* had published poems by PC at that point (see NOS 25 and 31). Regarding the project at Rot-Weiss-Rot, see NO. 21.

'*Todesfuge*': PC read, among other poems(?), 'Ein Lied in der Wüste' [A Song in the Desert], 'Schlaf und Speise' [Sleep and Food], 'Die Jahre von dir zu mir' [The Years from You to Me], 'Zähle die Mandeln' and 'In Ägypten'. Walter Jens recalled the reading of 'Todesfuge' as a 'disaster' (PC/GCL II Ger. 14/10).

32.1
Supplement

Dear Herr Celan,

it would be a great pleasure if you were to take part in the conference of 'Gruppe 47'. The conference will take place in Hamburg from 23 to 25 May. Participants will be arriving on 22 May. If you decide to come, please contact the office of Ernst Schnabel (director) at the Nordwestdeutscher Rundfunk. He will give you all further details.

> *Best wishes*
> *Hans Werner Richter*

Dear Paul! I hope you are coming. You do not need to worry so much about the accommodation costs—just scrape together the travel money and come.

> *Best*
> *Yours*
> *Milo*

NOTE

Hamburg: The NWDR, one of the organizers, was based here; the conference took place in the Baltic town of Niendorf. See the photograph of the conference [*see Figure 1*].

33

Ingeborg Bachmann to Paul Celan, Vienna, 10 July 1952

Vienna, 10 July 1952.

Dear Paul,

I have decided not to wait any longer for a letter from you. But try to write to me soon, please, for I do very much want to know how you are! From Munich, I also went to Stuttgart and spoke to Dr Koch, who was very unhappy that you declined. He had already arranged a reading for you that would probably have been very important. Dingeldey, the director of Verlagsanstalt, wanted to make your acquaintance. You absolutely must write to Koch, so that these translations and perhaps the volume of poems will come out. And please do not forget that the publisher of the Frankfurter Hefte is very interested.

And above all: send Rowohlt the manuscript immediately. Naturally, I did not send mine, as I do not want anyone to 'play us off' against each other and repeat the Niendorf situation. It was not my fault, and you blamed me for it— how would you condemn me now? So you must understand why I cannot send the manuscript. I will finish with Rowohlt once and for all in the next few days.

I saw Nani and Klaus again. I found it very difficult to tell them about you and those days in Germany, all the more because I do not know what you think of it now that some time has passed. Even I do not quite understand what led to all the tension. But I can see clearly that our first conversation crushed all my hopes and efforts of the last year, and that you managed to hurt me better than I ever hurt you. I do not know if you realize today what you said to me, at a time when I had firmly resolved to win you back, to go into the 'jungle' with you, in whatever form, and I simply do not understand how a few days later, when I already knew that you were going to someone else, you could accuse me of never being with you in this German 'jungle'. Tell me, how can I be with you when you have long since left me? It chills me so deeply to think that this had already happened long ago and I did not sense it, that I was so unsuspecting.

But I want to give this friendship on which you have decided a chance. It will not be free of confusion for a long time, any more than your friendship for me can be.

And so, now too, I am with you with all my heart.

Ingeborg.

Nani is <u>furious</u>* because I did not bring back the manuscript, but gave it to you. Please send us one soon.

Furthermore, I <u>urgently</u> need the last poems, about ten to twelve, for a programme and for *Die Furche*. Prof. Fiechtner just called me again and asked about them. 'Wasser und Feuer' and 'Mache mich bitter' [Make Me Bitter] should be among them, yes?

* She truly reproached me quite terribly!

NOTES

GLA D90.1.2827/7: *tw. letter w/hw. corrections and a hw. addition, ALCO, envelope missing.*

Dr Koch: The editor-in-chief of Deutsche Verlags-Anstalt had shown interest in a volume of PC's poems in Niendorf, and subsequently arranged the publication of *Mohn und Gedächtnis*.

that you declined: The reading instead took place on 17 or 18 July 1952, when PC and GCL passed through Stuttgart on the way to Austria.

Dingeldey: Literary director of Deutsche Verlags-Anstalt in 1952.

translations: Deutsche Verlags-Anstalt had offered PC a commission to translate Malraux's *La condition humaine* [The Human Condition].

volume of poems/the manuscript: *Mohn und Gedächtnis*.

Frankfurter Hefte—the publisher: PC told GCL on 2 June 1952 that he had applied for one of the poetry volumes planned by the publisher for the autumn. The left-Catholic journal with socio-political and literary contributions, founded by Walter Dirks and Eugen Kogon in 1945, published numerous poems by IB in the first half of the 1950s, beginning with 'Früher Mittag' [Early Afternoon] (Issue 12, 1952, p. 952).

Rowohlt: Unknown.

cannot send the manuscript: Draft of *Die gestundete Zeit* [Borrowed Time].

last poems: There are no indications that PC had sent poems recently; regarding the plans for Rot-Weiss-Rot and *Die Furche*, see NOS 21 and 30.

all my heart: Handwritten ending.

34
Ingeborg Bachmann to Paul Celan, Vienna, 24 July 1952

Vienna, 24 July 1952.

Dear Paul,

you must know how frustrating it is to wait for mail. Can you really not write to me? Perhaps my letter was not a very wise one, but in a situation that is becoming ever darker and more oppressive, I cannot keep a distance from what is oppressing me. It is a summer without end, and I ask myself: what is to happen after all that?

For a moment, I thought—because Nani and Klaus were under that impression—that you would come to Graz, but, if my intuition is not mistaken, you will not. I do, however, hope that you will accept Hansen-Löve's invitation to Vienna. The Austrian College intends for you to fly over. (You do know that you can do that?!) But you will only receive this invitation for October in the autumn, after Hansen returns from America.

M. D. tells me that Frankfurter Hefte and Deutsche Verlagsanstalt are negotiating with you; he expects DVA to publish your poems. How much of this is true, what is actually happening?

I plan to go to Italy with my sister in late August or early September, during my holiday—just for a few days, but I am all the happier because she is so looking forward to getting out of Carinthia for a change.

There is deathly silence in Vienna at the moment—and that is the best thing about it; there is no longer any explanation for my estrangement from the city. I could go to Paris in August, to a congress, but you will understand that I do not feel like sitting around with some people or other about things that are not my concern. That would seem like a betrayal of Paris. I would like to come alone another time.

You know that I do not want to stay here any longer, and that, in Germany, I entertained the idea of going to Hamburg or to the sea; but I do not have the courage to work towards a change, and that would be necessary. I am dropping every ball I am thrown, and so I suppose I shall have to stay. This state of helplessness and weakness feels both pleasant and terrible. But that too is the wrong way to describe it, and does not quite express the reason for my attitude.

I am trying to write a little; it is going worse and more laborious. Did I not ask you once if I could send you something? Perhaps you could help me.

But it would be more important to me to receive a letter in which you write about yourself, even if you do not answer mine. I think I can bear being passed over.

Write to me, please!

Ingeborg

NOTES

GLA D 90.1.2827/8: *tw. letter w/hw. corrections, envelope missing.*

to Graz: PC spent the second half of July in Austria with GCL. As well as seeing Demus and Maier, he visited Hölzer in Graz.

invitation for October: Hansen-Löve had invited PC on 29 May 1952 to a reading at the Institut für Gegenwartskunde [Institute of Contemporary Studies]; it did not take place (PCE).

DVA: *Mohn und Gedächtnis* was published by Deutsche Verlags-Anstalt, who had the final manuscript (dated 30 June 1952) by the time the letter was written. PC received the letter of confirmation on 7 August 1952.

Italy: On 8 Setpember 1952, IB went via Rome to Positano, south of Naples, for a holiday.

congress: Unknown.

send you something: IB only sent PC manuscripts of poems on two occasions (see NOS 39 and 98).

35

Ingeborg Bachmann to Paul Celan, Vienna, 15 August 1952 (?)

Dear Paul,

please, could you not send your poems? *Die Furche* and the station need them urgently! It would be enough if you put together a volume for Klaus and Nani—like the old one—then I will copy out the requested poems and return the volume to Nani and Klaus.

Ingeborg
Vienna, 15 August

NOTES

GLA D 90.1.2826/6: tw. letter w/hw. corrections and a hw. addition (date), envelope missing.

Die Furche *and the station*: See NOS 30 and 21.

15 August: Assigned to 1951 by the archive.

the old one: Regarding the typescript of *Der Sand aus den Urnen*, see NO. 25n.

36

Ingeborg Bachmann to Paul Celan, Positano, 16 September 1952

Positano, 16.IX.52.

Dear Paul,

perhaps a letter from you arrived in Vienna in the last few days—and I am not there.

I came to Italy with my sister, expecting quite a lot from this trip; I hoped it would take my mind off things, that it would make me feel lighter, that I would be relieved of the pressure of recent months. But, if anything, it has got worse. This country is making me ill, and I now want to return sooner than I had planned.

I had, in fact, originally meant to write to you and ask if you could come over here. But then I was too convinced that you would absolutely not. Now it is too late, and the year will end soon with the usual work in Vienna and no changes. I am thinking of Paris a great deal again, but, as I know how little you wish for me to come, I keep suppressing it. I fear everything there that belongs to the past, and I fear being even lonelier there than I am here and at home.

Please try, if you have not already done so, to write to me again.

Ingeborg

NOTES

GLA D 90.1.2827/9: *hw. letter, envelope missing.*

Positano: See NO. 34n.

37
Paul Celan to Ingeborg Bachmann, dedication in Mohn und Gedächtnis, *Paris, March 1953*

For Ingeborg,

a little jug of blue.

Paul

Paris, March 1953.

NOTES

LIB: *hw. dedication on the flyleaf of* Mohn und Gedächtnis *(Stuttgart: Deutsche Verlags-Anstalt, 1952).*

'*Mohn und Gedächtnis*': Reading traces: pp. 41–2 (cycle title 'Gegenlicht' [Counter-Light] until pp. 49–50 ('Kristall'), creases at the top right corners, presumably to mark this section. Inserted: part of a hw. railway map, torn off a larger piece, showing the stations Karlsruhe, Mannheim and Frankfurt. A second copy of this edition in the LIB does not contain any dedication; wipe mark on p. 46. Regarding the copy of the second edition, see NO. 67.

a little jug of blue: See 'Marianne' (line 9) in the same volume.

March: The volume already appeared on 17 December 1952 as a Christmas gift for friends of the publisher, but most of the printing was in early January 1953.

38
Ingeborg Bachmann to Paul Celan, Vienna, 29 June 1953

Vienna, 29 June 1953.

Forgive me for only thanking you for the poems today. I could not pluck up the courage.

Now Nani and Klaus have been telling me a great deal about Paris, and it no longer seems so difficult to write this letter.

In August I shall be leaving Vienna for Italy, and I will not return.

For me, the poems are the most precious thing I will take with me.

I wish you the best of luck, and I know that it will come to you now.

Ingeborg

NOTES

GLA D 90.1.2828: *hw. letter, ALCO, envelope missing.*

poems: *Mohn und Gedächtnis.*

Paris: Nani and Klaus Demus (married since December 1952) visited PC and GCL in Paris in the spring of 1953 [*see Figure 6*]; the plan for an Austrian anthology of poems probably also came about there.

leaving Vienna: The German composer Hans Werner Henze, whom IB had met at the Gruppe 47 conference in the autumn of 1952 (at Burg Berlepsch, near Göttingen), invited her to Ischia on 7 July 1953 to live near him. She was never again to take up lasting residence in Austria.

in May: See NO. 29.1.

39

Ingeborg Bachmann to Paul Celan, Vienna, 18 July 1953

Vienna, 18 July 1953.

Dear Paul,

Nani and Klaus tell me you are compiling an anthology of Austrian poetry. I would be happy to send you something, but please do not feel obliged to include a poem of mine. Only do so if you feel you can justify it. Whatever you decide, I will accept it.

The only condition is this: there has to be a note somewhere that the poem is taken from the 'studio' volume *Die gestundete Zeit* (Franfurter Verlagsanstalt, 1953). The poems will be appearing in that volume in September.

Mail will be forwarded to me from my Carinthia address (Klagenfurt, Henselstrasse 26) in the coming months. I shall still be in Vienna until 1 August.

I wish you a good summer.

Ingeborg

Enclosed: *the poems 'Botschaft', 'Sterne im März', 'Fall ab, Herz, vom Baum der Zeit', 'Einem Feldherrn' and 'Grosse Landschaft bei Wien'.*

NOTES

> *GLA D 90.1.3105/1*: *tw. letter including four cpys w/hw. corrections ('Botschaft' [Message],* *'Sterne im März' [Stars in March], 'Fall ab, Herz, vom Baum der Zeit' [Fall, O Heart, from* *the Tree of Time] and 'Einem Feldherrn' [To a Commander], the second and third poems with* *pencilled-in question marks, possibly added by PC?); GLA D 90.1.3104 (ass. supplement):* *cpy 'Grosse Landschaft bei Wien' [Great Landscape near Vienna], envelope missing.*

> *anthology of Austrian poetry*: The project was never realized. Thirteen authors sent poems between July and September 1953: Hans Carl Artmann, Ingeborg Bachmann, Christine Busta, Klaus Demus, Jeannie Ebner, Herbert Eisenreich, Michael Guttenbrunner, Ernst Kein, Andreas Okopenko, Wieland Schmied, Helmut Stumfohl, Hanns Weissenborn and Herbert Zand. 'Grosse Landschaft bei Wien' was one of those on PC's shortlist (together with poems by Artmann, Busta, Demus, Schmied, Stumfohl and Zand).

> *in September*: The volume was published in December 1953 (see NO. 42).

40

Nani and Klaus Demus with Ingeborg Bachmann
to Paul Celan and Gisèle Celan-Lestrange, 1 August 1953

[*Nani Demus*] *1 August 1953.*

We are together to bid farewell—it is Inge's last day in Vienna. We are drinking to the next meet-ing, some day in Paris, in a darkly beautiful location known only to the 'initiated'. [*Klaus Demus*] *None of us know how things will continue; we hardly even know the fabric from which they will be made. But perhaps we shall be able to say that it was always enjoyable. An occasional forever, as full of unfathomable places as this one—far removed from the here and now. Those who sail on the rivers see, white as wheat, the coasts of the world into the image of the night*—The wall is wholly black now, but may it be light when you come. The glasses are empty, but they will be full when you come.
[*Nani Demus*] *Faithfully*:
Nani—*Klaus*—Ingeborg

[*Nani Demus*] *Tout mon cœur à Gisèle.*

NOTES

GLA D 90.1.1341: *hw. postcard to*: '*Monsieur/Paul Celan/Tournebride/GRAND-BOURG./par Evry-Petit-Bourg/Seine-et-Oise/FRANKREICH*', *Vienna, 2 August 1953, from*: [*Nani Demus*] '*Inge, Nani, Klaus*'/[*in place of a sender*] '*Ehemalige Hofstallungen, Weinstube an der schwarzen, hohen Mauer* [*Former court stables, wine tavern by the black, high wall*]', *ALCO*.

Inge's last day in Vienna: On 2 August 1953, IB travelled via Klagenfurt to Ischia, where she arrived on 8 August.

Tout mon cœur à Gisèle: My heartfelt greetings to Gisèle.

41

Ingeborg Bachmann to Paul Celan, San Francesco di Paola, 2 September 1953

San Francesco di Paola
Casa Elvira Castaldi
<u>FORIO d'ISCHIA</u>
(Napoli)   San Francesco di Paola, early
(until 12 October)   September.

Dear Paul,

could you please tell me fairly soon which poem you intend to use for your anthology? Frankfurter Verlagsanstalt write that they are giving away a few manuscripts for a different German anthology, and I think it would not be good if one of those also happened to be printed in yours. But, naturally, you have the first choice.

I am going to Germany in mid-October, and could perhaps also come to Paris briefly in November. But I cannot entirely say what lies ahead. I feel so well here that I do not want to think about what will be. I am living in a little old farmhouse, completely alone, in a wild, beautiful area known as the 'burnt sea', and sometimes I wish I never had to return to 'Europe'.

Ingeborg

NOTES

GLA D 90.1.3105/2: tw. airmail letter w/hw. corrections to: '[*tw.*] M. Paul Celan/ ~~Tournebride, Grand-Bourg/PAR EVRY-PETIT-BOURG (Seine-et-Oise)~~ [*replaced in unknown handwriting by:* 5 rue de Lota/Paris 16ᵉ]/FRANCIA', *Ischia, 2 September 1953, from:* 'Bachmann, San Francesco di Paola, Casa Elvira Castaldi,/FORIO d'ISCHIA, Napoli, Italia', *Every-Petit-Bourg, 7 September 1953.*

San Francesco di Paola [. . .] *FORIO d'ISCHIA (Napoli)/'burnt sea'*: See NO. 38n. IB lived in a sub-village of Forio in the north-western part of the island, near the 'mare bruciato'.

your anthology: See NO. 39.

a different German anthology: In *Deutsche Gedichte der Gegenwart* [Contemporary German Poems]: 'Fall ab, Herz', 'Psalm' and 'Beweis zu nichts' [Proof of Nothing] (Georg Abt ed. [Gütersloh: Bertelsmann, 1954], pp. 308–11).

70

to Germany: To the autumn conference of Gruppe 47 in Bebenhausen, near Tübingen (22–24 October 1953).

to Paris: See NO. 29n.

42

Ingeborg Bachmann to Paul Celan,
dedication in Die gestundete Zeit, *Rome (?), December 1953*

For Paul—

exchanged in order to be consoled
  Ingeborg
  December 1953

NOTES

GLA LPC: hw. dedication on the flyleaf of 'Die gestundete Zeit. Gedichte' (Frankfurt: studio Frankfurt in der Frankfurter Verlagsanstalt, 1953).

'*Die gestundete Zeit*': Reading traces: p. 12 ('Paris'): lines in the margins beside line 9f., which were changed in later editions ('Entzweit ist das Licht,/und entzweit ist der Stein vor dem Tor' [Divided is the light,/and divided is the stone before the gate]). Presumably IB had originally planned to include a dedication card, see the insert in IB's copy of *Der Sand aus den Urnen* (see NO. 2n): 'For Paul—/Exchanged in order to be consoled/Ingeborg/In December 1953'. On p. 28 there had originally been a note with IB's address: 'Ingeborg Bachmann/Klagenfurt/Henselstr. 26/Österreich'. Regarding further supplements, see NOS 74 and 119 (BC III). It was probably this copy that was originally accompanied by a handwritten copy of IB's 'Im Gewitter der Rosen' [In the Storm of Roses] on a strip of paper (see NO. 53). Concerning the copy of the second edition, see NO. 68.

exchanged in order to be consoled: Line 8 [*getauscht, um getröstet zu sein*] from PC's 'Aus Herzen und Hirnen' [From Hearts and Brains]. In the IBE, there is a handwritten copy of the poem with sketches by IB on the back (from the abandoned novel *Stadt ohne Namen?, MAN/ANL folder 11, p. 1 = HKA 2–3.2 247 H²**).

43

Ingeborg Bachmann with Heimito von Doderer and Hanns Winter
to Paul Celan, Vienna, 7 January 1955

To the poet we have lost here, and who will gain himself over there—as we firmly believe!—the
warmest greetings! Heimito von Doderer

7.I.55

Just now Herr von Winter told me so much about the meeting in Paris. It made
me very happy! Ingeborg

All good people here love you and send their greetings along with ours. I think often and
with pleasure of traduttore-traditore and the subsequent conversations. Warmest regards

Hanns Winter

NOTES

GLA D 90.1.1361: hw. postcard (Vienna, Stephansdom) to: '[hw. by Winter] Monsieur/Paul
    Celan/Poste restante/Rue de Montevideo/<u>Paris 16^e</u>/France', Vienna, 8 January 1955.
Hanns Winter/conversations: It is unknown how the Austrian translator knew PC.
traduttore-traditore: (the) translator, (is) a traitor—an Italian saying. [Trans.]

44

Ingeborg Bachmann and Paul Celan, conversation notes,
Wuppertal, between 11 October 1957 and 13 October 1957

[*Ingeborg Bachmann*]
When are you leaving?
And when are you coming back?

[*Paul Celan*]

———

I am going to Düsseldorf <u>today</u> around eight.

I am coming back tomorrow morning

I sometimes go on other occasions too.
I can think: you can often come back.

NOTES

MAN/ANL folder 10, p. 9: hw. *conversation notes on the back of the programme for the 11th conference of the Wuppertaler Bund from 11 October 1957 until 13 October 1957*: '*Literary Criticism—Critically Viewed*'.

Wuppertal: After four years without contact, it is unlikely that IB's and PC's simultaneous participation at the conference of the Wuppertaler Bund [Wuppertal Federation], originally founded in 1945/46 as the 'Gesellschaft für geistige Erneuerung' [Society for Intellectual Renewal], was agreed upon in advance. On 13 October 1957, PC and IB took part in a round-table discussion with Hans Magnus Enzensberger, Peter Huchel, Walter Jens and Hans Mayer (see MSS 176). Regarding a later conference, see NOS 135.1 and 142. An envelope deposited by PC at IB's hotel marked 'Fräulein Ingeborg Bachmann/Hotel Kaiserhof' (with the room number '308' added, presumably by a third party) has also survived (*MAN/ANL folder 1, p. 3*); its contents, however, could not be identified.

Düsseldorf: The reason for this trip is unknown.

45

Paul Celan to Ingeborg Bachmann, Paris, 17 October 1957 (?)

Read this, Ingeborg, read this:

For you, Ingeborg, for you—
'Weiss und Leicht'

Sicheldünen, ungezählt.

Im Windschatten, tausendfach: du.
Du und der Arm,

mit dem ich nackt zu dir hinwuchs,
Verlorne.

Die Strahlen. Sie wehn uns zuhauf.
Wir tragen den Schein, den Schmerz und den Namen.

Weiss,
was sich uns regt,
ohne Gewicht, was wir tauschen.
Weiss un Licht: Lass es wandern.
Die Fernen, mondnah, wie wir. Sie bauen.
Sie bauen die Klippe,
an der sich das Wandernde bricht,
sie sammeln
Lichtschaum und stäubende Welle.
Das Wandernde, klippenher winkend.
Die Stirnen winkt es heran,
die man uns lieh,
um der Spiegelung willen.

Die Stirnen.
Wir rollen mit ihnen dorthin.
Stirnengestade.

    Schläfst du jetzt?
Schlaf.
Meermühle geht,
eishell und ungehört,
in unseren Augen.

'White and Light'

Sickle dunes, uncounted.

In the slipstream, thousandfold: you.
You and the arm
with which I grew towards you naked,
lost one.

The rays. They blow us in droves.
We bear the glow, the pain and the name.

White
is what moves before us,
weightless is what we exchange.
White and light: let it roam.
The distant ones, close to the moon, like us. They build.
They build the cliff
on which that which roams breaks,
they gather
light-foam and spraying wave.

That which roams, beckoning from the cliffs.
It beckons
the brows
we were lent
for the sake of the reflection.

The brows.
We roll there with them.
Brow-shores.

    Are you asleep now?
Sleep.
Sea mill turns
ice-bright and unheard,
in our eyes.

Further poems enclosed: undedicated typescripts of 'Nacht', 'Stilleben mit Brief und Uhr', 'Ich komm' and 'Matière de Bretagne'.

NOTES

MAN/ANL ser. n. 25.202 a, p. 15: hw. reading request (front of an A3 sheet folded to A4); p. 16: hw. poem (= HKA 5.2.171/325 H³ᵃ); unpublished supplements: MAN/ANL ser. n. 25.202a, p. 17 ('Nacht' [Night], ts. w/a hw. correction dated '17.X.57', = HKA 5.2.211/325 H³ᵈ), p. 18 ('Stilleben mit Brief und Uhr' [Still Life with Letter and Clock], ts. w/hw. corrections, = HKA 5.2.96/325 H³ᵃ), p. 19 ('Ich komm' [I Come], ts., = HKA 5.2.194/325 H⁴ᵃ) and p. 20 ('Matière de Bretagne' [Matter of Britain], ts., = HKA 5.2.217/326 H¹ᵃ).

poems enclosed: Concerning further documents, see NO. 66n.

46

Paul Celan to Ingeborg Bachmann, Paris, 18 October 1957

'Rheinufer'
(Schuttkahn II)

Wasserstunder, der Schuttkahn
fährt uns zu Abend, wie haben,
wie er, keine Eile, ein totes
Warum steht am Heck

.   .   .   .

Geleichtert. Die Lunge, die Qualle
grüßt eine Glocke, ein brauner
Seelenfortsatz erreicht
Den helligkeitswunden Hauch.

'Rhine Bank'
(Rubble Boat II)

Water hour, the rubble boat
ferries us in the evening, we are,
like it, in no hurry, a dead
'why' stands at the stern.

.   .   .   .

Lightened. The lung, the jellyfish
greets a bell, a brown
soul extension reaches
the brightness-sore breath.

Paris, 18 October 1957.

NOTES

*MAN/ANL ser. n. 25.202 a, p. 14 and MAN/ANL folder 3, p. 5 (ass. envelope): hw. poem
(= HKA 5.2. 227 and 326) to: 'Fräulein Ingeborg Bachmann/ Pension Biederstein/ München
23/ Biedersteinerstrasse 21 a/ Allemagne', Paris 18 October 1957.*

Schuttkahn II: Second version or later variant of 'Schuttkahn' from *Sprachgitter* (6
October 1957, see NO. 66n).

47
Paul Celan to Ingeborg Bachmann; Paris, 20 October 1957

'Köln, Am Hof'

Herzzeit, es stehn
die Geträumten für
die Mitternachtsziffer.

Einiges sprach in die Stille, einiges schwieg,
einiges ging seiner Wege.
Verbannt und Verloren
waren daheim.

.   .   .   .   .   .

Ihr Dome.
Ihr Dome ungesehen,
ihr Wasser unbelauscht,
ihr Uhren tief in uns.

'Cologne, Am Hof'

Heart-time,
the dreamt ones stand for
the midnight numeral.

Some things spoke in the silence, some things were silent,
some things went their way.
Banished and Lost
were at home

.   .   .   .   .   .

You cathedrals.
You cathedrals unseen,
you waters unlistened to,
you clocks deep in us.

Paris, Quai Bourbon, Sunday 20 October 1957,
    2:30 p.m.—

NOTES

*MAN/ANL ser. n. 25.202 b, p. 8 and MAN/ANL folder 3, p. 6 (ass. envelope): hw. poem (=
    HKA 5.2. 231/326 H²) to: 'Mademoiselle Ingeborg Bachmann/Pension Biederstein/
    München/Biedersteinerstrasse 21 a/Allemagne', Paris, 20 October 1957.*

Köln, am Hof: After the conference in Wuppertal, PC met with IB on 14 October
1957 in Cologne, where he stayed at a hotel on the road *Am Hof*, located near the
cathedral and the banks of the Rhine. The road leads from the archbishop's
palace ('Hof' [Court]) to the square in front of the town hall; the area had been
assigned to the city's Jews in the Middle Ages. The street name became a sort of
code word between IB and PC (see NOS 68 and 118). Further document for the
poem in the IBE: ts., dated 'Paris, on 20 October 1957' (*MAN/ANL ser. n. 25.202
a, p. 10, = H1a*); see also NO. 66n.

Quai Bourbon: From the quay at the banks of the Ile Saint-Louis, one can view the Ile
de la Cité with Notre-Dame and the right bank of the Seine.

48
Paul Celan to Ingeborg Bachmann, Paris, 23 October 1957

23 October 1957.

I can understand, Ingeborg, that you are not writing to me, cannot write to me,
will not write to me: I realize I am not making it easy for you with my letters and
poems, even less than before.

Just tell me this: should I write to you and send you poems? Should I come
to Munich (or somewhere else) for a few days?

You must understand: I could not have acted <u>differently</u>. If I had acted differently, it would have meant denying you—I cannot do that.

Be calm, and do not smoke too much!

Paul

NOTES

*MAN/ANL folder 3, p. 7: hw. letter, envelope not identified (MAN/ANL folder 8, p. 2 or 3?:
p. 2 to: 'Mademoiselle Ingeborg Bachmann/Pension Biederstein/<u>München</u>/Biedersteiner-
strasse 21 a/<u>Allemagne</u>', on the back in unknown handwriting: 'Benjamino Joppolo/I
<u>Gobernanti</u>'; p. 3 to: 'Mademoiselle Ingeborg Bachmann/Pension Biederstein/<u>München</u>/Bie-
dersteinstr. 21 a/<u>Allemagne</u>', airmail; stamps torn off.*

Benjamino Joppolo: No work with the title *I Gobernanti* by the Italian anti-Fascist writer and dramatic adviser Beniamino (!) Joppolo could be identified.

letters: Since the resumption of the relationship in Wuppertal, PC seems not only to have sent poems. Accompanying letters may have been lost; at least one letter postmarked 16 October 1957 is certain from IB's reaction (see NO. 52) and the envelope (*MAN/ANL folder 3, p. 4*).

49
Paul Celan to Ingeborg Bachmann, Paris, 25 October 1957

25.X.57.

Today there is a postal strike, today there cannot be any letter from you.

In a French newspaper I see the maxim: 'Il est indigne des grands cœurs de répandre le trouble qu'ils ressentent.

And yet! Here:

———————

Two hours later:

One last thing, it must not go unsaid:

That line '. . . you know where it was pointing' must be completed thus: into life, Ingeborg, into life.

Why I <u>spoke</u> about all that: to take away the feeling of guilt that awoke in you when the world sank away from me. To take it away from you forever.

You should, you must write to me, Ingeborg.

NOTES

MAN/ANL folder 3, pp. 8–9: hw. airmail letter to: '[tw.] Mademoiselle Ingeborg Bachmann/ Pension Biederstein/<u>MÜNCHEN</u>/Biedersteinerstrasse 21 A/<u>ALLEMAGNE</u>', Paris, 25 October 1957.

25.X.57: PC's letter may have contained 'In die Ferne' [Into the Distance] as a supplement (ts. and hw., MAN/ANL ser. n. 25.202 c, pp. 10 and 11, HKA 5.2, 233 and 326, H^3 and H^4).

'*Il est* [. . .] *ressentent*': The source of the quotation—'It is unworthy of great hearts to spread the confusion they feel'—could not be identified. It is taken from 'Lucie, nouvelle épistolaire' by Clotilde de Vaux, published in 'Complément de la Dédidace' for her friend Auguste Comte's work *Système de politique* (*Œuvres* [Paris, 1969], VOL. 7, p. *xxviii*).

'. . . *you know where it was pointing*': Is PC quoting from a lost letter?

<u>*spoke*</u>: PC is presumably referring to a lost letter or telephone conversation in which he had given an account of an open conversation with GCL (see NO. 52).

50
Paul Celan to Ingeborg Bachmann, Paris, 26–27 October 1957

In Mundhöhe, fühlbar:
Finstergewächs.
(Brauchst es, Licht, nicht zu suchen, bleibst
das Schneegarn, hältst
deine Beute.
Beides gilt:
Berührt und Unberührt.
Beides spricht mit der Schuld von der Liebe,
beides will da sein und sterben.)

Blattnarben, Knoten, Gewimper.
Äugendes, tagfremd.
Schelfe, wahr und offen.

Lippe wusste. Lippe weiss.
Lippe schweigt es zu Ende.

At mouth level, palpable:
Dark-loving plant.

(you need not look for it, the light, you remain
the snow trap, you hold
your prey.

Both apply:
Touched and Untouched.
Both things speak of love with guilt,
both things want to exist and to die.)

Leaf scars, tubercles, cilia.
Things eyeing, alien to day.
Husk, true and open.

Lip knew. Lip knows.
Lip hushes it to an end.

26th–27th October 1957.

NOTES

MAN/ANL ser. n. 25.202 a, p. 7 and MAN/ANL folder 3, p. 10 (ass. envelope): tw. poem (= HKA 5.2 238/326 H⁴ᵃ) to: Mademoiselle Ingeborg Bachmann/Pension Biederstein/ MÜNCHEN/Biedersteinerstr. 21 A/ALLEMAGNE', Paris, 27 October 1957 (airmail rate).

In Mundhöhe: See NO. 66n.

51
Ingeborg Bachmann to Paul Celan, Munich, 28 October 1957

I WILL WRITE TODAY IT IS DIFFICULT FORGIVE ME

INGEBORG

NOTE

GLA D 90.1.2829/1: telegram to: 'Paul Celan, 29 bis rue de Montevideo Paris 16ᵉ', Munich, 28 October 1957, 11³⁸ and Paris, 28 October 1957, 12⁴⁰.

52

Ingeborg Bachmann to Paul Celan, Munich, 28–29 October 1957

Monday 28 October 1957
Munich

Paul,

your first letter arrived ten days ago. Since then I have meant to reply every day, but keep failing to because of my hours of desperate conversations with you.

What short cuts I will have to take in this letter! Will you understand me nonetheless? And as you read this, will you also imagine the moments in which I have only the poems to look at, or only your face, or Nous deux encore?!

I cannot ask anyone for advice, you know that.

I am grateful to you for telling your wife everything—'sparing' her would mean becoming even guiltier, and also belittling her. Because she is the way she is, and because you love her. But do you realize what her acceptance and her understanding mean for me? And for you? You must not leave her and your child. You will answer that it has already happened, that she is already abandoned. But please, do not leave her. Do I have to explain why?

If I have to think of her and the child—and I will always have to think of them—I will not be able to embrace you. That is all I know. The addition, you say, must be 'Into life'. That is true for the dreamt ones. But are we only the dreamt ones? And has there not always been an addition, and have we not already despaired at life, even now, when we think it is a matter of a step—a step out, a step over, a step together?

Tuesday: now I no longer know how to continue. I was awake until four in the morning trying to force myself to carry on writing, but I could not touch the letter anymore. Dearest Paul. If only you could come at the end of November! I wish for it. May I? We must see each other now.

Yesterday, in a letter to the Princess, I had to write a few words about you, 'warm' words, so as not to be evasive. I used to find that easier, in spite of everything, because I was so happy to be able to speak or write your name. Now I almost feel I must ask you for forgiveness if I do not keep your name to myself.

But we already know how we will fare among the others. Yet that will no longer restrict us.

When I came to Donaueschingen a week ago, I suddenly felt a desire to say everything, to <u>have to</u> say everything, as you had to in Paris. But you had to, and I was not even allowed to; I am free and lost in this freedom. Do you know what I mean by that? But that is simply one thought from a long chain of thoughts, a chain that binds me.

You told me you were forever reconciled with me, I will never forget that. Do I now have to worry that I will make you unhappy again, that I will bring destruction again, for her and you, and for you and me? I cannot comprehend being so damned.

Paul, I shall send the letter off in this state; I had longed to be much more precise.—

I meant to tell you in Cologne, to ask you if you could read my 'Lieder auf der Flucht' again; I was at my wits' end during that winter two years ago, and accepted my rejection. I no longer hoped to be acquitted. To what end?

Ingeborg

Tuesday evening:

This morning I wrote: we have to see each other now.

That is the imprecision I already felt, and which you must still forgive. For I cannot go back on what I said: you must not leave her and your child.

Tell me if you think it is irreconcilable with that for me to want to see you, and to tell you so.

NOTES

GLA D 90.1.2829/2: hw. airmail letter to: '[tw.] *M. Paul Celan/29 bis Rue de Montevideo/* P a r i s 1 6*ᵉ/France*', Munich, 29 October 1957.

ten days ago: Probably in the envelope postmarked 16 October 1957 (see NO. 48n).

Nous deux encore: Poem by Henri Michaux, see PC's translation 'Noch immer und wieder, wir beiden' [Still and Once Again, the Two of Us] (fair copy 17 December 1957). He had bought the book, published in 1948 in Paris, in August 1957. IB also owned a copy of this edition (LIB); as PC noted in May 1960, she placed it visibly in her library (PCPC).

your wife: Gisèle Celan-Lestrange.

your child: Claude François Eric.

'Into Life': See NO. 49.

the dreamt ones: See line 2 of 'Köln, Am Hof' (NO. 47).

Tuesday: 29 October 1957.

Princess: In early 1954, IB met Marguerite Caetani, Princess of Bassiano, editor of the international literary journal *Botteghe Oscure: An International Review of New Literature*, which she had founded in Rome in 1948. A poem by PC had appeared in 1956 in Issue 17 ('Vor einer Kerze' [Before a Candle], pp. 358f.). The journal first published poems by IB in 1954 in Issue 14 ('Lieder von einer Insel' [Songs from an Island], 'Nebelland' [Fog-Land], pp. 215–19), then in 1957 in Issue 19 ('Hôtel de la Paix', 'Nach dieser Sintflut' [After This Flood], 'Liebe: Dunkler Erdteil' [Love: the Dark Continent], 'Exil' [Exile], 'Mirjam', pp. 445–9). Regarding Issue 21, see NO. 58n.

Donaueschingen/to have to say everything: IB attended the premiere of Henze's *Nachstücke und Arien* on 20 October 1957 at the Donaueschinger Musiktage, having contributed to the work with her texts 'Aria I' and 'Aria II'. IB never told the composer about her relationship with PC.

'Lieder auf der Flucht': [Fugitive Songs] A poem (XII) from the final cycle of *Anrufung des Grossen Bären* [Invocation of the Great Bear]; in its form and content, it alludes to PC's poem 'Ins Nebelhorn' [Into the Foghorn] from October 1950.

53

Paul Celan to Ingeborg Bachmann, Paris, 31 October–1 November 1957

31 October 1957.

Today. The day with the letter.

Destruction, Ingeborg? No, certainly not. Rather: the truth. For this, here too, is surely the opposite principle: because it is the basic principle.

Passing over many things:

I will be coming to Munich in late November, around the 26th.

Returning to what was passed over:

I do not know what all this means, I do not know what I should call it—destiny perhaps, fate and calling; searching for names is pointless, I know <u>that</u> is how it is, forever.

It is the same for me as for you: being allowed to speak and write down your name without struggling with the shudder that comes over me—for me, in spite of everything, that is joy.

You also know: when I met you, you were both for me: the sensual <u>and</u> the spiritual. The two can never separate, Ingeborg.

Think of 'In Ägypten'. Every time I read it, I see you step into this poem: you are the reason for living, not least because you are, and will remain, the justification for my speaking. (And I suppose this is what I was referring to that time in Hamburg, without quite realizing how true my words were.)

But that alone, my speaking, is not even the point; I wanted to be silent with you too.

A different area in the dark:

Waiting: I considered that too. But would that not also mean waiting for life to accommodate us in some way?

Life is not going to accommodate <u>us</u>, Ingeborg; waiting for that would surely be the most unfitting way for us to be.

Be—yes, we can and are allowed to do so. To be—be there for another.

Even if it is only a few words, alla breve, one letter, once a month: the heart will know how to live.

(And yet—one concrete question that you must answer quickly: when are you going to Tübingen, and when to Düsseldorf? I have also been invited there.)

Do you know that I can speak (and write) again now?

Oh, there is still so much I have to tell you, some of them things that even you would barely suspect.

Write to me.

Paul

P. S. Strangely enough, I had to buy the *Frankfurter Zeitung* on the way to the national library. And stumble across the poem you had sent me together with *Die Gestundete Zeit*, written on a strip of paper, by hand. I had always interpreted it for myself, and now I found it greeting me again—in such a context!

I.X.57.

Forgive me, Ingeborg, forgive my stupid postscript of yesterday—perhaps I must never think or speak in such a way again.

Oh, I was so unjust towards you all these years, and the postscript was probably a relapse that was supposed to come to my aid in my helplessness.

Is 'Köln, Am Hof' not a beautiful poem? Höllerer, whom I recently gave it to print in *Akzente* (was I allowed to?), called it one of my most beautiful ones. Through you, Ingeborg, through you. Would it ever have happened if you had not spoken of the 'dreamt ones'? A single word from you—and I can live. And to think that I now have your voice in my ear again!

NOTES

MAN/ANL folder 3, pp, 11–14 (1st letter), folder 3, p. 3 (ass. continuation on a letter from '1.X. [instead of *XI*] *57') and folder 3, p. 15 (envelope): hw. partial letters to: 'Mademoiselle Ingeborg Bachmann/Pension Biederstein/<u>München</u>/Biedersteinerstrasse 21 A/<u>Allemagne</u>',*

Paris, 2 November 1957 (airmail rate).

26th: PC was in Munich from the 7th to the 9th during a visit to Germany (only actually 3–11 December 1957) (PCPC).

the sensual and the spiritual: the original phrase *das Geistige* connotes both intellectual and spiritual qualities. [Trans.]

'In Ägypten': See NO. 1.

Hamburg: After the conference in Niendorf (see NO. 32).

Tübingen [. . .] *Düsseldorf*: Concerning PC's reading in Tübingen, see NO. 56; on 5 May 1958, he read in Düsseldorf at the invitation of the city's Volkshochschule [Adult Education Centre].

Frankfurter Zeitung/*the poem*: A later letter (NO. 98) includes a piece of paper torn out of the *FAZ* with IB's 'Aria I' and 'Aria II', preceded by a brief reference to the premiere of Henze's *Nachtstücke und Arien* [Night Pieces and Arias] at the 1957 Donaueschinger Musiktage (31 October 1957); both poems are set in the piece. 'Aria I' is a version of 'Im Gewitter der Rosen', which was evidently included with NO. 42, extended by one stanza. See the version sent later (NO. 98).

'Köln, Am Hof': See NO. 47.

Höllerer [. . .] *Akzente*: PC gave the poem to the writer and literary scholar, whom he and IB had probably known since 1954, on 21 October 1957 for the bimonthly journal he edited (PCPC, see NO. 72).

'dreamt ones': Line 2 of 'Köln, Am Hof', see NO. 47.

54
Paul Celan to Ingeborg Bachmann, Paris, 2 November 1957

'Allerseelen'
2.XI.57.

Was hab ich getain?
Die Nacht besamt, als könnt es
noch andere geben, nächtiger als diese.

Vogelflug, Steinflug, tausend
beschriebene Bahnen. Blicke,
geraubt und gepflückt. Das Meer,
gekostet, vertrunken, verträumt. Eine Stunde,
seelenverfinstert. Die nächste, ein Herbstlicht,
dargebracht einem blinden
Gefühl, das des Wegs kam. Andere, viele,
ortlos und schwer aus sich selbst: erblickt und umgangen.
Findlinge, Sterne, schwarz und voll Sprache: benannt
nach gebrochenem Schwur.

Und einmal (wann? auch dies ist vergessen):
den Widerhaken gefühlt,
wo der Puls den Gegentakt wagte.

'All Souls' Day'

What did I do?
Inseminated the night, as if there
might still be others, nightlier than
this one.

Bird's flight, stone's flight, a thousand
traced paths. Gazes,
robbed and picked. The sea,
tasted, drunk away, dreamt away. An hour,
soul-darkened. The next one, an autumn light,
offered to a blind
feeling that came along the way. Others, many,
placeless and heavy from within themselves: espied and evaded.
Foundling rocks, stars, black and full of language: named
after a broken oath.

And once (when? this too is forgotten):

felt the barb
where the pulse ventured the offbeat.

NOTES

MAN/ANL ser. n. 25.202 a, p. 8 and folder 8, p. 1 (ass. envelope): hw. poem (= HKA 5.2, 253/327 H³) to: '*Mademoiselle Ingeborg Bachmann/Pension Biederstein/<u>München</u>/ Biedersteinerstrasse 21 A/<u>Allemagne</u>*', Paris, 3 [*November*] 19[*57*].

<u>*Allerseelen*</u>: This title replaced the crossed-out title '<u>Bericht</u>' [Report]. A further document for the poem is located in the IBE: cpy, dated 'Paris, on 2 November 1957' (*MAN/ANL ser. n. 25.202 a, p. 9 = HKA H²ᵃ*); see also NO. 66n.

foundling rocks: The original word *Findling*, which normally simply means 'foundling', is also a geological term referring to a glacial erratic, a piece of rock differing in size and type from the rock of its immediate environment, having been brought there by glacial movements. As the geological term in English lacks the ambiguity of the German, but it is known from PC's reading notes (where he wrote down the definition) that he specifically intended this meaning (see the commentary on this poem in Paul Celan, *Die Gedichte* [The Poems], Barbara Wiedemann ed. [Frankfurt: Suhrkamp, 2003], p. 660), the non-existent but comprehensible phrase 'foundling rock' has been chosen as a compromise. [Trans.]

55
Paul Celan to Ingeborg Bachmann, Paris, 5 November 1957

As Lines so Loves oblique may well
Themselves in every Angle greet:
But ours so truly Parallel,
Though infinite can never meet.

Therefore the Love which us doth bind,
But Fate so enviously debars,

on 5 November 1957.

Is the Conjunction of the Mind,
And Opposition of the Stars.
/Andrew Marvell, The Definition
of Love p. 77./

A brief message, Ingeborg, that might pre-empt your reply: today I received a letter from Tübingen suggesting the first week of December, which I will accept. The journey will then probably pass through Frankfurt, where I plan to collect my fee from Fischer for a small translation I am currently working on, and I can be in Munich on the 29th or the 30th. I can stay for a few days, three or four—tell me if you still want me to.

Gisèle knows that I plan to visit you, she is so brave!

I will not leave, no.

And if you do not want me to visit you from time to time, I will also try to comply with that. But you must promise me one thing: to write to me, send me news, once a month.

I sent you three books yesterday, for the new apartment. (It is so unjust that I have so many books and you have so few.) I do not know the stories of Rabbi Nachman at all, but it was a real book, it had to belong to you; and in any case, I love Buber.

Did you already know the English anthology? I may already have had it when you were in Paris—I lost it later on, at any rate. Then, in the train, the one separating, I opened an English anthology I had been given in Wuppertal and re-read a poem I used to love very much: 'To His Coy Mistress'. I then tried to translate it in the first days after my return; it was difficult, but in the end it was there, except for a few lines I still need to straighten out—then you will receive it. Read the other poems by Marvell too, he is probably the greatest next to Donne. And the others too, they all deserve it.

I have made a change to the All Souls' Day poem; it now reads:

Findlinge, Sterne, schwarz und voll Sprache: benannt
nach <u>zerschwiegenem</u> Schwur.

Foundling rocks, stars, black and full of language: named
after an oath <u>silenced to pieces</u>.

NOTES

MAN/ANL folder 3, pp. 16–17: hw. airmail letter to: 'Mademoiselle Ingeborg Bachmann/

Pension Biederstein/Münchenl Biedersteinerstrasse 21 A/Allemagne, Paris, 6 *November 1957* [*see Figure 13*].

Marvell: PC quotes the two final stanzas from the anthology *Metaphysical Lyrics and Poems of The Seventeenth Century: Donne to Butler* (Herbert J. C. Grierson comp. and ed. [Oxford: Oxford University Press, 1956], pp. 77–8; LPC). On p. 74 are translation attempts for Marvell's 'To His Coy Mistress'. A newspaper clipping with an article by E. E. Duncan-Jones—'The Date of Marvell's "To His Coy Mistress"'— (*Times Literary Supplement*) is also enclosed.

December: Changed from 'January'.

a small translation: PC's translation *Notizen zur Malerei der Gegenwart* [Notes on Contemporary Painting] of a short essay by the French abstract painter Jean Bazaine (Paris, 1953), was only published in 1959 (Frankfurt: S. Fischer).

Gisèle [. . .] *brave*: Concerning the trip, see NO. 53. GCL's 'bravery' is demonstrated by her diary entries from January 1958 (PC/GCL II, 92/3; see NO. 216).

three books: The third book gift could not be identified.

Buber: *Die Geschichten des Rabbi Nachman. Ihm nacherzählt von Martin Buber* [The Tales of Rabbi Nachmann, Retold by Martin Buber] (sixth edition; Frankfurt: Rütten & Loening, 1922, LIB and LPC). PC was a passionate reader of the philosopher and storyteller; he had a copy of *Mohn und Gedächtnis* sent to him as early as 1954, and met him in person on 14 September 1960.

English anthology: *The Oxford Book of English Verse 1250–1918*, Sir Arthur Quiller-Couch ed. (Oxford: Clarendon Press, 1939), with a date of purchase in unknown handwriting ('London Feb 1951'; LIB). PC did not have a copy of his own; he borrowed it for a time from his friend, the English teacher Guy Flandre (reading traces from PC).

anthology/in Wuppertal: PC may already have received the anthology *Gedichte von Shakespeare bis Ezra Pound* [Poems from Shakespeare to Ezra Pound], Hans Hennecke ed. (Wiesbaden: Limes, 1955), in which he also made translation sketches for the poem named in the following (p. 82, LPC), during his first stay in Wuppertal in 1955.

'To His Coy Mistress'/Donne: PC later gave IB a fair copy of his translation 'An seine stumme Geliebte' (5 January 1958, *MAN/ANL ser. n. 25.202 c, p. 1r/v-2*), as well as hw. translation sketches (17–30 October 1957; *25.202 c, pp. 3–8*). It was only in 1968 that PC translated John Donne's 'The Curse' (as 'Der Fluch').

56

Paul Celan to Ingeborg Bachmann, Paris 7 November 1957

on 7 November 1957.

May I send you two translations, completed a few days ago, at the request of my Wuppertal hostess (Frau Klee-Pályi), who is editing a French anthology for Limes?

It is not much, I know, but your eyes will rest on them for a few moments.

Yesterday, as we are to move house in a few days, I had to rummage about among all sorts of old documents. In doing so, I stumbled on a pocket calendar from 1950. Under 14 October I had written: Ingeborg. It was the day you came to Paris. On 14 October 1957 we were in Cologne, Ingeborg.

You clocks deep in us.

Paul

I have arranged the reading in Tübingen for 6 December, so I can visit you beforehand or afterwards—please, you decide.

Enclosed: *translations of Antonin Artaud, 'Prayer' and Gérard de Nerval, 'The Cydalises'.*

NOTES

MAN/ANL folder 3, p. 18: *hw. letter*; *MAN/ANL ser. n. 25.202 b, pp. 6–7 (unpublished supplements)*: *ts., each with the note 'Translated by Paul Celan'; envelope not identified (see NO. 48).*

two translations [. . .] anthology: The two translations enclosed appeared in the volume *Anthologie der französischen Dichtung von Nerval bis zur Gegenwart* [Anthology of French Poetry from Nerval to the Present], Flora Klee-Pályi ed. (Wiesbaden: Limes, 1958), pp. 17 and 277), as did PC's translations of 'Epitaph' and 'The Last Poem' by Robert Desnos (pp. 318–21). The Hungarian-Jewish graphic artist and translator Flora Klee-Pályi, a survivor of the concentration camp in Theresienstadt, had lived in Wuppertal since 1927. PC stayed with her (at Boltenbergstrasse 10) during the conference of the Wuppertaler Bund in October 1957 (see NO. 44). Working primarily for the dissemination of modern French and German poetry, she had been in contact with PC in this capacity since 1949.

You clocks deep in us: Final line of 'Köln, Am Hof' (see NO. 47).

Tübingen: PC read in the university's old hall [*Alte Aula*] for the bookshop Buchhandlung Osiander.

57

Ingeborg Bachmann to Paul Celan, Munich, 7 November 1957

Thursday

This week is too dire, and I almost fear that I shall not finish my letter before it is over. I am completely exhausted from work, Paul, forgive me, I truly am. I am trembling with weakness, but it will be better at the start of the next week! I cannot write a letter to you in ten minutes!

Thank you for everything—you know.

Ingeborg

I will still be at this guesthouse until 1.XII after all.

NOTES

GLA D 90.1.2829/3: *hw. letter to*: '[*tw.*] *M. Paul Celan/29 bis, Rue de Montevideo/P a r i s 16ᵉ/France*', Munich, 8 November 1957.

This week is too dire: In September 1957, IB's meanwhile financially unsustainable situation as a freelance writer forced her to take a permanent position as dramatic adviser at the Bayerisches Fernsehen in Munich, a department of the Bayerischer Rundfunk; she saw it as 'forced labour' (letter to Hermann Kesten, 3 September 1957, Literaturarchiv Monacensia, Munich). In addition, she was under pressure to finish *Der gute Gott von Manhattan* [The Good God of Manhattan] by the deadline.

this guesthouse: Pension Biederstein, Biedersteiner Strasse 21a. The move to the apartment in Franz-Joseph-Strasse 9a, also in Schwabing and planned for 1 December 1957, was delayed until the 16th.

58

Paul Celan to Ingeborg Bachmann, Paris, 9 November 1957

29bis rue de Montevideo

from 20.XI.: <u>78 rue de Longchamp, Paris 16^e</u>

on 9 November 1957.

Ingeborg, dear!

A letter, today too—I cannot help it, even though I tell myself that I am only causing confusion, that I am addressing things you may prefer to remain unmentioned. Forgive me.

The day before yesterday I went to see the Princess, and we immediately spoke about you (as we did during my first visit); it made me glad that I was allowed to speak your name with a free heart—the Princess kept referring to 'Ingeborg', and finally I said it too: Ingeborg.

If I understood her correctly, you have written a 'play' ('une pièce'): could I read it, can you send it to me?

And then, in my impetuousness, I did something that may have gone far beyond what I should have done: the Princess spoke of the German contributions for the spring issue of *B.O.*, and I had the idea (not entirely without premeditation, I must confess) of suggesting that the two of us, you and I, select the texts. That was rather brazen, forgive me—you can, after all, make the selection by yourself, as you presumably have in the past, so what do you need me for? Do not be angry, Ingeborg, what burst out of me so abruptly was simply this desire to come to you, which suddenly (or not so suddenly) sensed a chance, in something unchallengeable, and did not want to be robbed of this chance, at least <u>this</u> chance.

The Princess agreed—I had taken her by surprise, after all—but the choice is yours: if you do not want it to happen, we can put everything back into balance.

Botteghe Oscure: that promises a little darkness and security—could we not join hands here and exchange a few words?

Tomorrow you will be moving into your new apartment: could I come soon and help you find a lamp?

Paul

NOTES

MAN/ANL folder 3, pp. 19–20 and folder 3, p. 1 (ass. envelope): hw. airmail letter to: 'Mademoiselle Ingeborg Bachmann/ <u>München 13</u>/ ~~Franz-Josephstr. 9 A~~/ <u>Allemagne</u>/ [in unknown handwriting: z. Zt. Fremdenheim/ Biederstein/ Biedersteinerstr. 21. A.]'; Paris, [xx.xx.] 1957 [see Figure 15].

<u>78 rue de Longchamp, Paris 16^e</u>. The first apartment bought by PC and GCL.

first visit: Date unknown (contrary to PC/B.O., p. 14).

German contributions [. . .] *select the texts/darkness and security*: The German portion of Issue 21 (1958, LPC: a number of printing errors corrected) was, though it is not stated there, indeed put together by IB and PC (except for 'Fragmente' by Rezzori, pp. 379ff., provided by Moras but, likewise, proofread by PC). There were six further authors and one translator: Georg Heym with the poem 'Der Tod des Schauspielers' [The Actor's Death] (p. 370), Nelly Sachs with eight poems ('Siehe Daniel' [Behold Daniel], 'Schon schmeckt die Zunge Sand im Brot' [The Tongue Already Tastes Sand in the Bread], 'Und du riefst und riefst' [And You Called and Called], 'Das Kind' [The Child], 'Kein Wort birgt den magischen Kuss' [No Words Holds the Magic Kiss], 'Staubkörner rede ich' [I Speak Grains of Dust], 'Röchelnde Umwege' [Gasping Detours], 'Ach dass man so wenig begreift' [Oh, Why Does One Understand So Little]; pp. 371ff.), Arthur Rimbaud with 'Das trunkene Schiff' [The Drunken Boat], German translation by Paul Celan (pp. 375ff., see NO. 99), Walter Höllerer with six poems ('Vogel Roc' [Roc Bird], 'Bein und Eisen' [Leg and Iron], 'Eiben' [Yew Trees], 'Für eine flüchtige Freundin' [For a Fugitive (Female) Friend], 'Antlitz, geflochten' [Countenance, Woven], 'Gläsern' [Made of Glass]; pp. 408ff.), Günter Grass with 'Der Kuckuck' [The Cuckoo] (Act II of *Onkel, Onkel* [Uncle, Uncle]; pp. 413ff.) and Hans Magnus Enzensberger with six poems ('Gespräch der Substances' [Conversation of the Substances], 'Die grossen Erfindungen' [The Great Inventions], 'Memorandum', 'Plädoyer für einen Mörder' [Plea for a Murderer], 'Das Ende der Eulen' [The End of Owls], 'Trennung' [Separation]; pp. 435ff.). The title of the journal (literally meaning 'dark shops' or 'dark deals') cites the address of the publisher's office in Rome, the Palazzo Caetani in the Via Botteghe Oscure 32.

59

Ingeborg Bachmann to Paul Celan, Munich, 14 November 1957

Munich, 14 November 1957

Paul, I am not in the new apartment yet—I still have to wait until 1 December. The landlady called yesterday and said there was already a letter for me there, the first one from 'Montevideo'. It came just now, and it was from you; all that could be read on the Paris postmark was the clear word Montevideo.

There are so many letters I should answer, and thank you for, as well as the splendid books, and I shall do so by replying to your letter of today right away, all right!?

(Nonetheless: I am glad whenever you come—whether to Tübingen in late November or early December!) I will be staying in Munich without interruption until shortly before Christmas. I cannot go away, for I have too much work and my new work is still too new.

The pièce to which the Princess referred is the English translation of *Die Zikaden*. But perhaps you know that radio play.

It will be very good if you help her; I always hesitate to make such decisions, but this time, in the spring, she did not have anyone to help her, and I wanted to get Klaus involved with *B.O.* and also mention a few good names. Aside from all that, I have the sincerest admiration for the Princess, which you will understand when you know her better. I am only glad that you intend to advise her.

'Allerseelen' is a wonderful poem. And 'Köln, am Hof'. . . you must write to me when you must. I have not yet told you that I sometimes feared for your poems during the last two or three years; now I have no more fear. We shall speak to each other of many other things in three weeks—I am too helpless alone.

I sometimes speak to you in Paris as if you were alone there, and I often fall silent when I admit that you exist along with everything there, and that I exist along with everything here. But then we shall have clarity and no more confusion—and go in search of the lamp!

Ingeborg

NOTES

GLA D 90.1.2829/4: *hw. airmail letter to*: '*M. Paul Celan/29 bis, Rue de Montevideo/ PARIS 16ᵉ/FRANCE, Munich, 15 November 1957.*

'*Montevideo*': Rue de Montevideo, PC's address in Paris until the end of November 1957.

splendid books: See NO. 55.

Tübingen: See NO. 56.

Die Zikaden: IB had already finished the work [The Cicadas] during the winter of 1954/55 in Naples (first broadcast: 5 March 1955, NWDR). BBC3 broadcast an English version on 30 July and 1 August 1957.

Klaus [. . .] *B.O.*: Issue 19 (1957) included Demus' poems 'Meerstern' [Sea Star], 'Vorüber zieht am Himmel' [Passing in the Sky] and 'Gipfelkalmen' [Calm Moments on the Mountain Peak(s)] (pp. 455–9).

60
Paul Celan to Ingeborg Bachmann, Paris, 16 November 1957

Paris, on 16 November 1957.

Today another letter came from you: many thanks.

A request: could you already write to the Princess now and tell her that you are prepared to help her, together with me, to select the German texts? And please also tell her to send a few copies of *B.O.* to H. M. Enzensberger (STRANDA, Norway). (I have already asked her, but she may have forgotten it in the meantime.)

Should I ask Walter Jens for a small prose piece for *B.O.*? And perhaps you could tell me which other people you have in mind. We can discuss everything else in Munich. As you are letting me decide, I shall go there <u>after</u> the reading in Tübingen, i.e. on 7 or 8 December.

I am moving house on Monday; when you write to me, please use the new address:

78 rue de Longchamp, Paris 16^e
(Tel.: Poincaré 39-63)

Lamp-searchingly

Paul

NOTES

MAN/ANL folder 3, pp. 21–2: hw. letter to: '*Mademoiselle Ingeborg Bachmann/Pension Biederstein/München/Biedersteinerstrasse 21 A/Allemagne*', Paris, 16 November 1957.

Enzensberger: PC explained the request by pointing out that the German poet, living in Norway at the time, could make the journal known through radio broadcasts in Germany (18 October 1957, PCE). PC had met him in April 1955 in Paris; the friendship between Enzensberger and IB only became closer towards the end of the 1950s.

Jens: PC and IB had first met the Tübingen-based writer and philologist in Niendorf in 1952 (see NO. 32.1), then again in Wuppertal.

61
Ingeborg Bachmann to Paul Celan, Munich, 16 November 1957

Paul, dear,

I wrote that you can come any time. But now I must ask you after all not to come in November.

Please come after Tübingen, i.e. after 4 December. I will be freer then.

It is Saturday evening, I am barely getting out of the house and am trying to finish one piece of work after another, but it is all going so slowly. I went to the English Garden for a quarter of an hour to get some air; there are small lakes there that remind me of the city park in Vienna and the bridge where we stood together, spellbound.

Ingeborg

NOTES

GLA D 90.1.2829/5: *hw. letter to*: '*M. Paul Celan/78, rue de Longchamp/PARIS 16ᵉ/ FRANCE*', *Munich, 18 November 1957*.

after Tübingen: After PC's reading (see NO. 56).

Saturday: 16 November 1957.

city park in Vienna: See NO. 4.

62
Ingeborg Bachmann to Paul Celan, Munich, 22 November 1957

Thursday

It was seven years ago that we last celebrated your birthday together. Foolish and forlorn.

But now I shall sit beside you for a while and give your eyes kisses.

I was going to send you something in Paris, but then I felt that I cannot possibly send you anything <u>there</u>. You would have to conceal it or cause pain once more.

I have your present ready for you here, and you can look for it when you visit me. (Our last letters crossed—to think that this is possible again, or even for the first time!) I am thinking of you, Paul, and you think of me!

Ingeborg

NOTES

GLA D 90.1.2829/6: *hw. express letter to*: '*M. Paul Celan/78, rue de Longchamp/PARIS 16ᵉ/FRANCE*', *Munich, 22 November 1957 and Paris, 23 November 1957*.

seven years ago: They celebrated PC's 30th birthday together, on 23 November 1950, shortly before IB left Paris.

there: The resumption of the love affair between IB and PC in September 1957 put a great strain on his marriage with GCL; hence, IB did not want to send a present to their home at rue de Longchamp.

63
Paul Celan to Ingeborg Bachmann, Paris, 23 November 1957

on 23 November 1957.

Just one line, to thank you, with all my heart, for everything.

To think that we had to hound our hearts to death in the past over such trifles, Ingeborg! Whom were we obeying, tell me, whom?

But now I am coming soon, not for long; for one day, for another—if you want and allow me to.

Let us then go in search of the lamp, Ingeborg, you and I, us.

Paul

NOTE

MAN/ANL folder 3, pp. 23–4: hw. letter to: 'Mademoiselle Ingeborg Bachmann/Pension Biederstein/München/Biedersteinerstrasse 21 A/Allemagne', postage stamp removed.

64
Ingeborg Bachmann to Paul Celan, Munich, 2 December 1957

2 December

When are you coming, dear Paul? Send me a telegram from Tübingen so that I can pick you up. (To Franz Josephstrasse 9a, Munich 13)

Only a few more days now . . .

Ingeborg

NOTES

GLA D 90.1.2829/7: hw. letter to: 'M. Paul Celan/78, Rue de Longchamp/PARIS 16²/FRANCE', Munich, 4 December 1957.

Tübingen: See NO. 56.

Franz Josephstrasse 9a: See NO. 57n.

65
Paul Celan to Ingeborg Bachmann, Stuttgart, 5 December 1957

Thursday

The day after tomorrow, <u>Saturday</u>, I will be in Munich—visiting you, Ingeborg.

Could you come to the station? My train will arrive in Munich at <u>12.07</u>. If you cannot come, I will be pacing up and down outside your house in the Franz-Josephstr. half an hour later.

Tomorrow I shall be in Tübingen (address: Hotel Lamm or Osiander Bookshop).

Two more days, Ingeborg.

Paul

NOTES

MAN/ANL folder 1, p. 11 and folder 3, p. 25 (ass. envelope): hw. express letter to: 'Fräulein/Ingeborg Bachmann/<u>München</u>/~~Franz-Josephstr. 9-A~~ [replaced in unknown handwriting by: Pension Biederstein/Biedersteiner Str. 21a]', Stuttgart, 5 December 1957; '[on the back in unknown handwriting] Empf. Bachmann Franz-Josephstr. 9a/noch nicht eingezogen zur Zeit [not yet moved in]/Pension Biederstein', Munich, 5 December 1957.

Stuttgart: PC was visiting his friends Hanne and Hermann Lenz (Birkenwaldstrasse 203).

66
Paul Celan to Ingeborg Bachmann: dedication for a group of 21 poems from Sprachgitter, *Munich (?), between 7 and 9 December 1957 (?)*

For Ingeborg

NOTE

MAN/ANL ser. n. 25.170 N 8000: hw. dedication on a double page as a cover for N 8001–8030 with ts. of 'Zuversicht' [Confidence] (HKA 5.2., 90 H²ᵉ), 'Stilleben mit Brief und Uhr' (96 H²ᵃ), 'Unter ein Bild von Vincent van Gogh' [Under a Picture by/of Vincent van Gogh] (108 H²ᵐ), 'Heimkehr' [Homecoming] (112 H²ᵃ), 'Heute und morgen' [Today and Tomorrow] (127 H²ᵐ), 'Schliere' [Streak] (139 H²ᶜ), 'Unten' [Below] (119 H³ᵃ), 'Stimmen' [Voices] (67 H⁹ᵃ), 'Sprachgitter' [Speech Grille] (188 H¹ᶜ), 'Tenebrae' [149 H²ᵉ), 'Blume' [Flower] (156 H³ᵃ), 'Weiss und Leicht' [White and Light] (171 H²ᵃ), 'Schneebett' [Snow Bed] (also cpy, 194 H²ᵃ/=ᶜ), 'Matière de Bretagne' (217 H²ᵃ), 'Windgerecht' [Fit for the Wind] (201 H¹ᶜ), 'Nacht' (also cpy, 212 H¹ᵃ/=ᶜ), 'Schuttkahn' [Rubble Boat] (225 H¹ᶠ), 'Köln, Am Hof' (231 H¹ᶠ), 'In die Ferne' (also cpy, 233 H²ᵃ/=ᶜ), 'In Mundhöhe' [At Mouth Level] (also cpy, 238 H³ᵃ/=ᶜ) and 'Allerseelen' [All Souls' Day] (also cpy, 253 H¹ᵉ/ᶠ), preceded by a list of these titles dated to 2 December 1957 (46f.); the bundle of papers was presumably handed over in Munich.

67

Paul Celan to Ingeborg Bachmann, dedications for 23 poems
in Mohn und Gedächtnis, *Munich (?), between 7 and 9 December 1957 (?)*

f. y.

above the poems 'Nachts ist dein Leib' [At Night Your Body], 'Erinnerung an Frankreich' [Memory of France], 'Nachtstrahl' [Night Ray], 'Die Jahre von dir zu mir', 'Lob der Ferne' [In Praise of Distance], 'Das ganze Leben' [The Whole of Life], 'Corona', 'Auf Reisen' [On Travels], 'In Ägypten', 'Brandmal' [Brand], 'Wer sein Herz', 'Kristall', 'Nachts, wenn das Pendel', 'So schlafe . . .', 'So bist du denn geworden' [And So You Have Become], 'Die feste Burg' [The Mighty Fortress], 'Der Tauben weisseste' [The Whitest of Doves], 'Aus Herzen und Hirnen', 'Landschaft', 'Stille!', 'Wasser und Feuer' and 'Zähle die Mandeln'.

& f. y.

above the poem 'Sie kämmt ihr Haar'.

NOTES

GLA D 95.12.1: hw. dedications (each in top left corner) on pp. 8, 24, 27–30, 33, 43–4, 48–50, 55–9, 68, 72–4 [76], as well as 70 in Mohn und Gedächtnis *(second edition; Stuttgart: Deutsche Verlags-Anstalt, 1954).*

'*Mohn und Gedächtnis*': The volume was given to the GLA by Christine Koschel. Regarding the copy of the first edition, see NO. 37.

f. y.: For you [originally f. D., *für Dich*].

68

Ingeborg Bachmann to Paul Celan, dedication in
Die Gestundete Zeit, *Munich* (?), *between 7 and 9 December 1957* (?)

Munich, Am Hof
      Ingeborg

NOTES

GLA LPC: *hw. dedication on the back of the flyleaf of* Die Gestundete Zeit. Gedichte, *second edition* (*Munich: Piper, 1957*). *The book was presumably handed over in Munich.*

Munich, Am Hof: Though this refers to the title of 'Köln, am Hof', an actual address, it does not appear to be an address itself. It has been left untranslated, however in order to retain the reference. [Trans.]

Reading traces: p. 9 ('Abschied von England'), ellipses at bottom (the final line in the first edition, 'Alles bleibt unbesagt' [Everything remains unmentioned], is missing); p. 12 ('Paris'), line in margin beside line 9f., underlining in line 14 ('fliehende' [fleeing]); p. 32 (blank), note by PC with ellipses: 'Beweis zu nichts' (the poem from the first edition is missing); p. 37 (second part of 'Psalm', exclamation mark and double line in the margin beside the first stanza, which only deviates from the first edition in this edition ('Da alles eitel ist:—vertrau dir nicht mehr/und übernimm kein Amt./Verstelle dich nicht mehr,/um der Blossstellung zu entgehen' [As all is vanity:—have no more faith in yourself/and take on no duty./Do not simulate/to avoid being exposed]. Inserted: between pp. 30 and 31 a newspaper clipping with 11 of IB's translations of poems by Giuseppe Ungaretti, some deviating from the book edition (see NO. 188): 'Universum' [Universe], 'Sich gleich' [Equal to Itself], 'Eine andere Nacht' [A Different Night], 'Einsamkeit' [Solitude], 'Trennung', 'San Martino del Carso', 'Zerknirscht' [Remorseful], 'Brüder' [Brothers], 'Wache' [Keep Watch], 'In Memoriam', 'Schlafen' [Sleep] (*NZZ*, 3 December 1960). Concerning the copy of the first edition, see NO. 42.

69

Paul Celan to Ingeborg Bachmann, Frankfurt am Main, 9 December 1957

Frankfurt, Monday night

Ingeborg, my dear Ingeborg—

I cast another look out of the train, you had looked around too, but I was too far away.

Then it came and choked me, so wildly.

And then, when I went back to the compartment, something very strange happened. It was so strange that I entrusted myself to it, for a very long stretch of the journey—I shall describe it to you here as it came to me—but you must already forgive me for acting in so uncontrolled a fashion.

So, I was back in my compartment and took your poems out of my briefcase. I felt I was drowning in something completely transparent and bright.

When I looked up, I saw the young woman who had the window seat take out a copy of *Akzente*, the last issue, and start leafing through it. She leafed and leafed, and my eyes could follow her leafing, because they knew that your poems and your name would come. Then they came, and the hand that had been leafing paused. And I saw that there was no more leafing, that her eyes were reading, again and again. Again and again. I was so grateful. Then I thought for a moment that it could be someone who had heard you read, who had seen you and recognized you.

And then I wanted to know. And asked. And said that it had been you, before.

And invited the lady, a young writer who had sent a manuscript to *Desch* in Munich, who also, she told me, wrote poems, to have a coffee with me. Then I heard how much she admired you.

I hardly said anything careless, Ingeborg, but I think she had already guessed; it was an experience for her.

Then I gave her my two volumes of poetry and asked her to read them only after I had left the train.

She was a young woman, maybe thirty-five; I suppose she knows now, but I do not think she will tell people. I really do not think so. Do not be angry with me, Ingeborg. Please do not be angry.

It was so strange, it was so completely out of our world—the person to whom I owe the experience will have known who was sitting in front of her. Say something about it, one word—please!

Now I also think you could send this woman your greetings, here is her address:

> Margot Hindorf
> Cologne-Lindenthal
> Dürener Str. 62

Send me a line in Paris, I will be there on Wednesday.

In Frankfurt, it was eight o'clock, I immediately called Frau Kaschnitz—no one answered. I shall try it again tomorrow morning.

I have to see you again, Ingeborg, for I love you.

Paul

I am staying with Christoph Schwerin here: our books are standing side by side.

NOTES

MAN/ANL folder 2, pp. 8–10: hw. letter, envelope missing.

Frankfurt, Monday night: Coming from Munich, PC arrived in Frankfurt on 9 December 1957. Between then and 11 December, he met with representatives of the publishers S. Fischer, Insel and Suhrkamp (PCPC), one of the issues being the publication of translations of Char's 'Hypnos' in the journal *Die Neue Rundschau*.

your poems: Presumably the new copy of *Die gestundete Zeit*.

Akzente: IB's four poems 'Nach dieser Sintflut', 'Hôtel de la Paix', 'Exil' and 'Liebe: Dunkler Erdteil' had just appeared in Issue 6 (pp. 491–5), which also featured contributions from Hilde Domin, Gert Kalow, Heinz Piontek and Wolfdietrich Schnurre. Both IB and PC had published in the 'journal for poetry', founded by Walter Höllerer and Hans Bender, since its first year (1954).

volumes of poetry: *Mohn und Gedächtnis* and *Von Schwelle zu Schwelle* [From Threshold to Threshold].

Hindorf: No publications were found under this name. In her only letter to PC, she thanks him for his New Year's greetings, expresses her admiration for his poems and continues: 'And only now do I know that I not only love Ingeborg Bachmann, but was also able to grasp her essence. These were great gifts; they let me forget my loneliness and filled my soul with a joyous sound.' (Cologne, 26 December 1957, PCE)

Kaschnitz: PC met the German writer Marie Luise Kaschnitz near Paris in 1948; in 1949, she arranged the first publication of his poems in Germany, which later led him to ask her to hold the eulogy at the Büchner Prize ceremony. IB had maintained a strong friendship with her since her first visit to Rome; in her poetics lecture 'Über Gedichte' [On Poems], IB referred to Kaschnitz's anti-war poem 'Bräutigam Froschkönig' [Bridegroom Frog Prince] (IBW 4, 206–08).

Schwerin: The son of the officer Ulrich-Wilhelm, Count of Schwerin, who had taken part in the attempt to assassinate Hitler on 20 July 1944, was working as an editor at S. Fischer Verlag at the time. PC had made his acquaintance in the summer of 1954 in connection with a publication of Char's poems. The volumes he saw in Schwerin's Frankfurt apartment at Raimundstrasse 21 were almost certainly IB's *Die gestundete Zeit* and *Anrufung des Grossen Bären*, as well as PC's *Mohn und Gedächtnis* and *Von Schwelle zu Schwelle*.

70
Ingeborg Bachmann to Paul Celan, Munich, 11 December 1957

Wednesday

Paul, dear,

here in the hotel I only have this crumpled-up paper, everything else is in the Franz Josephstrasse with the candlestick. This afternoon I picked up your letter there. That story is a strange and beautiful one; now it belongs to us. Why should I be angry? But I will not write to the woman, forgive me—I cannot add anything of worth. (And I find it difficult to write to others.)

In the evening, Monday evening, I went to Piper with the black penny in my hand, and everything went well; I was also able to move to a hotel at once—I will be staying here (it is called Blaues Haus) until Friday morning.

The telephone was changed today; the number, which will stay the same, is: 337519. You can cross out the other one.

Every day is now full of echoes. But you must not neglect Gisèle because of me. Not out of duty, but out of liberation. Whom will we have to thank for everything?

Ingeborg

NOTES

GLA D 90.1.2829/8: hw. letter to: '*M. Paul Celan/78, Rue de Longchamp/PARIS 16ème/ FRANCE*', Munich, 12 December 1957 [*see Figure 14*].

candlestick: See line 9 of PC's 'Ein Tag und noch einer' [One Day and Another] (NO. 73).

this woman: Margot Hindorf.

Piper: IB's Munich publisher since *Anrufung des Grossen Bären* (1956).

Blaues Haus: IB stayed at this hotel (Hildegardstrasse 1), rich in tradition, because, for unknown reasons, she could not move into the new apartment in the Franz-Joseph-Strasse (see NO. 57n).

71
Paul Celan to Ingeborg Bachmann, Paris, 12 December 1957

PLEASE DO NOT GIVE MORAS POEMS YET SEE YOU SOON

PAUL

NOTES

MAN/ANL folder 3, p. 26: telegram to: '*Ingeborg Bachmann, Franzjosephstr 9a Muenchen*', Paris, 12 December 1957, 12⁴⁹ and Munich, 12 December 1957.

Moras: The publicist and translator, co-founder and co-editor of *Merkur*, had also, since 1954, been on the editorial staff of the yearbook *Jahresring*, published by PC's publisher on behalf of the Bundesverband der Deutschen Industrie [Federal Association of German Industry]. PC himself sent him 'Stimmen' for *Jahresring* shortly before Christmas 1957 (VOL. 58–9, pp. 198f., there also IB's *Der gute Gott von Manhattan* on pp. 91–138). PC and IB had together met Moras in Munich (PCE).

72

Paul Celan to Ingeborg Bachmann, Paris, 12 December 1957

Paris, Thursday

I visited Frau Kaschnitz the day before yesterday; I gave her your letter and your roses, they were red, dark, there were seven of them. And the same number, the same kind, from me. She placed them together.

Tell me if we should meet again in Cologne after Bremen (26 January), for longer.

I just sent you a telegram asking you to hold on to the poems that were meant for Moras for a while: Höllerer, who will be printing the Cologne poem in the next issue of *Akzente*, wanted a few more; I promised him some, and I want it to be the finest, I shall tell you tomorrow which ones.

As Huchel has not got in touch, I will write to him that I am giving everything away; then there will be enough for Moras too.

At Suhrkamp, where everyone was very friendly, I met Hans Hennecke. I had to tell him that I had come from Munich, he wanted to know if I had seen you, I said yes. Then I also had to give him your address.

A letter came from Enzensberger: the Princess has still not sent him the copies of *B.O.* she had promised.

Should we tell him to send poems already for this issue? I will certainly ask Nelly Sachs to contribute.

Ingeborg, Ingeborg.

I am so full of you.

And know, finally, what your poems are like.

Say something about the events in the train to Frankfurt.

NOTES

MAN/ANL folder 1, pp. 6–7, folder 1, pp. 4–5 (ass. continuation, from 'Ingeborg, Ingeborg') and folder 3, p. 27 (ass. envelope): 2 hw. letter parts to: 'Fräulein/Ingeborg Bachmann/<u>München</u>/Franz-Joseph Str. <u>9a</u>/<u>Allemagne</u>', Paris, 12 December 1957.

roses [. . .] *seven*: See the second stanza of PC's 'Kristall'.

Bremen: PC would have informed IB through the telephone about receiving the Bremen Literature Prize. PC only stayed with IB in Munich for three days (28–30 January 1958, PCPC).

Akzente: The poems sent to Höllerer on 12 December 1957—'Schneebett', 'Windgerecht', 'Matière de Bretagne', 'Nacht', 'Allerseelen' and 'In Mundhöhe' as well as 'Köln, Am Hof' (see NO. 53)—appeared in the February 1958 issue (Issue 1, pp. 18–24, LPC).

Huchel: PC had given the German poet the poems 'Schneebett', 'Windgerecht', 'Matière de Bretagne' and 'Nacht' for his East Berlin journal *Sinn und Form* [Sense and Form] during the conference in Wuppertal (NO. 44). Because PC heard from others that the publication date was yet to be fixed, he informed Huchel on 12 December 1957 that he had decided to publish the poems in *Akzente* instead.

Hennecke: PC met the German publicist and translator on 10 December 1957 (PCPC).

copies [. . .] *promised*: See NO. 60.

Sachs: The German-Jewish poet, born in Berlin, had lived in Stockholm since 1940; her involvement with *Botteghe Oscure* gave PC occasion to resume their correspondence from 1954.

73

Paul Celan to Ingeborg Bachmann, Paris, 13 December 1957

Paris, 13.XII.57

'Ein Tag und noch einer'

Föhniges Du. Die Stille
ging mit uns mit wie ein zweites,
deutliches Leben.

Ich gewann, ich verlor, wir glaubten
an düstere Wunder, der Ast,
gross an den Himmel geschrieben, trug uns, wuchs
in die Mondbahn, ein Morgen
stieg ins Gestern hinauf, wir holten
den Leuchter, ich weinte
in deine Hand.

'One Day and Another'

Foehn-windy you. The silence
went along with us like a second,
clear life.
I gained, I lost, we believed
in ominous miracles, the branch,
writ large upon the sky, bore us, grew
into the moon's orbit, a tomorrow
ascended into yesterday, we fetched
the candlestick, I cried
into your hand.

NOTES

MAN/ANL ser. n. 25.202 b, p. 4: hw. poem (=HKA 5.2 235/326 H⁵), envelope missing.

One Day and Another: See 'for one day, for another' in NO. 63. Further documents of the poem in the IBE: a ts. dated 'Paris, on 13 December 1957'. (*MAN/ANL ser. n. 25.202 b, p. 5 = HKA H⁴ᵃ*) and an undated ts. (*MAN/ANL ser. n. 25.202 b, p. 11 = HKA H²*).

74
Ingeborg Bachmann to Paul Celan, Munich, 16 December 1957

Monday evening

Paul, your roses were there when I moved in, so now almost nothing is missing—just the ink for this letter. Then the money came, and I really am very glad about it because of Christmas and the start here. Thank you!

The poem just came; you wrote it on the 13th, on Friday, the day I moved in with the candlestick (for I still had to wait that long).

I am tired and happy in the apartment, have to work a great deal, but it no longer irks me.

Ingeborg

P. S.

I shall write to the editors of *B.O.* about Enzensberger tomorrow; the Princess cannot do anything herself, and I would not burden her with it. Include Enzensberger if there is still room, but I think there is already too much.

I am going home on Wednesday morning.

NOTES

GLA D 90.1.2829/9: hw. letter to: 'M. Paul Celan/78, Rue de Longchamp/ PARIS 16ème/ FRANCE', Munich, [1]7 December 195[7], from '[. . .] Klagenfurt, Henselstr. 26, Österreich'.

when I moved in: Into the apartment at Franz-Joseph-Str. 9a.

the money: The dedicated copy of *Die gestundete Zeit* originally contained the receipt for a postal order for 400 DM, sent on 11 December 1957 from Frankfurt (see NO. 42n BK III) on p. 46.

the poem: 'Ein Tag und noch einer'.

75

Paul Celan to Ingeborg Bachmann, dedication in offprint with translations of poems by Apollinaire, Paris, Christmas 1957

For Ingeborg, Christmas 1957

Paul

NOTE

LIB: *hw. dedication (p. 5) in offprint with PC's translations of three poems by Guillaume Apollinaire ('Salome', 'Schinderhannes', 'Der Abschied'* [The Farewell]), *from* Die Neue Rundschau, *2 (1954), pp. 1–5 [pagination in book, pp. 316–21], envelope missing.*

76

Ingeborg Bachmann to Paul Celan, Munich, 27 December 1957

Munich 27.XII.1957

You shall at least have a letter before the year is out! The books arrived exactly on the 24th and were placed under the tree. They are so lovely!

Today I bought a nice candle for the candlestick. I had to return quickly from Klagenfurt because of some work. Forgive me that I am only writing this. I have to work a great deal in the next few days.

I received a surprise call from Vienna (!)—they want me to read there in two weeks. I have agreed, but will travel there fearfully, just for 1 or 2 days. I wish I could undo it. Please accompany me in your thoughts so that the ugliness there cannot touch me! Our time there is my only protection.

But how are you living at the moment? Let me know.

Ingeborg

NOTES

GLA D 90.1.2829/10: *hw. letter to*: '*M. Paul Celan/78, Rue de Longchamp/<u>PARIS 16ème</u>/ FRANCE*', *Munich, 28 December 1957.*

The books: The only known gift is the offprint of Apollinaire poems dedicated to IB.

because of some work: Probably in connection with her work for Bavarian television.

Vienna: The invitation to the reading on 11 January 1958 at the Kleines Theatre in the Josefstadt district.

77

Ingeborg Bachmann to Paul Celan, Munich, 1 January 1958

Dear Paul,

I have just written to Günter Eich and H. Heissenbüttel for *B.O.*, as the Princess wrote to me today that she needs the manuscripts by 15.I. (If you have already done so too, it does not matter.) But please: to whom else?!

It is so cold here. And all the work has been piling up at once these last few days.

Ingeborg

Do you want to ask Holthusen, or shall I? Do not forget Jens, possibly Grass.

NOTES

GLA D 90.1.2837/1: *hw. letter to*: '[*tw.*] *M. Paul Celan/78, Rue de Longchamp/<u>PARIS 16e</u>/FRANCE*', *Munich, 1 January 1958.*

Eich: PC and IB made the German poet's acquaintance in Niendorf in 1952. IB was close friends with Eich and his wife Ilse Aichinger until 1962.

Heissenbüttel: IB knew the publishing reader, radio editor and author of experimental texts from Gruppe 47 conferences.

the Princess wrote to me today: Part of Caetani's letter (in English) reads: 'We have not received any manuscripts yet and as I wrote Celan we would like everything by Jan. 15 at latest—' (undated, IBE).

Holthusen: The poet and influential critic had recommended IB for the study trip to Harvard in the summer of 1955; he only commented publicly on her poems some time after that ('Kämpfender Sprachgeist. Zur Lyrik Ingeborg Bachmanns' [Fighting Language Spirit: The Poetry of Ingeborg Bachmann], in *Merkur*, June 1958, pp. 563–84). PC learned of Holthusen's SS membership through Hanne Lenz; he rightly judged his review of *Mohn und Gedächtnis* as influenced by Claire Goll's accusations of plagiarism ('Fünf junge Lyriker II', *Merkur*, May 1954, pp. 378–90; see NO. 89n).

Grass: IB first met the writer, painter and illustrator at the Gruppe 47 conference in Berlin in May 1955; he illustrated her Büchner Prize speech *Ein Ort für Zufälle* [A Place for Coincidences] ([Berlin: Wagenbach, 1965] = quarto book 6; LPC with note from PC on flyleaf: 'from Klaus Wagenbach/5.3.65' and reading traces on p. 52). IB and Henze participated in his electoral initiative for Willy Brandt in 1965. PC first met Grass during the latter's Paris years (1956–59); he supported Grass during his work on *Die Blechtrommel* [The Tin Drum], and Grass subsequently supported him in the context of the Goll affair.

78
Paul Celan to Ingeborg Bachmann, Paris, 2 January 1958

2.1.58.

Ingeborg, dearest, what can I say?

You are going to Vienna, my heart will accompany you, do not worry—go to Nani and Klaus. (You can call Klaus at Belvedere—Austrian Gallery:

72-64-21 or

72-43-58)

When are you going to Berlin, when to Hamburg, Kiel, etc.? Please tell me, I have to know. On the 26th I am going to Bremen, that will probably take a few days— shall we meet in Cologne on the way back, if you are also up there?

Come, Ingeborg.

Paul

Did the little calendar and the two notebooks arrive?

Botteghe Oscure:

Günter Eich and Holthusen have not sent the Princess anything yet—can you ask them for contributions, or shall I? You must answer this question immediately, as the Princess wants the texts by 15 January.

So far I have only received contributions from Nelly Sachs, Höllerer, Enzensberger. No reply from K. L. Schneider (Heym estate) or Heissenbüttel. I will write to both of them again.

Can you think of anyone else?

Shall I send you copies of the contributions received—at what address?

Please answer quickly.

NOTES

MAN/ANL folder 4, pp. 1–2: hw. letter, envelope not identified (possibly MAN/ANL folder 8, p. 4 to: 'Mademoiselle/Ingeborg Bachmann/München 13/Franz-Josephstrasse 9a/ Allemagne', airmail.

to Vienna: See NO. 76.

Austrian Gallery: Demus was working as an art historian at the Austrian Gallery of nineteenth- and twentieth-century art, located at Schloss Belvedere, Vienna.

Berlin [. . .] Hamburg, Kiel: Reading trip; the individual dates could not be ascertained.

Sachs, Höllerer, Enzensberger: Höllerer sent his contribution on 19, Sachs on 21 and Enzensberger on 26 December 1957 (PCE).

K. L. Schneider (Heym estate): The Hamburg Germanist, active in the resistance against the Nazis in his student days, was preparing an edition of Heym's works (estate in the Hamburg State Library). IB and PC first met Schneider in Wuppertal (see NO. 44).

79

Paul Celan to Ingeborg Bachmann, Paris, 3 January 1958

on 3 January 1957.

Just a few lines, Ingeborg, to answer your *Botteghe* letter—or, rather, to augment the answers in the letter I wrote you yesterday.

Last night the 'highlight' or our German section arrived: an unpublished poem by Georg Heym, Der Schauspieler.

So far the following have sent contributions:

Nelly Sachs
Höllerer
Enzensberger

Are you giving the Princess any poems? I will probably contribute 'Das Trunkene Schiff', but I am not especially pleased to be appearing in a selection partly being made by me.

Following your suggestion, I have written to Jens./I had already asked him for some short prose in Tübingen, but he did not have any; today I asked him for a fragment of his as yet unfinished drama (of whose existence I learned this morning)./

I wrote to Grass a few days ago, and to Heissenbüttel for the second time yesterday. No answer yet.

I could, if you consider it a good idea, write to Schroers, who would proba-bly have something. I would even be quite glad to do so.

Please send me a quick response!

Yours

Paul

So you will tell Günter Eich and Holthusen to send something—is that all right? It would be best to send a copy to me for the corrections.

NOTES

MAN/ANL folder 3, p. 2: hw. letter, envelope not identified (see NO. 78). The letter was accompanied by the poems 'Aber' [But] and 'Entwurf einer Landschaft' [Sketch of a Landscape] (see NO. 80).

'*Das Trunkene Schiff*': PC's German translation of Arthur Rimbaud's poem 'Le Bateau ivre' [The Drunken Boat]. [Trans.]

<u>*Jens*</u>: Jens sent a first evasive reply on 7 January 1958 (PCE); the text could not be identified.

<u>*Grass*</u>: On 30 December 1957 (PCE).

Schroers: PC and IB had first met the writer, publicist and publishing reader in Niendorf in 1952. As a reader at Deutsche Verlags-Anstalt, he contributed to the publication of *Mohn und Gedächtnis*.

80
Ingeborg Bachmann to Paul Celan, Munich, 6 January 1958

6.1.58.

My dear,

now we are suddenly having to exchange letters about other people's manuscripts. But I am taking it with good humour—since we started writing to each other again, I am content with anything.

I wrote to Eich, he has <u>nothing</u>. Holthusen probably has nothing either, but he will call me. I have not had any response from Heissenbüttel yet either. Do not forget Jens, and possibly Grass. That will probably be enough.* I will also speak to Klaus in Vienna on 11 January—perhaps one could publish something of his too. What do you think? Please write to me about it at his address in Vienna, for I already have to leave here on Friday, and will be reading on Sunday afternoon at 5; I am telling you so precisely because I so want you to think of me, and take away my fear.

The posthumous Heym poem would naturally be very important.

Please do <u>not</u> send me any copies; I am in agreement with everything, and we have already decided on the names in any case.

I will now also write to Martin Walser, whose work I value, and it would be good to have a little more prose.

I am already looking forward to the calendar, but it has not arrived yet.

I am saving up my thanks for your poems because they do not fit into this letter, which must be sent off quickly!

Ingeborg

*with Sachs, Enzensberger, Höllerer.

NOTES

GLA D 90.1.2837/2: hw. *express letter to*: '*M. Paul Celan/78, Rue de Longchamp/<u>PARIS 16ème/FRANCE</u>*', *Munich, 7 January 1958 and Paris, 8 January 1958.*

write [. . .] *Vienna*: Not found.

reading [. . .] *at 5*: See NO. 76.

Walser: PC and IB knew the German novelist from the conference in Niendorf. PC later wrote about him: 'Walser is one of Germany's best pen-pushers and, along with Enzensberger, is one of the mainstays of Suhrkamp Verlag' (27 May 1966, PC/GCL 445).

calendar: Not found.

poems: The IBE contains two poems written shortly beforehand that were sent either with NO. 79 or separately (folding marks): 'Aber' (31 December 1957, ts.: *MAN/ANL ser. n. 25.202 b, p. 12 = HKA 5.2, 245, H⁴ᵃ*) and 'Entwurf einer Landschaft' or 'Landschaft' (3 January 1958, cpy and hw. draft: *MAN/ANL ser. n. 25.202 c, p. 9* and *MAN/ANL ser. n. 25.202 a, p. 12 = HKA 5.2, 257, H¹ᵇ and H⁴*).

81
Paul Celan to Ingeborg Bachmann, Paris, 7 January 1958

'Eine Hand'

Der Tisch, aus Stundenholz, mit
dem Reisgericht und dem Wein.
Es wird
gegessen, geschwiegen, getrunken.

Eine Hand, die ich küsste,
leuchtet den Mündern.

'A Hand'

The table, made of hour-wood, with
the rice dish and the wine.
There is
eating, silence, drinking.

A hand I kissed
gives light for the mouths.

———

Paris, on 7 January 1958.

NOTE

MAN/ANL ser. n. 25.202 b, pp. 9–10: hw. poem on an envelope (= HKA 5.2. 244/327 H²ª)
to: 'Mademoiselle Ingeborg Bachmann/<u>München 13</u>/Franz-Josephstrasse 9<u>a</u>/<u>Allemagne</u>',
Paris, 7 January 1958 (envelopes identical).

82

Ingeborg Bachmann to Paul Celan, 8 January 1958

Dear,

another letter of yours just arrived. And it occurred to me that I could still send express letters to ask Ernst Schnabel and Walser. I have just done so, for we will not have any prose otherwise. I am not so sure about Schroers, for pragmatic reasons—there are a few others who should have their turn first. But if you already want to have him this time nonetheless . . .

I do not have any poems, but perhaps some prose; that is still uncertain, however, for I have so much to do at the moment that I do not know whether I am coming or going.

<u>You</u> absolutely must give the Princess something, for you are not the editor but the one who was asked before all the others; collecting the other contributions is simply a friendly favour to her. So I think your reservations are quite unjustified.

I shall write to Eugene Walter now and tell him roughly what to expect.

After the 15th we can write normal letters again, thank God.

Ingeborg

NOTES

GLA D 90.1.2837/3: tw. letter w/hw. corrections and additions to: '[tw.] M. Paul Celan/78, Rue de Longchamp/<u>Paris 16ème</u>/France', Munich, 8 January 1958.

But if [. . .] *this time* [. . .] *After* [. . .] *thank God*: All added by hand.

<u>You</u> *absolutely must* [. . .] *before all the others*: Concerning PC's involvement, see NO. 58n.

Walter: The American journalist, writer and translator was editor of *Botteghe Oscure*.

83

Paul Celan to Ingeborg Bachmann, Paris, 11 January 1958

Saturday

You are reading now

I am thinking of your voice.

NOTES

MAN/ANL folder 1, p. 12 and folder 4, p. 5 (ass. envelope): hw. letter to: 'Fräulein Ingeborg Bachmann/ Münch‌en 13/ Franz-Josephstrasse 9a/ Allemagne', Paris, 11 January 1958.

You are reading now: See NO. 76.

84

Ingeborg Bachmann to Paul Celan, Vienna, 13 January 1958

Monday, 13.I.58.

Paul,

a page from Vienna. Everything was so strange here that one can barely describe it. Worse than expected, yet better than can be expected.

Nani and Klaus are happy about us, and have proved the finest and most sincere friends to me—in all those problematic hours. Before I leave, let me wave to you. Be good to me!

Ingeborg

NOTES

GLA D 90.1.2830/1: hw. letter to: 'M. Paul Celan/78, Rue de Longchamp/ Paris 16ème/France', Vienna, 14 January 1958.

Vienna: See NO. 76.

85

Ingeborg Bachmann to Paul Celan, Munich, 18 January 1958

Saturday
18—1—58

The Proust arrived. How lovely!! (But how you are spoiling me!)

That evening when you called again, I kept thinking how you had asked me: should I come? You do not know what it means to me to be asked like that. I suddenly had to cry, simply because this exists for me and I never had it before.

I wish you a good journey, be happy and do not let any of the petty things that are always there lessen your joy. I will give some more thought to the location and write to you in Bremen. This time I will protect you!

Ingeborg

NOTES

GLA D 90.1.2830/2: hw. letter to: M. Paul Celan/78, Rue de Longchamp/*PARIS*/France', *Munich, 19 January 1958* [*see Figure 17*].

The Proust arrived: The three-volume edition in the LIB does not contain any dedication: *A la recherche du temps perdu*, Pierre Clarac and André Ferré comp. and ed. (Paris: Bibliothèque de la Pléiade, 1954).

called: 14 January 1958, both calls noted (PCPC).

Bremen: Regarding the prize ceremony, see NO. 72.

86

Paul Celan to Ingeborg Bachmann, Paris, 21 January 1958

Tuesday

I am leaving the day after tomorrow, Ingeborg, then staying in Cologne until Saturday morning—I plan to call you on Friday around ten o'clock in the morning.

I will definitely send you a telegram from Bremen (or Hamburg) when I am finished with everything.

Would it not be simplest if I came to Munich?

Forgive my haste (and the ugly paper)

Paul

Think about whether we should perhaps meet somewhere in the middle. That could be Würzburg, Frankfurt, Heidelberg, etc. Or Freiburg im Breisgau, Basel, Strasbourg.

But I could also come to Munich, with one of the fast trains.

I do not know my address in Bremen; evidently the guesthouse of the senate (or something like that)

NOTES

MAN/ANL folder 4, pp. 11–12: *hw. airmail letter to*: '*Mademoiselle Ingeborg Bachmann/ München 13/Franz-Josephstrasse 9a/Allemagne*', *Paris, 21 January 1958*.

Cologne/Hamburg: PC was in Germany from 23 until 30 January 1958. In Cologne, he met his friends Heinrich Böll and Paul Schallück on 24 January 1958 (PCPC). Concerning the prize ceremony in Bremen, see NO. 72; regarding the stay in Hamburg, see NO. 88.

ugly paper: A sheet from a lined pad.

Munich: See NO. 72n.

87

Ingeborg Bachmann to Paul Celan, Munich, 26 January 1958

I AM THINKING OF YOU

INGEBORG

GLA D 90.1.2830/3: telegram to: '*Paul Celan, Gaestehaus des Senats Bremen*', *Munich, 26 January 1958, 14^{19} and* [*Bremen*] *26 January 1958, 14^{23}*.

26 January 1958: IB had received the Bremen Literature Prize the same day. PC presumably gave IB the text of his Bremen speech in Munich (*cpy, MAN/ANL ser. n. 25.202 b, pp. 2–3*).

88
Paul Celan to Ingeborg Bachmann, Hamburg, 27 January 1958

TOMORROW TEN-THIRTY-THREE

PAUL

NOTE

MAN/ANL folder 4, p. 6: telegram to: '*Ingeborg Bachmann, Franzjosephstr. 91 Muenchen/13*', *Hamburg, 27 January 1958, 18^{12} and* [*Munich*] *27 January 1958, 18^{56}*.

89
Ingeborg Bachmann to Paul Celan, Munich, 2 February 1958

Sunday evening

Paul,

the work that had been such an ordeal and a burden for me is finished. And now you shall have your letter right away before my eyes fall shut.

Regarding the latest Goll accident: I implore you, let this business die in your heart, then I believe it will also die outside. It often seems to me as if persecutions can only harm us for as long as we are prepared to let ourselves be persecuted.

The truth lets you rise above it, and so you can wipe it away from above.

I am to receive 'Facile'? It truly turned out to be simple and easy, and I did not have to think for a moment that I was afraid. After Cologne I was very much afraid. Now I am not.

My final worry concerns not us but, rather, Gisèle and you, and that you might not find the way to her beautiful, heavy heart. But you will see once more, and be able to dispel the darkness for her too. This is the last time I shall speak of the matter, and you do not have to reply.

After you left, I enjoyed working for the first time in a while—even the monotonous task of typing out text for hours was a joy to me, and I am as eager as anything.

Is that not good too? Now I shall soon be off to Tübingen. On your trail.

Ingeborg

NOTES

GLA D 90.1.2830/4: hw. letter to: 'M. Paul CELAN/78, Rue de Longchamp/PARIS 16ème/FRANCE', Munich, 3 February 1958.

work: Der gute Gott von Manhattan.

Goll accident: In his eulogy, Erhart Kästner had mentioned Yvan and Claire Goll as relevant influences on PC's work. Contary to Kästner's promise, this passage was not changed for the partial publication of the speech in the *FAZ* of 31 January 1958. Since 1953, Claire Goll had accused PC of plagiarizing the last works of her late husband Yvan Goll in *Mohn und Gedächtnis*; in fact, the similarities with PC's early works came about afterwards through the editing of Goll's poems— some of them only fragmentary—by his widow, who was in possession of *Der Sand aus den Urnen*. In addition, she used PC's unpublished translations of three French-language volumes of Goll's poems for her own translations (see NO. 179).

'Facile': This enigmatic word (Fr. and It. 'easy') also appears in the second chapter of *Malina* (IBW 3, 195). PC had translated the poem 'Nous avons fait la nuit' [We have Made the Night] (see NO. 93) from Paul Éluard's volume *Facile* (first edition, with erotic photographs by Man Ray [Paris: Editions GLM, 1935]). No copy exists in the LIB.

Cologne: See NO. 47n.

Tübingen. On your trail: As part of a reading trip, IB read at the Buchhandlung Osiander in Tübingen on 4 February 1958 in the same series as PC (see NO. 56).

90

Paul Celan to Ingeborg Bachmann, Paris, 8 February 1958

8.2.58.

May—the reading in Düsseldorf—is a long way off, I am not sure I can wait so long; I shall try to write my way through all that time.

Strange, this time I translated something from Russian, I think it is the poem of the Revolution, here it is (forgive me, I sent the original to Fischer Verlag, you are only getting a copy)—tell me, if you can, whether you like it, I pull out a few peculiar stops in it . . .

The second, translated yesterday, is a poem by Yesenin, one of his most beautiful.

Did you receive 'Facile'? Tell me.

I would be very happy if you could send me a copy of the radio play!

You know, Ingeborg, you know.

Paul

Enclosed: translations of Alexander Block, 'Die Zwölf' [The Twelve] and Sergei Yesenin, 'In meiner Heimat leb ich nicht mehr gern' [I No Longer Enjoy Living in My Homeland].

NOTES

MAN/ANL folder 4, p. 7: hw. letter; unpublished supplements: MAN/ANL ser. n. 25.171 N 8034–8054, cpy (Block) and 25.171 N 8055, dated 7 February 1958 in top right corner, ts. w/hw. corrections (Yesenin), envelope missing.

Düsseldorf: Date unclear.

the *poem of the Revolution*: PC translated Block's cycle of poems *The Twelve* in a few days (2–4 February 1958, PCPC).

Yesenin: PC collected his Yesenin translations in the selection *Gedichte* [Poems] (Frankfurt: S. Fischer, 1961); there is no dedicated copy in the LIB.

radio play: *Der gute Gott von Manhattan* was written in the summer and autumn of 1957 (first broadcast on 29 May 1958).

91
Paul Celan to Ingeborg Bachmann, Paris, 12 February 1958

12.2.58.

A request, Ingeborg:

send Gisèle your two volumes of poetry—I told her you would.

Paul

NOTES

MAN/ANL folder 4, p. 8: *hw. letter, envelope not identified (see NO. 78).*

volumes of poetry: *Die gestundete Zeit* and *Anrufung des Grossen Bären* (see NO. 217).

92
Ingeborg Bachmann to Paul Celan, Munich, 17 February 1958

17 February 1958

Paul, I am scarcely able to write, to answer. So much work, so much weariness and exhaustion. I will send the books today or tomorrow!

The translation of 'The Twelve' was a great surprise; I mean, it is very good—and daring, but very good because of that! One can only love the Yesenin poem. But when I read the final line, I involuntarily thought 'fall' again instead of 'roll'. Fall strikes me as better and, especially when repeated, more urgent.

After Tübingen and Würzburg—both places were very welcoming—I caught the flu, and now the foehn wind has been blowing for a few days, great warmth and madness in the air. I am dejected, but only because of that.

Ingeborg

NOTES

GLA D 90.1.2830/5: *hw. letter to*: '*M. Paul Celan/78, Rue de Longchamp/PARIS 16ème/FRANCE*', Munich, 17 February 1958.

books: *Die gestundete Zeit* and *Anrufung des Grossen Bären*.

'*The Twelve*': See supplement with NO. 90.

Yesenin poem: 'I No Longer Enjoy Living in My Homeland' (see supplement with NO. 90).

Tübingen and Würzburg: Stops on the reading trip (see NO. 89n.); in Würzburg, IB read at the Dante-Gesellschaft on 3 February 1958.

93
Paul Celan to Ingeborg Bachmann, Paris, 27 February 1958

27.2.1958

Paul Eluard

Nous avons fait la nuit

Die Nacht ist begangen, ich halte deine Hand,
ich wache, ich stütz dich
mit all meine Kräften.
Ich grabe, tiefes Gefurch, deiner Kräfte
Stern in den Stein: deines Körpers
Gütigsein—hier

soll es keimen und aufgehn.
Ich sage mir deine
Stimmen vor, beide, die heimliche und
die von allen gehörte.
Ich lache, ich seh dich
der Stolzen begegnen, als bettelte sie, ich seh dich, du bringst
den Umnachteten Ehrfurcht entgegen, du gehst
zu den Einfachen hin—du badest.
Leise
stimm ich die Stirn jetzt ab auf die deine, stimm sie
in eins mit der Nacht, fühl jetzt
das Wunder dahinter: du wirst mir
zur Unbekannt-Fremden, du gleichst mir, du gleichst
allem Geliebten, du bist
anders von Mal zu Mal.

The night is spent, I hold your hand,
I wake, I support you
with all my powers.
I dig, deep furrows, the star of your powers
into the stone: the benevolence
of your body—may it
sprout and blossom here.
I speak your
voices, both of them, the secret one
and the one heard by all.
I laugh, I see you
meeting the proud one as if she were begging, I see you, you show
awe before the deranged, you go
to the simple—you bathe.
Quietly
I now match my brow with yours, match it
in oneness with the night, I now feel
the miracle behind it: you become

an unknown stranger, you resemble yourself, you resemble
all that is loved, you are
different every time.

NOTES

MAN/ANL ser. n. 25.202 b, p. 13 and MAN/ANL folder 4, p. 9 (ass. envelope): hw. poem
translation (= published text, GW IV 812–813, first edition 'Insel-Almanach' 1959, p. 32),
to: 'Mademoiselle Ingeborg Bachmann/ <u>München 13</u>/ Franz-Josephstrasse 9<u>a</u>/ <u>Allemagne</u>',
Paris, 4 March 1958.

27.2.1958/Paul Eluard: The date corresponds to that of the fair copy; the translation
from *Facile* (see NO. 89) was published by 24 December 1957. PC had already
translated poems by the French-Jewish surrealist poet in Bucharest, but this is the
only one he published.

94

Ingeborg Bachmann to Paul Celan, Munich, 4 March 1958

Paul, I did not go to Berlin. I fell ill directly after we spoke (flu, middle ear infection)—and now things are finally a little better. The climate here does not agree
with me at all. At the end of the week I can step out into the open again. And I
am only going to Berlin on the 19th. I just wanted to tell you finally, but do not
worry!

Write how you have been. Just whether everything is going well, whether you
are working, my dear.

Ingeborg
Tuesday, 4 March 1958

NOTES

GLA D 90.1.2830/6: hw. letter to: 'M. Paul Celan/ 78, Rue de Longchamp/ <u>PARIS 16ème</u>/
FRANCE', Munich, 5 March 1958.

Berlin: Concerning the reading trip, see NO. 78. IB made up for the cancelled reading on her next Berlin visit (see NO. 96), when she went to accept the award of the Berlin senate on Henze's behalf.

95
Paul Celan to Ingeborg Bachmann, Paris, 14 March 1958

HOW ARE YOU THE RADIO PLAY IS SO BEAUTIFUL AND TRUE YOU KNOW IT YES THE BRIGHT AND THE BRIGHTEST INGEBORG I THINK OF YOU ALWAYS

PAUL

NOTES

MAN/ANL folder 4, p. 10: telegram to: '*Ingeborg Bachmann, Franz-Josephstr. 9a München 13*', *Paris, 14 March 1958, 11^{05} and [Munich], 14 March 1958, 11^{41}.*

RADIO PLAY: The duplicate of *Der gute Gott von Manhattan* requested in NO. 90 was not found; see, however, the dedicated copy of the print, NO. 108.

96
Ingeborg Bachmann to Paul Celan, Munich,
after 23 March 1958 and on 3 April 1958

Late March

Paul,

I will not write a great deal here, in this letter. I have been completely empty since Berlin, completely worn out from running to this office and that, for there is a stamp missing in my passport and I am supposed to leave, to be 'expelled' in April. But today the radio 'stepped in', and perhaps everything will turn out all right. These terms and this world! Still, the shock was so great that I do not feel like staying here much longer, and I will probably turn down the position at the radio too. I cannot do it, I have found that out during these last few days, though I do not know yet how things will continue. I cannot.

And on top of that—and above all—my dejection over the political developments in Germany.

3 April: everything should turn out all right with the papers after all.

I am going away for a week now, over Easter, and looking forward to fresh air and the countryside.

My dear, now the sun is even shining, and it will soon be May. We should look forward to that. I often say to myself out loud that are you thinking of me. You must also say to yourself out loud that I am thinking of you.

Ingeborg

NOTES

GLA D 90.1.2830/7: *hw. letter to*: '*M. Paul Celan/78, Rue de Longchamp/PARIS 16ème/FRANCE*', *Munich, 3 April 1958*.

since Berlin: IB probably returned to Munich from Berlin on 23 March 1958 (IBE).

stamp/papers: Formalities to extend her expired visitor's visa for West Germany (IBE).

radio: As the governing body of Bavarian television (see NO. 57n).

position: A permanent position for IB at the Bayerischer Rundfunk was planned, but did not transpire.

Germany: The discussion about equipping the German army with nuclear weapons; IB had just signed a petition in the Munich newspaper *Kultur* (1 April 1958) for people active in culture entitled 'Niemals Atomwaffen für Deutschland!' [Nuclear Weapons for Germany—Never!] (see NO. 122n).

away for a week: Destination unknown.

May: PC was in Germany from 4 until 8 May 1958, and met IB in Munich on 7/8 May 1958 (PCPC/GCL). Taking place exactly 10 years after their encounter in Vienna, the meeting seems to have coincided with a change in the character of their relationship.

97

Paul Celan to Ingeborg Bachmann, Paris, 6 June 1958

Paris, 6 June 1958.

Troubled times, Ingeborg. Troubled, eerie times. How could it have been otherwise—it was already there. Do this or that? One tries to answer, decides on the one or the other and feels the grip of the vice.

I have worked a great deal these last few days, in spite of everything, with no hope of return. Eighteen poems by Ossip Mandelstamm have been translated, I will send them to you in the next few days. The new volume of poems is also nearly finished. All that—to what end?

Follow your heart, Ingeborg, keep it awake, always and everywhere.

And write a few lines.

Paul

NOTES

MAN/ANL folder 4, p. 13, MAN/ANL ser. n. 25.202 a, p. 13 (ass. envelope): hw. airmail letter to: 'Mademoiselle Ingeborg Bachmann/München 13/Franz-Josephstrasse 9a/ Allemagne', Paris, 6 June 1958.

Troubled times/worked: PC's poems 'Ein Auge, offen' [An Eye, Open] and 'Oben, geräuschlos' [Above, Soundless], written just before the letter, mirror the critical political situation not only in Germany but also in France (the risk of war due to the Algerian crisis); the same can be said of 'Welt' [World], written slightly later (*MAN/ANL ser. n. 25.170, pp. 8031–3*, probably given to IB in Paris at the end of June).

Mandelstamm: PC began translating poems by the Russian-Jewish poet Ossip Mandelstam on 11 May 1958: 'Dein Gesicht' [Your Face], 'Es tilgen' [They Erase], 'Petropolis', 'Diese Nacht' [This Night], 'War niemands Zeitgenosse' [Was No One's Contemporary], 'Das Wort bleibt ungesagt' [The Word Remains Unspoken], 'Silentium', 'Schlaflosigkeit' [Sleeplessness], 'Venedigs Leben' [The Life of Venice], 'Der Tannen' [Of the Pines], 'Keine Worte' [No Words], 'Diebsvolk' [Pack of Thieves], 'Meine Zeit' [My Time], 'Die Priester' [The Priests], 'Der Schritt der Pferde' [The Walk of the Horses], 'Die Muschel' [The Sea Shell], 'O Himmel, Himmel' [O Heaven, Heaven] and 'Die Luft' [The Air] (IBE, see NO. 102).

Ossip Mandelstamm: Though the common transliteration is 'Mandelstam', PC consistently writes 'Mandelstamm', emphasizing the German meaning 'tribe (or root) [*Stamm*] of the almond [*Mandel*]', referring to his Jewish descent. [Trans.]

volume of poems: Concerning the last poems for *Sprachgitter*, see NO. 103.

98
Ingeborg Bachmann to Paul Celan, Paris, 23 June 1958

Monday 23 June 1958

Paul,

I am in Paris (no one knows)—but are you here too—or still in Germany? I have to speak to you. Please can you come on Wednesday at 4 p.m. to <u>Café George V</u>, I cannot think of anything better offhand, it is next to the Métro station of the same name. If you are not here on Wednesday, I will write to you again and ask you to come another day.

And please, if you meet any acquaintances, do not tell them I am here.

That does not apply to Gisèle, of course.

Wednesday is my birthday; 10 years ago we had my 22nd.

When you called me, I did not yet know how everything would turn out. But I know that you will try to understand me, to help me whether you have any advice or not. As long as you are there, looking at me for a few hours—

Ingeborg

Enclosed: the poem '*Wohin wir uns wenden im Gewitter der Rosen*'.

NOTES

GLA D 90.1.2830/8: hw. letter to: 'M. Paul CELAN/78, Rue de Longchamp/<u>PARIS 16ème</u>',Paris, 24 June 1958; supplement: cpy; the letter may have contained further supplements (higher postage fee), but it cannot have been the newspaper clipping mentioned in NO. 53 and stored with this letter (different folding marks).*

Paris: IB explained the reasons for her trip to her parents on 15 June 1958 as follows: 'I am going to Paris now, but without anyone knowing, because I need peace to work until 1 September.' IB left Munich on 18 June 1958 and stayed at Hôtel Parisiana, 4, Rue Tournefort, 5e (IBPE).

Germany: PC was in Wuppertal, Düsseldorf and Frankfurt with GCL (14–20 June 1958).

Café George V: IB and PC did indeed meet there at 4 p.m. on 25 June 1958 (PCPC).

my 22nd: See NO. 1n.

'Wohin wir uns wenden im Gewitter der Rosen': [Wherever We Turn in the Storm of Roses] Original version (*MAN/ANL 317/1409*) of the poem 'Aria I', which had been set to music by Henze (see NO. 53n).

99
Paul Celan to Ingeborg Bachmann, dedication in offprint of Arthur Rimbaud,
'Das trunkene Schiff', Paris, June 1958

For Ingeborg—
      Paul

NOTES

LIB: *hw. dedication (p. 375) in Arthur Rimbaud, 'Das trunkene Schiff', Paul Celan trans., Estratto da Botteghe Oscure, 21, pp. 375–8.*

June 1958: Probably given to IB during her stay in Paris in late June. Concerning the publication, see NO. 58n. The IBE contains a typescript dated 8 September 1957 (*MAN/ANL ser. n. 25.173 N 8083–92*).

100

Ingeborg Bachmann to Paul Celan, Naples, 16 July 1958

Naples, Via Generale Parisi 6
16 July 1958

Paul, I went on to Naples after all, because of the 'stay' for later in Munich, and so I shall be here until the end of summer. But I am sad and far away from everything, wherever I might be. I start working and only want to think about work, nothing else, and not look up. Sometimes I think there will be war; all the news and statements reveal more evil and madness than ever. What can we still do? Tell me. I am thinking desperately of you, then again of you during that afternoon on the Ile St Louis—it was as if we were in equilibrium, in the rain, and as if there were no need for a taxi to take us away.

I am glad that Gisèle and the child are around you and you around the two of them—a protection, insofar as there is any protection here.

And we—oh Paul, you know, but right now I cannot think of any words that would fully convey what holds us.

Ingeborg

NOTES

GLA D 90.1.2830/9: hw. letter to: '*M. Paul Celan/78, Rue de Longchamp/PARIS 16ème/ FRANCIA*', *Naples, 17 July 1958*.

Naples: IB went to Naples from Paris via Zurich and Munich in order to work undisturbed in Henze's apartment.

because of the 'stay': Unknown.

work: The libretto for Henze's *Der Prinz von Homburg* [The Prince of Hamburg], after Kleist, as well as *Das dreissigste Jahr* [The Thirtieth Year] (see NO. 187).

war: See NOS 96 and 97.

Ile St Louis: On 30 June 1958 (PCPC).

101

Paul Celan to Ingeborg Bachmann, Paris, 21 July 1958

21 July 1958

Ingeborg, your letter, your letters came, today.

Where are things leading with us, I do not know; so many terrible things are happening.

Take these two Yesenin poems, I enjoyed translating them, now the veils are closed again.

Il y aura toujours l'Escale

Paul

We are going out to the country, for a week.

Enclosed: translations of Sergei Yesenin, 'The spring rain weeps its last tear' and 'You fields, too many to count'.

NOTES

MAN/ANL folder 5, p. 18: hw. letter, envelope missing; *MAN/ANL cod. ser. n. 25.202 b, pp. 14 and 15 (ass. supplements)*: ts. w/hw. corrections.

your letter, your letters: Is one letter missing?

Yesenin poems: The texts of the two translations deviate both from their first publication (in *Merkur*, Issue 8, 1959, pp. 719f. and 718f.) and, later, in *Gedichte* (see NO. 90n, pp. 18f. and 17).

Il y aura toujours l'Escale: 'There will always be L'Escale', presumably referring to the wine tavern L'Escale on Ile Saint-Louis (1, rue des Deux-Ponts, 4e). *Escale* also means 'stopover port', and Celan probably intended this double meaning (he had originally written 'escale' instead of 'Escale').

out to the country: See NO. 219.

102

Ingeborg Bachmann to Paul Celan, Naples, 10 August 1958

Via Generale Paris 6 (please: Parisi!)
Napoli, 10 August 1958

Paul, dear.

One of those dead Sundays. I am looking through the Mandelstamm again and reading the last Yesenin poems. '. . . you do not sing any leaf from the branch'. But I am writing all the same, and am timidly glad about it; it is going slowly, nothing is final and finished yet. Aside from that, nothing. Almost indifference in this solitude. One day like the next. No people. Hans works next door, now and again we go to the cinema at the weekend like everyone here. It is a decent enough life, one needs so little once one has understood. It will only be a breather anyway, one of the few we are afforded. And the 'solution' I was looking for, and may some day be tempted to look for again, probably does not exist. One is wary of asking questions when there is so much outright senselessness. What authority can you think of? And so there is no one I can ask to protect you—I realize that too. That I only have my arms to place around you when you are there, only a few words to tell you something, a piece of paper to send my name to you in Paris. Oh, Paul.

Ingeborg

Gisèle wrote such a kind letter, also about your days in the country. What is Eric up to? Could he not call me some time? On his little telephone.

NOTES

GLA D 90.1.2830/10: *hw. airmail letter to*: 'M. Paul Celan/78, Rue de Longchamp/ <u>PARIS</u> <u>16ème</u>/FRANCIA', Naples, 11August 1958.

the Mandelstamm: The IBE contains a bundle of papers, presumably given to IB in Paris at the end of June, with transcriptions of 24 poems *(MAN/ANL ser. n. 25.172*, partly deviation from the first publications and *Gedichte*); in addition to the 18 poems named in NO. 97, there were 'Man gab mir' [I Was Given],

'Gestrafft' [Tightened], 'Nein, nicht den Mond' [No, It Was Not the Moon], 'Der Dämmer, herbstlich' [Dusk, Autumnal], 'Nachts' [At Night], as well as 'Nicht Triumph' [Not Triumph]; these, PC did not publish. Regarding the book edition, see NO. 154.

Yesenin poems: 'Ihr Äcker, nicht zu zählen' [You Fields, Too Many to Count] and 'Der Frühlingsregen weint' [The Spring Rain Weeps], with line 22 of the latter quoted by IB.

Gisèle: See NO. 219.

103
Paul Celan to Ingeborg Bachmann, Paris, 1 September 1958

Paris, 1 September 1958.

Are you still in Naples, Ingeborg? (As I recall, you were planning to return to Munich in September.)

My August was empty, except for four poems; September will probably bring much excitement; my mood is not the best.

Neske was here about two weeks ago, because of the recording, I wrote you a rather foolish card—you are not cross, are you? How are you, Ingeborg, you and your work? You wanted to send me something—please do! (Should I send you the new poems—at what address?)

The Princess called me shortly after your departure; she then also wrote to you in Munich concerning the fees—did you receive the letter? Höllerer has not received his fee yet, and I fear the others are still waiting too. It is all very awkward for me; please write to the Princess and ask her to transfer the fees (which cannot be any smaller than those from *Akzente*) if she has not already done so. Forgive me for bothering you with this—I have the feeling that I am only in favour with the Princess to a modest extent.

Another thing: after being repeatedly asked by Karl Krolow, who has been living here for a few months, I told him you had been here, just for a moment, at a time when he was in Brussels. (He asked me so often that I supposed he might know from Böll, whom he met here. I heard from Neske that you were in Spain.)

Klaus will be coming in September, probably around the 14th; I am very much looking forward to this visit.

Do you think that there is already enough—imagine a few more poems as well as 'Engführung'—for a volume? Although the book could not come out before the spring, Fischer wants the manuscript now, i.e. by the end of September. It all seems so meagre to me!

Write me a few lines, Ingeborg!

Yours

Paul

NOTES

MAN/ANL folder 4, pp. 14–16: *hw. letter to*: '*Mademoiselle Ingeborg Bachmann/ ~~Via Generale Parisi 6/ Napoli/ Italie/ Prière de faire suivre!~~* [*Please forward*] / [*in unknown handwriting*] *Portovenere/(La Spezia) fermo posta/* [*in Henze's handwriting*] *Scrivimi/fin quando rimani la—/Affetuosità* [*Write to me how long you are staying there—Best wishes*] */ Hans*', *Paris, 1 September 1958 and Naples, 3 September 1958*.

Naples: See envelope. IB met with MF on the Ligurian coast in the late summer of 1958.

four poems: In August, PC wrote 'Bahndämme, Wegränder, Ödplätze, Schutt' [Railway Embankments, Waysides, Wastelands, Rubble], 'Sommerbericht' [Summer Report], 'Niedrigwasser' [Low Water] and 'Ein Holzstern' [A Wooden Star]. Unlike all other poems for *Sprachgitter* except 'Engführung' [Stretto], there are no manuscripts or typescripts of these four in the IBE (see NOS 66 and 97n). PC does not mention the translations he produced at the same time: Mandelstam's 'Der Sterne Einerlei' [Monotony of the Stars] and 'Die Städte, die da blühn' [The Cities That Bloom There] (both 4 August 1958) and Yesenin's 'Fall nicht, Stern' [Fall Not, Star] (12 August 1959).

excitement: Is PC referring to the publication of 'Das trunkene Schiff' and *Die Zwölf* in September?

Neske [. . .] *recording*: PC had personally known the Fullingen-based publisher of philosophical and literary works, including some by Martin Heidegger, since

1957. The double album *Lyrik der Zeit* [Poetry of Our Time] Neske produced with recordings of IB, Heissenbüttel, Krolow and Eich as well as Arp, PC, Grass and Höllerer was published at the end of 1958 (PCE-Paris, see NO. 140).

card: Not found.

send me something: IB was working on *Das dreissigste Jahr*, but only sent something from it—'Alles'—on 1 February 1960 (see NO. 156).

departure: IB left Paris before mid-June 1958 (see date of NO. 100).

Princess / fees / letter: Writing from Rome (18 November 1958), Caetani informed IB that she was still waiting for the promised letter containing the list of German contributors: 'I am always waiting for a list with what I should pay the last issue with Germans' (written in English). The question of the outstanding authors' fees for *Botteghe Oscure* was still present in the correspondence as late as January 1960 (NO. 155), even though PC had 'already' noted on 17 October 1959: 'Finally!!!/(Fees *B.O.*)' (PCPC)

Akzente: See NO. 69n.

Krolow: PC and IB had already made the German poet's acquaintance in 1952 in Niendorf; between April and September, he stayed in Paris where PC saw him regularly (BC III).

Böll: PC had met the Cologne-based writer in 1952, and corresponded with him since 1957. Böll, one of IB's personal friends, came to Paris at the end of June, and met with PC on 24 June 1958 (PCPC).

Spain: The itinerary IB mentioned to others may have been intended to ensure that she could work undisturbed in Naples (see NO. 100n).

Klaus will be coming: He came on 10 September 1958 (PCPC).

'Engführung' / manuscript: No further poems were added to *Sprachgitter* after 'Ein Holzstern'; 'Engführung', begun in July and almost completed by September 1958, comes last in the volume as a cycle in its own right. PC only sent the manu-cript to S. Fischer Verlag on 3 November 1959.

104
Ingeborg Bachmann to Paul Celan, Munich, 5 October 1958

Munich, 5 October 58

Paul, dear Paul,

I have been silent for so long, yet thought of you so much; for during a time when I could only have written you a letter that would not have conveyed what was really happening, it seemed more honest to remain silent. But it was still very painful for me, if only because I was so afraid for you all in these recent days of unrest in Paris!

This August and September: full of doubts, and the new thing that has happened. You remember, one afternoon when we were leaving rue de Longchamp, drank a Pernod, and you made a joke—asking whether I had fallen in love. At the time I had not, and some time later it happened in such a strange way, though I must not call it that. A few days ago I returned from a short trip to Carinthia . . . no, I have to start differently, and say it quickly. In the last few days here, the first since returning to Munich, Max Frisch came to ask me if I could do it, live with him, and now it has been decided. I will stay in Munich for about another three months and then move to Zurich. Paul, if only you were here, if I could just speak to you! I am very glad, safe in warmth, love and understanding, and I am only sad sometimes about myself, because I cannot rid myself of a fear and doubt concerning myself, not him. I think I can tell you, for we know—that it is almost impossible for us to live with someone else. But as we know that, as we are not fooling ourselves and not trying to, something good can come about by making an effort every day, I do believe that now.

I would like to know your thoughts when you put this letter down. Think something good for me!

When are you coming? Should I meet you somewhere? Will you come here? Tell me! I can do it openly and will always be allowed to do so, and I am glad about that.

Send me your poems now, all the new ones! And say something!

Ingeborg

P. S.

About seven weeks ago I wrote to Eugene Walter again—I think everything is sorted out now, I did it even before your letter came. When my train was leaving Naples, I planned to get out in Rome and call on the Princess but I simply could not, could not, see people and all of that, and did not manage to do it. There is too much I do not want to do in Munich (I still have to work for the television for another four weeks), the people again, three months' worth of mail; I really do not know where my head is, I am getting everything confused.

But Klaus was here, came up the stairs just as I was putting down my suitcases, having just come from the station, and he was happy after Paris and Trier, that was nice; we had two evenings together before he had to go back to Vienna with some pictures. How often I was able to say 'Paul' . . .

I.

NOTES

GLA D 90.1.2830/11: *hw. letter to*: '*M. Paul Celan/78, Rue de Longchamp/PARIS 16ème/ FRANCE*', Munich, 6 October 1958.

days of unrest in Paris: Prior to the constitutional referendum in Paris and the vote in the colonies for their integration into a French community as independent states (both on 28 September 1958), there had been a new wave of terrorist attacks since mid-September by the FLN, a radical Algerian liberation movement.

new thing/Max Frisch: IB met the Swiss author at a performance of MF's *Biedermann und die Brandstifter* [Biedermann and the Arsonists] together with *Die grosse Wut des Philipp Hotz* [The Great Fury of Philip Hotz] by the actors of the Zurich Schauspielhaus in Paris on 2 and 3 July 1958 (the date 3 July 1958 appears in *Malina*, IBW 3, 254f.). From November 1958, IB lived with MF for four years. Their separation in the autumn of 1962 caused a mental breakdown on IB's part (see NO. 195).

rue de Longchamp: During her trip to Paris in late June/early July (see NO. 98), IB had also paid her first visit to the Celan family (see NO. 219).

Rome: Concerning the fees for *Botteghe Oscure* (see NO. 103).

Paris and Trier: In Trier, Demus had been awarded the Preis des Kulturkreises im Bundesverband der deutschen Industrie [Award of the Cultural Area in the

Federal Association of German Industry] (9 September 1958); following a visit to PC in Paris, he went to Munich on business (5–7 October 1958).

105
Paul Celan to Ingeborg Bachmann, Paris, 8 October 1958

Paris, 9 October 1958.

My dear Ingeborg!

I should think something good for you, you say—I am happy to do so, to do so in the same way that your letter, which radiates such unmistakable goodness, shows me. Security, warmth, love and understanding: you speak of these, and the mere fact of being able to speak of them proves to me that they must be there for you. Perhaps, I am thinking to myself, you should not stay in Munich for so long: three months are a long time.

Were you also able to work? Do not forget that you wanted to send me something, prose or poems.

I am telling my heart to wish you happiness—and it does so, gladly, of its own accord: it can hear you hoping and believing.

Paul

NOTES

MAN/ANL folder 4, pp. 17–18: hw. airmail letter to: '*Mademoiselle Ingeborg Bachmann/ München 13 / Franz-Josephstrasse 9a / Allemagne*', *from* '*Paul Celan, 78 Rue de Longchamp / Paris 16ᵉ*', *Paris, 8 October 1958.*

9 October: See the postmark!

106

Ingeborg Bachmann to Paul Celan, Munich, 26 October 1958

Sunday, 26/10/1958

Paul,

thank you! You already saw further, told me—I do not know why—that I should go sooner, and now I really am leaving Munich soon, on 15 November. I long for order and quiet, and here everything is restless, too many trivialities, so many disturbances that I feel more strongly every day.

I will first have an apartment to myself in the city (Zurich, c/o Honegger-Lavate, Feldeggstrasse 21), but later be closer, out in the country.

I have had some difficult times, with many doubts, much despairing, but one can only bring these fears into real life and solve them there, not in one's thoughts.

But you have not told me when you are coming, when we can see each other. You did not send the poems! Please do not pull your hand away from me, Paul, please do not.

And tell me how you have been, write about your days, I have to know where you stand.

Your beautiful, your kind letter, once again, and my still feeling joy about it many times—not 'silence'.

Ingeborg

NOTES

GLA D 90.1.2830/12: hw. letter to: 'M. Paul Celan/78, Rue de Longchamp/<u>PARIS 16ème</u>/ FRANCE', Munich, 26 October 1958.

poems: See NO. 103.

107

Ingeborg Bachmann to Paul Celan, Zurich, 20 November 1958

Feldeggstrasse 21
c/o Honegger
Zurich/Switzerland
Tel: 34 97 03
20 November 1958

Paul,

your birthday is near. I cannot make the post be exact to the day and the hour, but we can be.

It is so quiet here. Half an hour has passed since the first sentence, and last autumn is forcing its way into this autumn.

Ingeborg

NOTES

GLA D 90.1.2830/13: *hw. letter to*: 'M. Paul CELAN/78, Rue de Longchamp/<u>PARIS 16ème</u>/FRANCE', Zurich, 20 November 1958.

your birthday: His thirty-eighth, on 23 November 1958.

be exact: See NO. 1.

108

Ingeborg Bachmann to Paul Celan, dedication
in Der gute Gott von Manhattan, *Munich* (?), *November 1958*

Paul, for you.

Ingeborg
November 1958

NOTE

GLA LPC: hw. dedication on the flyleaf of Der gute Gott von Manhattan. Hörspiel *(Munich: Piper, 1958, = Piper Bücherei 127), envelope missing.*

109

Paul Celan to Ingeborg Bachmann, dedication in Arthur Rimbaud,
Bateau ivre/Das trunkene Schiff, *Paris, 24 November 1958*

For Ingeborg—

Paul
Paris, 24.XI.1958.

NOTES

LIB: hw. dedication on the flyleaf of Arthur Rimbaud, Bateau ivre/Das trunkene Schiff,
Paul Celan trans. (Wiesbaden: Insel-Verlag, 1958), envelope missing.

24.XI.1958: The dating directly after PC's birthday suggests a reaction to a birthday
present (NO. 108?). The translation, produced in late July 1957, had already been
published in early September 1958 (see the first edition, NO. 99). PC also enclosed
two copies of Demus' *Das schwere Land* [The Heavy Land] (PCPC, see NO. 111).

110

Paul Celan to Ingeborg Bachmann, Paris, 1 December 1958

on 1 December 1958.

Dear Ingeborg,

a request: tell me whether you have written to the Princess, or, more specifically,
whether you have mentioned the figures of the individual fees. For they have not

been transferred to this day. This is more than awkward for me. But before sending a letter to Rome, I at least wanted to ask you for more details.

All the best!

Paul

NOTES

MAN/ANL folder 4, pp. 19 and 21 (ass. envelope): hw. letter to: 'Mademoiselle Ingeborg Bachmann/Zürich/Feldeggstr. 21/bei Honegger/Suisse', Paris, 1 December 1958.

fees: Letter with this heading noted in PCPC (see NO. 103).

111

Ingeborg Bachmann to Paul Celan, Zurich, 2 December 1958

Feldeggstrasse 21
Zurich, 2 December 1958

Dear Paul,

I wrote to the Princess; I did, however, receive a letter from Rome first, containing a sentence I find hard to understand: ' . . . I am waiting for a hit (?) with what I should pay for the last issue with Germans. I long to get this in order . . .' And I wrote because of Nelly Sachs in particular, and hope to receive an answer from her soon and find out what kind of difficulty there is, if any.

Thank you for *Das trunkene Schiff* and the poems by Klaus!

(I think I shall write to Eugene Walter again too; it is a mystery what has happened this time.)

It is still difficult for me to step out of here, out of the new situation, with letters and things, to think of everything, sometimes I am very tired, and you also seem to have fallen silent; I am trying to understand it, I want us to resolve the difficulties in conversations, as we sometimes did last year.

Ingeborg

NOTES

GLA D 90.1.2830/14: *hw. letter to*: '*M. Paul Celan/78, Rue de Longchamp/PARIS 16ème/ FRANCE*', *Zurich, 2 December 1958.*

for a hit (?): IB read Caetani's barely legible handwriting as 'hit' instead of 'list' (see NO. 103n).

'. . . *I am waiting for a hit* (?) [. . .] *I long to get this in order* . . .': In English in the original. [Trans.]

poems by Klaus: PC had helped to initiate the publication of Demus' collection of poems *Das schwere Land* (Frankfurt: S. Fischer, 1958). A dedicated copy is located in the LIB: 'Inge von Herzen/Dez. 1958 Klaus'.

112
Paul Celan to Ingeborg Bachmann, Paris, 2 December 1958

2.XII.58.

Dear Ingeborg,

I have copied out an account of my reading in Bonn for you. (The letter was written by a student.) Please, tell me what you think.

Paul

NOTES

MAN/ANL folder 4, p. 20: *hw. letter; folder 14, p. 9 (ass. Supplement)*: *ts. w/hw. lines in margin, envelope missing.*

reading in Bonn: Reading on 17 November 1958 at the University of Bonn. PC had been corresponding with Jean Firges, the first doctoral student to write a dissertation on his work ('Die Gestaltungsschichten der Lyrik Paul Celans ausgehend vom Wortmaterial' [The Morphological Layers in the Poetry of Paul Celan, Based on the Verbal Material] [Cologne, 1959]); the supplement is an excerpt from Firges' letter of 19 November 1958 (see PC/RH 58f.). Similar letters were sent on the same day to Höllerer, Böll, Schallück and Schroers (PCPC).

112.1
Supplement (Jean Firges, letter excerpt)

'. . . *others held the view that your announcements of the titles had a comical quality strongly reminiscent of Heinz Erhardt. (I do not agree with this opinion.) It was your pathos in the "Hosanna" part that attracted particular scorn. I encountered an unfair criticism after the reading in the form of a caricature. It showed a slave, bound and hunched, desperately trying to shake off his chains. Under the drawing (and this is the malicious part) was written: Hosanna to the son of David!*'

NOTES

Heinz Erhardt: Popular German comedian of the 1950s and 1960s.

"Hosanna" part: Lines 155–65 of 'Engführung'; the text under the picture refers to Matthew 21:9.

113
Ingeborg Bachmann to Paul Celan, Zurich, 10 December and 23 December 1958

10.XII.58

Paul,

I am thinking about your question and this letter cannot write down everything I am thinking, only say something starting at the end. I do not think there is any answer, for you or from you, to this report; it belongs in the bin. We know these people exist, in Germany and elsewhere, and it would indeed be surprising if they had all suddenly disappeared. The question is, rather: having entered a room full of people one has not chosen oneself, whether one is still prepared to read for those who do want to listen, and are ashamed of the others. This is practically the only way to do anything, to decide anything.

I do not know how to rid the world of evil, or whether one is simply supposed to endure it. But you are there and are having an effect, and the poems have an effect of their own and help to protect you—that is the answer and a counter-balance in this world.

23 December:

Christmas is so near, I must hurry up. A parcel came from you and Gisèle this morning; I shall put it under the Christmas tree tomorrow, and not open it before then. Last week I sent you one, and hope very much that it will reach you safely and on time. Shortly after New Year I will be visiting my parents for a few days; there are a few things to discuss. My brother is planning to do his next practical training in Israel. He had the idea all by himself, and that makes me happy for some reason and no reason at the same time.

I will be thinking of you all tomorrow. Of Eric, who will truly make the evening. That is difficult for us.

> With love.

> Ingeborg

P. S. The Princess wrote to me; she sent Nelly Sachs 100 dollars, paid for the Heym and is now sending the others cheques too. But please tell me if you have received anything yet! I will write her a few words anyway without waiting for your reply, to bring everything in order again; I am doing so because she asks me to remind her of everything, so it is only natural.

I.

NOTES

GLA D 90.1.2830/15: hw. express letter to: 'M. Paul Celan/78, Rue de Longchamp/*PARIS 16ème*/FRANCE', Zurich, 23 December 1958.

practical training: Part of Heinz Bachmann's geology studies.

Princess/100 dollars: Regarding the fees for *Botteghe Oscure*, see NO. 103.

114

Ingeborg Bachmann to Gisèle Celan-Lestrange and Paul Celan,
dedication card accompanying a present, Christmas 1958 (?)

Pour Gisèle, pour Paul

Ingeborg

NOTES

BC III/2 without location number: originally inserted between pp. 24 and 25 of Anrufung des
Grossen Bären (*Munich: Piper, 1956*) (*p. [2] by PC: 'Cologne, October 1956.', GLA
LPC; card lost, text according to BC*).

Pour Gisèle, pour Paul: The present accompanied by the note could not be identified.

115

Paul Celan to Ingeborg Bachmann, dedication in
Alexander Block, The Twelve, *Paris, Christmas 1958 (?),*
late January / early February 1959 (?)

For Ingeborg—

Paul

NOTES

LIB: hw. dedication in Alexander Block, Die Zwölf, *Paul Celan trans. (Frankfurt: S. Fischer,*
1958) (*[p. 1]*), *envelope missing.*

Block: See the words of thanks in NO. 117; the translation was published in 1958.
The book may have been a Christmas present (see NO. 113). This dedicated copy
cannot, however, have been the mail item sent to or received by IB which is
referred to in a note dated 6 February 1959 (PCPC); she would not have been in
possession of it on 8 February 1959 (a Sunday).

116

Paul Celan to Ingeborg Bachmann, Paris, 2 February 1959

on 2 February 1959.

Ingeborg, I am telling myself that the letter you said you would write has only failed to arrive because it is difficult for you to write it, i.e. because my flood of words on the telephone made it even more difficult than it already was. So please just write me a few lines, I know that you know what I am concerned with, in this nasty Bonn business too.

I am only going back to Germany in May—if you think there is something I can do for you, I would be happy to meet you somewhere to talk to you, perhaps in Strasbourg or Basel. Or would you rather come to Paris?

All the best, Ingeborg!

Paul

NOTES

MAN/ANL folder 5, p. 1: *hw. letter, envelope missing.*

Bonn business: See NO. 112.

Germany: PC was in Frankfurt from 17 to 20 March 1959 to read from *Sprachgitter* (19 March 1959, PCPC).

117

Ingeborg Bachmann to Paul Celan, Zurich, 8 February 1959

Zurich, 8 February 1959

Paul, the only reason I did not write the letter straight away was that I had a few difficult days here, with some excitement, and now the flu as well; nothing serious, but I do not feel up to anything, cannot work—and it was just going so well before. But now: inactivity, doubts and dejection once again.

I want to see you so very much, but I wonder whether Basel or Strasbourg would be right this time, the first time after the change in my life. Perhaps we should meet in Zurich? The reason is that things would be easier for Max if there were an encounter between the two of you; he already asked me some time ago not to exclude him. I am not sure I am explaining it very well—he knows what you mean to me, and will always approve of our meetings, in Basel, Paris or wherever; but I should not give him the feeling that I am using him to evade you, or you to evade him.

Tell me how you feel about it! I can imagine that it might not be easy, and perhaps even difficult for you to establish contact, but there could at least be some mutual acknowledgement. And you should certainly not worry that we might not have enough time for each other in Zurich.

I have not yet spoken to Max about our wish to meet again, as I want to have your answer first.

Please, Paul, leaving all that aside, let me say something else about the call— you only make things difficult for me when you begin to suspect that I might misunderstand something. For you must say whatever there is to say, whether it is rash or thought-out, it is all the same to me—both are always welcome and always equal.

The **Blok** is very beautiful, effortlessly wild and, in the German, an eruption that leaves the reader amazed. I am very happy about it, it is such a whole!

Now your poems will be published soon, poems from our time again. (Do not forget to see to the cover—it is so easy to get an unpleasant surprise.)

I am thinking of you so very much!   Ingeborg

NOTES

GLA D 90.1.2831/1: *hw. express letter to*: '*M. Paul Celan/78, Rue de Longchamp/ <u>PARIS 16ème</u>/FRANCE*', *Zurich, 9 February 1959 and Paris, 10 February 1959.*

encounter: A first encounter took place on 19 July 1959 (see NO. 135). It had presumably been avoided until then; PC only learned through others that IB and MF had been in Paris in early December 1958: 'A surprise (and not such a surprise): —saw Ingeborg two days ago at Café Odéon, with Max Frisch. Joy of the Zurichers, that greatest German prose writer is to marry greatest German poetess. (Frisch is getting divorced.) Heartening' (PCPC).

Blok: *Die Zwölf* (see NO. 115).

our time: Concerning *Sprachgitter*, whose fourth cycle contains the poems written to IB between October 1957 and January 1958, see NO. 124.

cover: PC considered the design very important; he had already expressed his wishes for *Sprachgitter* to Hirsch on 26 November 1958.

118
Paul Celan to Ingeborg Bachmann, Paris, 11 February 1959

Correspondence card.
To

Fräulein
Ingeborg Bachmann
in <u>Zurich</u>
Feldeggstrasse 38
c/o Honegger

Greetings from Vienna.　　　　*1ˢᵗ district, Am Hof.*

NOTES

MAN/ANL folder 5, p. 4: *hw. postcard, Paris, 11 February 1959.*

Am Hof: See 'Köln, Am Hof' (NO. 47). The card has no text other than IB's address, partly in Fraktur type (Gothic in print), 'as I learnt it from my mother many years ago' (to Hermann Lenz, PC/HHL 136).

119
Ingeborg Bachmann to Paul Celan, Zurich, 18 February 1959

Just a small essay that will be appearing in a music book; and because it will still take some time before I can show you the attempts, the current ones!

Enclosed: manuscript of the essay '*Musik und Dichtung*' [*Music and Poetry*], not preserved.

NOTES

GLA D 90.1.2831/20 and GLA D 90.1.2831 (ass. envelope): *hw. letter on picture postcard* (*Tarquinia, Tomba degli Auguri* [*Tomb of the Augurs*]) *to*: '*M. Paul Celan/78, Rue de Longchamp/PARIS 16ème/France*', *Zurich, 18 February 1959*.

Tomba degli Auguri: PC may have recalled this card when he wrote 'Mittags' [At Noon] on 30 April 1964 after a reading in Rome, where he also met MF (PCPC), and from where he went to see the important Etruscan necropolis Cerveteri.

small essay: First publication in the almanac *Musica Viva* (K. H. Ruppel ed. [Munich, 1959], pp. 161–6). It was presumably an offprint of this text that was originally inserted at the back of the dedicated copy of *Die gestundete Zeit* (see NO. 42; BC III).

attempts, the current ones: It is more likely that IB was referring to short stories (e.g. 'Jugend in einer österreichischen Stadt' for *Botteghe Oscure*, VOL. 23) than the completion of the libretto for *Der Prinz von Homburg* (for which Henze thanked her on 20 February 1959 after receiving it).

120
Paul Celan to Ingeborg Bachmann, Paris, 18 February 1959

18.2.59.

Ingeborg,

I sent you an old Viennese postcard a few days ago; I see now that the address was slightly incorrect—hopefully it reached you. (I found it at a bouquiniste's by the docks, almost the same spot where the poem occurred to me over a year ago.)

I would certainly like to come to Zurich, Ingeborg, perhaps in May. But perhaps the two of you will stop by here before then?

I am translating Mandelstamm; the volume will be published in the autumn, by Fischer.

Keep your head up, Ingeborg, write—and send me a few pages, if you can.

Klaus is reading at Fischer on the 26th, perhaps you could ask Frau Kaschnitz to go?

All the best, Ingeborg, all the best!

Paul

NOTES

MAN/ANL folder 5, pp. 2–3: hw. letter to: 'Mademoiselle Ingeborg Bachmann/<u>Zürich</u>/ Feldeggstrasse 21/bei Honegger/<u>Suisse</u>', Paris, 19 February 1959.

address: See the incorrect house number in NO. 118.

same spot/poem: See the location given with the date of 'Köln, Am Hof' in NO. 47.

Mandelstamm: PC had translated at least six poems since the start of the year, and on 18 February 1959 'Die Freiheit, die da dämmert' [The Freedom That Dawns There]. Concerning the book edition, see NO. 154.

Klaus [. . .] *Fischer*: Demus read from *Das schwere Land* at S. Fischer Verlag (see NO. 111n).

121

Paul Celan to Ingeborg Bachmann, Paris(?), 23 February 1959

Just a few lines, Ingeborg, to ask you if Hans Weigel, who now intends to augment his great achievements on behalf of new Austrian poetry with a bibliophilic anthology, has also contacted you or Piper. I have just received a request from Deutsche Verlagsanstalt (who, incidentally, did not pass up this opportunity to insult me in the most offensive manner . . .). I would be more than happy to turn down this 'honour', but that would only be of use if you did the same. So, please write me a few lines.

Paul

NOTES

MAN/ANL folder 5, p. 5: hw. letter, envelope missing.

Weigel/Deutsche Verlags-Anstalt/insult: The letter (14 February 1959) concerning poems for the anthology *Neue Lyrik* [New Poetry] (not published?), including 'Todesfuge', was forwarded to PC on 20 February 1959 by Gotthold Müller, managing director of the DVA (PCE). In his accompanying letter, he voiced his great disappointment at PC's change to S. Fischer Verlag.

Piper: See NO. 70.

122

Ingeborg Bachmann to Paul Celan, Zurich, 2 March 1959

from 15 March: Haus zum Langenbaum
Seestrasse
UETIKON, near Zurich
Tel: 92 92 13 (Zurich)

2 March 1959

Dear Paul,

I really do not think one can do anything about a review; it is not common to write letters, and as far as I know they do not get printed in any case. All one can do is try to draw a few people's attention to the book, which might help it to get some other reviews—assuming it does not anyway—to balance out the reception.

Yesterday I told Kuno Raeber (you may remember him) about the poems, as he does reviews for the radio. I will give Werner Weber the volume myself for the *Neue Zürcher Zeitung*. It will not always be easy to arouse interest, of course, and we know from experience how long it sometimes takes; my first volume was only reviewed a year after being published, and then only tentatively here and there, but time does work in favour of poems and will do so for Klaus' poems, I believe, and we are there, as well as other friends—and that has already helped a little in the short time so far. Moras will be publishing something again, and I could, if you think it is a good idea, write to Schwab-Felisch at the *FAZ*, asking him—specifically after this bigoted review—to print a poem by Klaus in the paper.

It was lovely to hear your voice; I am always glad to hear it coming out of the white box on my desk. In two weeks we are moving to a different apartment by the lake, near Zurich—it is so difficult to find something in the city. I rather doubt we will be able to leave here on 1 May and go to Rome, as I would have to finish the book before leaving, and it does not look as if I will.

It is so laborious, everything so doubtful, the many sentences and pages; simply managing not to lose sight of it already seems like an achievement.

I would like to come to Paris sooner, but it is the same as with you, I am stuck here at the moment—the house move is around the corner again—and you will have to be patient for a little longer, please. I will still write to you about the Char translation; I have not read all of it yet, and one can only really get through it bit by bit.

I have not heard from Weigel, and the publisher does not seem to have received any request. So I do not know what I should ask you to do. For I do want to say no, if it is at all possible and I am asked, after all this abuse; but on the other hand, I am wary of stirring up even more people who will only infuriate me senselessly, then prove impossible to confront. I am at a loss. Perhaps for now you could just decide for yourself.

Dear, so many things are painful, the very thought of it; but try to cast it all off as much as you can, it is not worth wasting energy on it.

If only you could come in May! . . .

Max sends his regards. He will also be very happy about it.

I am looking forward to your book—and every character!

Ingeborg

NOTES

GLA D 90.1.2831/2: *tw. letter w/hw. corrections to*: '*M. Paul Celan/78, Rue de Longchamp/ Paris 16ᵉ/France*', *Zurich, 3 March 1959*.

review/Klaus' poems: In his review 'Neue österreichische Lyrik' [New Austrian Poetry], Horst Bienek wrote the following about Demus' *Das schwere Land* (see NO. 111n): 'The difficulty of his poems does not stem from that poetic truth that often makes a genuine work of art "hard to understand", but rather his fleeting, uncontrolled associations. He is not lacking in verbal artistry, simply in poetic substance' (*FAZ*, 28 February 1959).

Raeber: IB was a friend of the Swiss writer and essayist, who likewise lived in Rome and Munich during the 1950s.

Weber: IB would have known the features editor at the *NZZ* (1951–73) primarily as a supporter and friend of MF; PC was in regular contact with him from 1959. Weber reviewed Demus' volume very unfavourably in the *NZZ* (17 March 1959).

first volume: The very first review of *Die gestundete Zeit* was the anonymous article printed in *Der Spiegel* on 18 August 1954, 'Bachmann. Stenogramm der Zeit' [Bachmann: Shorthand of Our Time] (pp. 26–9, with photograph on title page), which can be viewed as the harbinger of IB's early fame.

Moras: Moras published three poems by Demus in the almanac *Jahresring 1958/59*: 'Der Tiefe traumklar eingewachsen' [Grown into the Depths With Dream-Clarity], 'Im Gelb der Sonnen hängt' [In the Yellow of the Suns Hangs] and 'Einer Gestalt, oder zweier' [To a Shape, or Two] ([Stuttgart, 1958], pp. 35–7).

Schwab-Felisch: IB knew the features editor at the *FAZ* (1956–61) from Gruppe 47 conferences. PC had corresponded with him since 1958.

different apartment: See the address named above in the letter.

Rome: IB's and MF's plan was delayed owing to MF's illness (see NO. 132).

book: *Das dreissigste Jahr*.

to Paris: PC and IB did not see each other in 1959.

Char translation: Presumably 'Hypnos' (in *Neue Rundschau*, 4, 1958, pp. 565–601, but only published in February 1959). It is unclear when—if at all—IB received an offprint from PC. The book edition (René Char, *Poésies/Dichtungen* [Poems], Jean-Pierre Wilhelm ed., in collaboration with Christoph Schwerin [Frankfurt: S. Fischer, 1959]), containing PC's translations 'Einer harschen Heiterkeit' [Of a Harsh Gaiety] and 'Hypnos', is preserved in the LIB not as a dedicated copy from PC, but with René Char's signature. PC had met the French poet and resistance fighter in 1953, and been translating his poems since 1954.

abuse: Weigel had attacked IB because of the petition she had signed (see NO. 96) ('Offener Brief in Sachen Unterschrift' [Open Letter Concerning Signatures], in *Forum*, 54, June 1958, p. 218).

your book: *Sprachgitter*, see NO. 124. The sentence was completed by hand.

every character: The phrase '*jedes Zeichen*' is ambiguous; it could mean 'any sign (of life)', 'any signal' or 'any/every (written) character'. The last of these has been chosen because the reference to the book immediately preceding it appears to suggest that, though it is equally conceivable that a possible letter or telephone call is meant. [Trans.]

123
Paul Celan to Ingeborg Bachmann, Paris, 12 March 1959

on 12 March 1959.

Dear Ingeborg,

first and foremost, let me congratulate you on your prize. Some of those people are blind, but one of them must have seen—perhaps even several.

I have little to report. I experience a few slights every day, plentifully served, on every street corner. The last 'friend' to honour me (and Gisèle) with his mendacity was René Char. And why not? I translated him, after all (alas!), and so his gratitude, which I had been able to experience in the past, albeit in smaller doses, could not fail to be expressed.

Lies and baseness, almost everywhere.

We are alone and helpless.

Give Max Frisch my regards—

Be well and at ease—

Yours, Paul

NOTES

MAN/ANL folder 5, pp. 6–7: hw. letter to: '*Mademoiselle Ingeborg Bachmann/Zürich/ Feldeggstr. 21, bei Honegger/Suisse*', Paris, 12 March 1959.

prize: On 11 March 1959, the *FAZ* reported that IB's *Der gute Gott von Manhattan* had been awarded the Radio Play Prize of the War-Blind.

slights [. . .] *Char*: Unknown. PC had met with Char on 27 January 1959 (PCPC).

124

Paul Celan to Ingeborg Bachmann,
dedication in Sprachgitter, *Frankfurt am Main, 20 March 1959*

For Ingeborg

Frankfurt am Main, in the Palmengarten
On 20 March 1959.

Paul

NOTES

LIB: *hw. dedication on the flyleaf of* Sprachgitter (*Frankfurt: S. Fischer, 1959*); *nserted into*
the book are a ticket for the Frankfurt Palmengarten and a small dried twig, envelope missing.

Palmengarten: The collection of exotic plants, established in 1868, is located in the
Westend quarter of Frankfurt.

20 March 1959: The volume appeared directly beforehand (sending noted in PCPC,
see NO. 235).

125

Paul Celan to Ingeborg Bachmann, Paris, 22 March 1959

Paris, on 22.3.59

Did you receive the book, Ingeborg? (I sent it off on Friday from Frankfurt,
stupidly as printed matter and airmail—I hope it arrived safely.)

Strangely enough, I know in this moment that it has some weight.

Yours, Paul

NOTES

MAN/ANL folder 5, pp. 8–9: *hw. letter on picture postcard (Palmengarten Frankfurt) to*:

'*Mademoiselle Ingeborg Bachmann/ Uetikon bei Zürich/ Haus zum Langenbaum,/ Seestrasse/ Suisse*', *Paris, 23 March 1959.*

book: *Sprachgitter.*

Friday: 20 March 1959.

126

Ingeborg Bachmann to Paul Celan, Uetikon am See, 23 March 1959

DEAR PAUL THANK YOU FOR THIS TICKET TO GAIN ADMISSION
TO THE POEMS TO THE PALMENGARTEN TO NOUS DEUX ENCORE
THANK YOU FOR THESE POEMS

INGEBORG

NOTES

GLA D 90.1.2831/3: *telegram to*: '*Paul Celan, 78 Rue de Longchamp Paris 16*', *Uetikon am See, 23 March [1959], 11^{55}and Paris, 23 March 1959, 13^{30}.*

POEMS: *Sprachgitter* (see NOS 117n and 124).

TICKET [. . .] *PALMENGARTEN*: See NO. 124.

NOUS DEUX ENCORE: An allusion to Michaux's poem and PC's translation 'Noch immer und wieder, wir beiden' [Again and Yet Again, We Two].

127

Ingeborg Bachmann to Paul Celan, Zurich, 14 April 1959

Paul,

Tuesday or Wednesday then, whenever you want and can come! I will pick you up. Be sure to tell me the time of arrival or send a telegram, please!

And now I shall wait.   Ingeborg

                                                    14 April 1959

NOTES

GLA D 90.1.2831/4: *hw. letter to*: '*M. Paul Celan/78, Rue de Longchamp/ PARIS 16ème/ FRANCE*', *Männedorf (Zurich), 15 April 1959.*

Wednesday then: That is, on 23 April 1958; concerning the reason for the visit see NO. 197, which also mentions an attempted telephone conversation on 13 April 1959.

128

Paul Celan to Ingeborg Bachmann, Paris, 18 April 1959

                                                          15.4.59.

Dear Ingeborg,

I am sorry, I will not be able to come next week after all, only the week after that, for I have to go—I promised a long time ago—to England and visit an old aunt who is unlikely to forgive me if I let her down, as I have done before. Please do not be disappointed; if it suits you both, I can come around the end of April and stay for two or three days.

                              Yours

                              Paul

NOTES

MAN/ANL folder 5, p. 10: *hw. letter, envelope missing.*

15.4.59: See the letter to MF with the same date (NO. 199), which can only have been written on *18* April 1959; in the present case, IB's reply (NO. 129) indicates a mistake in the date. PC, however, also noted *both* letters in his diary under *15* April 1959.

aunt: The occasion for his visit to Berta Antschel, planned for 21 April 1959 but did not ultimately happen, was Passover, which began on 22 April 1959 (see NO. 199).

129
Ingeborg Bachmann to Paul Celan, Zurich, 20 April 1959

20-4-59

Dear Paul,

next week is just as good for us, I just wanted to tell you that quickly! Come when-ever is best for you. We do not have any plans, we are just working and wishing ourselves good weather for the days with you. But still, come soon.

Ingeborg

NOTE

GLA D 90.1.2831/5: hw. letter to: 'M. Paul Celan/78, Rue de Longchamp/ PARIS 16ème/ FRANCE', Männedorf (Zurich), 21 April 1959'.

130
Paul Celan to Ingeborg Bachmann, Paris, 22 April 1959

on 22 April 1959.

My dear Ingeborg,

I am afraid I am writing again, already today, to tell you that I will not be able to come next week either: we have had to postpone the trip to England for, in addi-tion to his whooping cough, which is still not completely gone, Eric has now caught a heavy cold. As well as that, I am being pressured by Fischer about the Mandelstamm translation—they want to have it by 15 May at the latest, so, really, I have to 'knuckle down' if I want to be on time and make sure the book comes out in the autumn. I have finished the translation, but not typed it up and, unfortunately, a few passages still need sorting out.

Will the two of you still be in Zurich around 20 May? Please do not be cross—you know how much I wanted to come.

Yours, Paul

NOTES

MAN/ANL folder 5, pp. 11–12: hw. letter to: '*Mademoiselle Ingeborg Bachmann/Haus zum Langenbaum/Seestrasse/<u>Uetikon bei Zürich</u>/Suisse*', *Paris, 22 April 1959, from*: '*Paul Celan, 78, rue de Longchamp,/Paris 16^e*'.

22 April 1959: Letter noted in PCPC.

trip to England: See NO. 128.

Mandelstamm translation: PC confirmed to Hirsch (S. Fischer Verlag) on the same day that he would be able to meet the deadline for the selection *Gedichte*.

131
Ingeborg Bachmann to Paul Celan, Uetikon am See, 16 May 1959

16-May-59

Dear Paul,

please forgive me for only writing now, after your telephone conversation with Max! I am glad you did not misinterpret my silence, for I was just completely out of action because of my illness; I have only just found a maid, and things are starting to get better with the household and looking after myself.

It is good that you are all coming. We are looking forward to it. I will go to the hotel now to choose the rooms. And on Thursday I will come and pick you up in Zurich. Please send a telegram beforehand.

I also wanted to say something about the risk of infection: it applies less to Gisèle and Eric than to you, as jaundice is primarily a 'men's illness', and the germs do not move through the air but are only passed on very directly, by eating from the same plate, etc., so that can be avoided. I am telling you this on the one hand to reassure you, but on the other hand so that you know I cannot entirely guarantee that nothing will happen. But it really does seem to be a rare illness, and one at least has to have the disposition for it. So, dear Paul, both things apply: we are looking forward to it and do not think it is dangerous, but we will not be cross for a moment and will understand completely if you have reservations.

I hope to provide good weather and some convenient little outings; Lake Greifen with the governor's house is nearby, a truly enchanted place, and a few other things besides.

Yes, do come!

Yours

Ingeborg

NOTES

GLA D 90.1.2831/6: *tw. letter w/hw. corrections, envelope missing.*

Thursday: 21 May 1959.

Lake Greifen with the governor's house: Lake and provincial capital east of Zurich, former seat of the governors.

132

Ingeborg Bachmann to Paul Celan, Uetikon am See, 31 May 1959

Uetikon, 31 May 1959

Dearest Paul,

how good that you did not come! On the Thursday when you were all planning to come, Max suddenly felt worse, and on Friday—10 days ago—he was taken to hospital. Now he is being partially drip-fed, is feeling very weak, and should not really even see me—we are, nonetheless, hopeful that in three weeks or so the good treatment will have restored him enough to leave for Chianciano, an Italian spa resort, the best or one of the best for liver treatment.

I am not well either, one reason probably being that I cannot do anything to help, that I am so superfluous; I cannot work either, even though I have more time for it than ever before. Now we have agreed—for this and other reasons—that I shall go ahead to Rome in about two weeks, find a small summer residence there in the Campagna, where it is cheaper, and from there I can get to Chianciano in two hours and visit Max.

Paul, what are we to do now? How and when could we see each other? At the moment, in this barren state that is continuing inside me, I have so few ideas. How long are you staying in Krimml? Even if you all came before or around 15 June, there would hardly be an opportunity for a conversation of the kind that you and Max would like; he is not allowed visitors, the door to his room has a window to speak through—it is just too miserable—and he is always so exhausted, and still will be for a long time. That is why I think it would be better for us to wait until the autumn, until he is both inwardly and outwardly restored.

So there is still the possibility of the two of us meeting, but I really must leave on the 15th or 16th, perhaps even on 14 June. I have looked at the map, hoping that your place would be closer, but it is very far off. Can you think of any solution? Give Gisèle and Eric many fond regards from me.

Oh Paul, I am utterly frozen—from the sudden temperature drop and various other things.

Ingeborg

NOTES

GLA D 90.1.2831/7: tw. letter w/hw. corrections to: '*M. Paul Celan/Gasthof Walderwirt/ <u>Wald bei Krimml</u>/(Land Salzburg)/Österreich*', *Zurich, 2 June 1959.*

Friday: 22 May 1959.

Chianciano: Thermal baths, south-east of Sienna.

Campagna: Countryside near Rome.

Krimml: See NO. 135.1n.

133

Ingeborg Bachmann to Paul Celan, Rome, 9 July 1959

Via della Stelletta 23
Roma
Tel: 56 30 39
  9 July 1959

Dearest Paul,

thank you for the telegram! And forgive me for not writing sooner, and now only writing so little. I cannot express myself clearly for emptiness and exhaustion, and it has been like this for weeks. Max was supposed to come to a sanatorium here, a liver treatment centre near Rome, but now he has to go to Germany first, to Bad Mergentheim. I received a letter from him today, he said you had been in Zurich and tried to reach him in Uetikon; but that he was visiting friends in Thalwil to pass the days between the hospital and the sanatorium. Max is coming here in August, so I will be staying here until 20 September; then, to earn a little money, I will go on an aeroplane trip and write something about it. I should be working in any case, but cannot; everything is breaking apart in my hands. Paul, we will speak some time. It is too difficult now, be patient with me.

Ingeborg

NOTES

GLA D 90.1.2831/8: tw. letter w/hw. corrections to: '*M. Paul Celan/Pension Chasté/Sils-Maria [instead of Sils-Baselgia]/Engadin/SVIZZERA*', *Rome, 9 July 1959.*

Via della Stelletta: The 'road of little stars' is in the city centre.

telegram: Not found.

Bad Mergentheim: Spa in northern Württemberg; MF broke off his treatment very abruptly (PC to Hildesheimer, 23 December 1959).

Thalwil: Village in the canton of Zurich.

aeroplane trip: IB was to write a report on a 'double world tour in a jet aircraft' for the SDR and the NDR (to Andersch, 16 June 1959, GLA); the trip was to be the 'first civil flight' to cover 'all 5 continents in 80 hours' (to Baumgart, 1 June 1959, Archiv Piper). Concerning her decision to refuse, see NO. 139.

134
Paul Celan to Ingeborg Bachmann, Sils-Baselgia, 15 July 1959

Pension Chasté, Sils (Engadin), on 15 July 1959.

My dear Ingeborg,

you are in Rome—please, could you ask the Princess why she did not pay the authors of the contributions for *Botteghe Oscure* I obtained for her? I certainly know that Grass, whom I met in Zurich, has not received his fee to this day. This has put me in an extremely awkward position, for I promised them payment.

Several letters to the truly insufferable Eugene Walter, including a registered one, have remained unanswered. Is this simply negligence, or—as I must sadly presume—something else? Please help me out of this unpleasant situation, please clarify things for me.

We are staying here until the 24th, then returning to Paris—not least to recover from so much holidays.

Like you, I am also not always well.

Fond regards

Yours

Paul

NOTES

MAN/ANL folder 5, p. 16: tw. letter w/ hw. corrections, envelope missing.

Sils/until the 24th: The mountain village Sils, in the Swiss Engadin, has two parts: Sils-Maria (see NO. 137), known as Nietzsche's sometime habitat, and Sils-Baselgia, where PC stayed until 23 July 1959 (see NO. 135.1).

pay the authors: See NO. 103.

Grass: PC probably met him around 1 July 1959, as both took part in a boat trip on Lake Zurich that day.

135
Paul Celan to Ingeborg Bachmann, Sils-Baselgia, 20 July 1959

My dear Ingeborg,

Max Frisch was here yesterday, unexpectedly; I was not prepared at all, some Zurich acquaintances had also come—the Allemanns—and the conversation was short; only a moment's worth of what he and I had hoped for.

I am—my last letter said it, in its stupid way—not well. Although I have translated 'La jeune Parque', I am at my wits' end with myself and everything again. What is the use of writing—and what is the use of someone who has made writing his life? And besides . . .

Before I wrote you the letter about the *Botteghe Oscure* fees I had written a different one—and not sent it; there it is now, with all its half-baked reflections and questions . . .

Perhaps you were right to accept the lectureship in Frankfurt, after all—we have <u>all</u> become deeply entangled in compromise, have we not?

But with your jet trip around the world, Ingeborg, things are perhaps a little different: allow me to say that something very deep within me is against it, and, because I am not remotely able to separate myself from it, asks you to think the whole thing over again; if you cannot, then you know I will reach the speeds up there in my thoughts and bring you back home safely.

We are going back to Paris in a few days—please write to me there! Write often!

Yours

Paul

NOTES

MAN/ANL folder 4, pp. 3–4, MAN/ANL folder 5, p. 17 (ass. envelope): *hw. airmail letter to*: '*Mademoiselle Ingeborg Bachmann/ Via della Stelletta 23/ Roma/ Italie*', *Sils Segl* [*xxx*], *20 July 1959*; *folder 5, pp. 13–15 (ass. supplement)*, *MAN/ANL folder 8, p. 5 (ass. envelope for supplement)*: *hw. letter to*: '*Mademoiselle Ingeborg Bachmann/ Via della Stelletta 23/ Roma/ Italie*', *from*: '*Paul Celan, Pension Chasté, Sils-Baselgia/ Suisse*', *unstamped*.

the Allemanns: PC knew Beda Allemann and his wife Doris from his time as lecturer at the ENS (Rue d'Ulm, 1957–58). In PC's will, the Swiss literary scholar, with whom he had met in Zurich on 30 June and 1 July 1959 (PCPC), was made responsible for the editing of his poems and translations (see NO. 234).

'*jeune Parque*': PC translated this famous philosophical poem by the French poet Paul Valéry between early January and 15 July 1959. His (and the first) German translation 'Die junge Parze' [The Young Fate] (see NO. 160) came about at the joint suggestion of Fritz Arnold (Insel-Verlag) and Peter Szondi (see also NO. 135.1).

writing: PC did not write any poems of his own between 'Bei Wein und Verlorenheit' [With Wine and Forlornness] (15 March 1959) and 'Es war Erde in ihnen' [There Was Earth in Them] (27 July 1959).

lectureship in Frankfurt: On 11 July 1959, the *FAZ* had reported on IB's lectures on poetics ('Frankfurter Vorlesungen') at the University of Frankfurt and initially sponsored by S. Fischer Verlag.

jet trip around the world: See NO. 133.

Paris: PC flew home from Sils-Baselgia via Zurich on 23 July 1959 (PCPC).

135.1
Supplement

Pension Chasté, Sils-Baselgia
on 11 July 1959.

My dear Ingeborg,

I was a little worried. But now less so, for you are in Rome, which is a kind of home, and, according to <u>my</u> Italian at least, you are living in the street of little stars . . .

We are here for a week, after long weeks of rain near Salzburg, a week's stay in Vienna, racing about for one day around Genoa (more precisely: Monterosso, which Lilly von Sauter had recommended to us as a deserted and very, very quiet place . . .), and three days of Zurich.

I tried calling you from Vienna, in the evening, but you were not there; it was probably because I was calling from the Westbahnhof, not the post office on Landstrasse.

I have been working a little; some devil wants me to translate 'La jeune Parque' now, instead of moving on with my own things, 460 out of 510 verses are done, and now may the devil or one of his close relatives help me get further!

Before your letter came, I read in the newspaper that you have been 'called' to teach in Frankfurt, at the university—my warmest congratulations! (But, between you and me: can one really teach that? Should one? 'Camerado, this is no book. Who touches this, touches a man!' I fear that the soul extensions extending to one's fingertips have long since been operationally removed from most people—in the name of human relations, incidentally . . .)

Ingeborg, do not fly too much! You know that we are 'chthonically fixated' . . . (By the way, as this little phrase was born in Wuppertal: has the 'Bund' invited you to come in October? Are you going?)

One request: please ask Princess Caetani why the fees for the contributions I obtained have not been transferred; Grass, whom I met in Zurich, has certainly not received his, and presumably the others have not either. (Please ask Enzensberger.) This is extremely awkward for me, and I am also wondering what is really behind it—for something or someone is definitely behind it!

I am sitting up here—may Nietzsche forgive me! (Do you remember that he wanted to have all anti-Semites shot? Now they probably come driving up in their Mercedes . . .)

Take care of yourself, Ingeborg—

I shall withhold the gentian from you, and am consequently

yours

with golden hawksbeard and many
rampions
Paul

NOTES

street of little stars: See NO. 133n.

weeks of rain [. . .] *Zurich*: PC stayed in Wald, near Krimml in the Salzburger Land, from 26 May to 28 June 1959, except for visits to Vienna (5–12 June 1959) and Innsbruck (22–24 June 1959). After spending a few days in Liguria, he went to Sils-Baselgia via Zurich (30 June–3 July 1959).

Sauter: Art historian, writer and translator, working at the French Cultural Institute in Innsbruck; probably made PC's acquaintance in early July 1948 in Innsbruck.

'called': In German, one refers to an invitation to take a university position as a *Ruf*, i.e. call.

human relations: In English in the original. [Trans.]

'Camerado [. . .] *man!'* / *chthonically* [. . .] *'Bund'*: The quotation from 'So long', the final poem in Walt Whitman's *Leaves of Grass* ([London: BPC, 1909], p. 460), also appears in the notes for the lecture 'Von der Dunkelheit des Dichterischen' [On the Darkness of the Poetic] which PC was intending to give before the Wuppertal Bund in October—thus speaking about poetics himself—but ultimately cancelled (MSS 130–152, esp. 138). At the 1957 conference of the Bund, which IB and PC both attended (see NO. 44), the topic of conversation was Sputnik I, launched shortly beforehand (MSS 106); here, by contrast, PC emphasizes the terrestrial.

soul extensions: See line 8 of 'Rheinufer. Schuttkahn II' (NO. 46).

fees: See NO. 103.

shot: PC still recalled this quotation from Nietzsche's letter of 4 January 1889 to his friend Franz Overbeck and his wife, signed 'Dionysos', on 21 December 1961: 'Nietzsche: it was very much in homage to him that I translated la Jeune Parque in Sils—and I remember the letter to Ingeborg written down there (up there!), in which I quoted the passage about shooting all anti-Semites' (DPC).

gentian [. . .] *rampions*: See the flower names (including rampion) in the story 'Gespräch im Gebirg' [Conversation in the Mountains], written that August (see NO. 165).

136

Paul Celan to Ingeborg Bachmann, Paris, 26 July 1959

on 26 July 1959.

Paris, once again—hopefully, it is not quite as hot in Rome as it is here . . .

Max Frisch was in Sils again last Wednesday. We took a walk on the Chasté peninsula for an hour (or more); it was, I think, a good conversation. He asked if you could perhaps help him by—he mentioned it—going up to the Engadin? And then: the air, the wealth of light, the larks, the naked rocks nearby. (Some time, when you come, you should go to Alp Grüm, which demonstrates with the utmost clarity that this earth was not necessarily created for humans.)

A request, Ingeborg: perhaps you could lay hands on this book in Rome:

Renato Poggioli, *Pietre di paragone*, Firenze 1939 (it contains a 'Commento a Mandelstam'). I ordered it months ago from Buchhandlung Flinker—without success. Please tell me to what address I can send your birthday book!

And also tell me what you are doing and thinking!

Yours

Paul

NOTES

MAN/ANL folder 5, pp. 19–20: hw. letter, envelope missing.

Paris: The letter is one of the first written after PC's return (DPC).

Wednesday: 22 July 1959.

Chasté: Peninsula in Lake Sils.

Alp Grüm: On 21 July 1959, PC made a trip to this railway station on the Bernina Line, located at an altitude of 2091 metres (PCPC).

Poggioli: The volume in question was a collection of essays primarily on Russian authors, but also on Kafka and others; the contribution on Mandelstamm was on pp. 113–32 (not in LPC).

Flinker: A German-language bookshop in Paris belonging to the Czernowitz-born Martin Flinker.

FIGURE 1. Ingeborg Bachmann and Paul Celan with Reinhard Federmann and
Milo Dor in 1952 at the conference of Gruppe 47 in Niendorf (IBPE).

FIGURE 2. Paul Celan, Vienna 1948 (Photo Studio Schulda-Müller, property of Eric Celan). Bachmann probably received the photograph for her birthday in 1948; it is also preserved in her estate (see NO. 1n).

FIGURE 3 (*left*). Ingeborg Bachmann, Vienna 1953, for the photo collage in *Stimmen der Gegenwart 1953* [Contemporary Voices 1953], Hans Weigel ed. (Vienna, 1953). Photograph by Wolfang Kudronofsky, IBPE.

FIGURE 4 (*right*). Ingeborg Bachmann, Munich *c.*1953. Photograph by Erika Sexauer, IBPE.

FIGURE 5 (*left*). Paul Celan with Nani Maier and Jean-Dominique Rey, Paris, Rue des Écoles, May 1951 (property of Jean-Dominique Rey).

FIGURE 6 (*right*). Gisèle Celan-Lestrange with Paul Celan and Klaus Demus, Paris, on the balcony of Celan's room in the Rue des Écoles, Spring 1953. Photograph by Nani Maier (property of Eric Celan).

FIGURE 7. Paul Celan, London, on Tower Bridge, February/March 1955. Cutting from the estate of Ingeborg Bachmann, originally with Nani and Klaus Demus on the right (see NO. 22 in PC/GCL II Fr., IBPE).

FIGURE 8. Paul Celan, Paris, apartment at rue Longchamps, 1958. Photograph by Gisèle Celan-Lestrange (property of Eric Celan).

FIGURE 9. Ingeborg Bachmann, reading at the prize-giving ceremony for the German Critics' Literature Prize, Berlin, 17 November 1961 (see NO. 193n). Photograph by Heinz Köster, IBPE.

FIGURE 10. Ingeborg Bachmann, Rome, 1962. Photograph by Heinz Bachmann, IBPE.

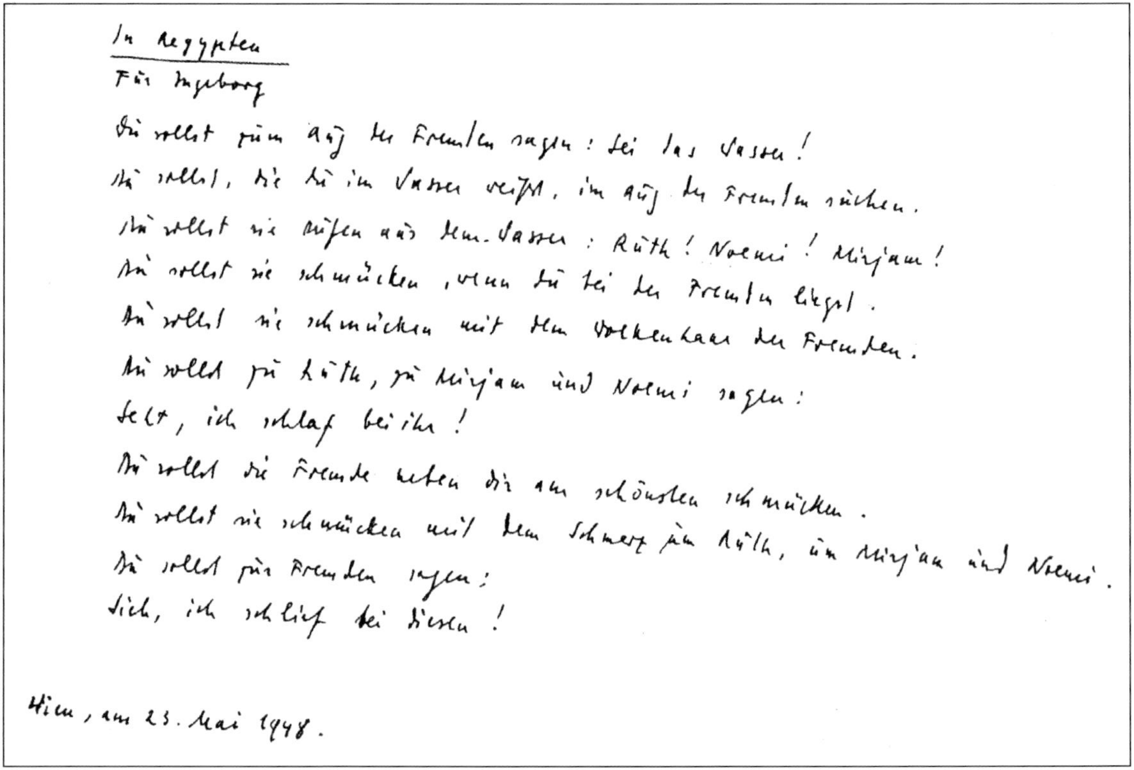

In Aegypten

Für Ingeborg

Du sollst zum Aug der Fremden sagen: Sei das Wasser!
Du sollst, die du im Wasser weißt, im Aug der Fremden suchen.
Du sollst sie rufen aus dem Wasser: Ruth! Noemi! Mirjam!
Du sollst sie schmücken, wenn du bei der Fremden liegst.
Du sollst sie schmücken mit dem Wolkenhaar der Fremden.
Du sollst zu Ruth, zu Mirjam und Noemi sagen:
Seht, ich schlaf bei ihr!
Du sollst die Fremde neben dir am schönsten schmücken.
Du sollst sie schmücken mit dem Schmerz um Ruth, um Mirjam und Noemi.
Du sollst zur Fremden sagen:
Sieh, ich schlief bei diesen!

Wien, am 23. Mai 1948.

FIGURE 11. Paul Celan, handwritten dedicatory poem 'In Ägypten' [In Egypt] for Ingeborg Bachmann (see NO.1, MAN/ANL).

Mäin 51.

Paul, Lieber,

es ist Ostermontag, und ich bin zum ersten Mal aufgestanden,
nach einer Krankheit, die nicht sehr arg war, die mir aber sehr
wichtig war, die mir fast wunderbar zu Hilfe gekommen ist. Dann ich
wusste nicht mehr, wie ich es hier und wie ich es hier mir recht
machen sollte. Der erste Fehler war, dass ich eine Woche mein altes
Wiener Leben weiterspielte, genaus so, als wäre nichts gewesen, dann
plötzlich verzweifelt und hysterisch abbrach und nicht aus dem Haus
wollte und dabei doch wusste, dass es so nicht immer bleiben könne,
und dann kam noch von aussen etwas dazu, das sehr schlimm war und
fast schlimmer als alles bisher. Dann kam meine Schwester und dann
diese Grippe. Jetzt ist es so still wie nach den Bombenabwürfen
im Krieg, wenn sich der Rauch verzogen hatte und man entdeckte,
dass das Haus nicht mehr stand und nichts zu sagen wusste; was
man auch sagen sollen?
Morgen werde ich vielleicht schon ausgehen, eine Arbeit suchen. Es
findet sich immer etwas. Das Telephon ist heute schon ganz still-
wie in einem heimli chen, heiteren Einverständnis.
Im Herbst komme ich vielleicht nach Paris. Es hat sich jedoch noch
nichts entschieden. Aber auch, wenn ich hierbleiben muss, will ich
nicht traurig sein. Ich habe soviel gehabt, soviel genommen, dass es
noch lange reichen könnte; aber auch, wenn es nicht reicht - man
kommt mit so wenigem aus. Später einmal werden wir sowieso nur wenig
Gepäck mitnehmen dürfen, vielleicht überhaupt keines.
Du erwartest ja nicht, dass ich heute schon etwa zu "uns" beiden sage,
ich kann jetzt nicht gut denken, ich muss zuerst wegkommen von allem,
nur fürchte ich, dass ich dann auch von Dir zu weit weg sein werde.
Schreibe mir bitte zuweilen. Schreib mir nicht zu vag,
erzähle ruhig, dass der Vorhang vor unserem Fenster schon wieder
angebrannt ist und uns die Leute zusehen von der Strasse.

Von Herzen

Deine

Lass die Nani innig grüssen von mir.
Milo Dor hat sich sehr gefreut.

4. Juli:

As lines so loves oblique may well
Themselves in every angle greet:
But ours so truly parallel,
Though infinite can never meet.

Therefore the Love which us doth bind,
But Fate so enviously debars,
Is the Conjunction of the mind,
And opposition of the stars.
(Andrew Marvell, the Definition of Love
l. 33).

am 5. November 1957.

Eine kurze Nachricht, hoffend, mit der ich
vielleicht keiner vorkommt zuvorkomme: heute kam
ein Brief aus Tübingen, man schlägt mir die
erste Dezemberwoche vor, ich werde annehmen.
Die Reise geht dann wohl zunächst über
Frankfurt, wo ich bei Fischer für das Honorar
für eine kleine Übersetzung, an der ich jetzt
arbeite, abholen will, am 29. der 30. kann
ich in München sein. Ich kann ein paar
Tage bleiben, bei oder wieder, sag, ob Du's
noch willst.

Zürile weiß, daß ich zu Dir fahren will,
sie ist so tapfer!

Ich werde nicht weggehen, nein.

Und wenn Du nicht willst, daß ich von

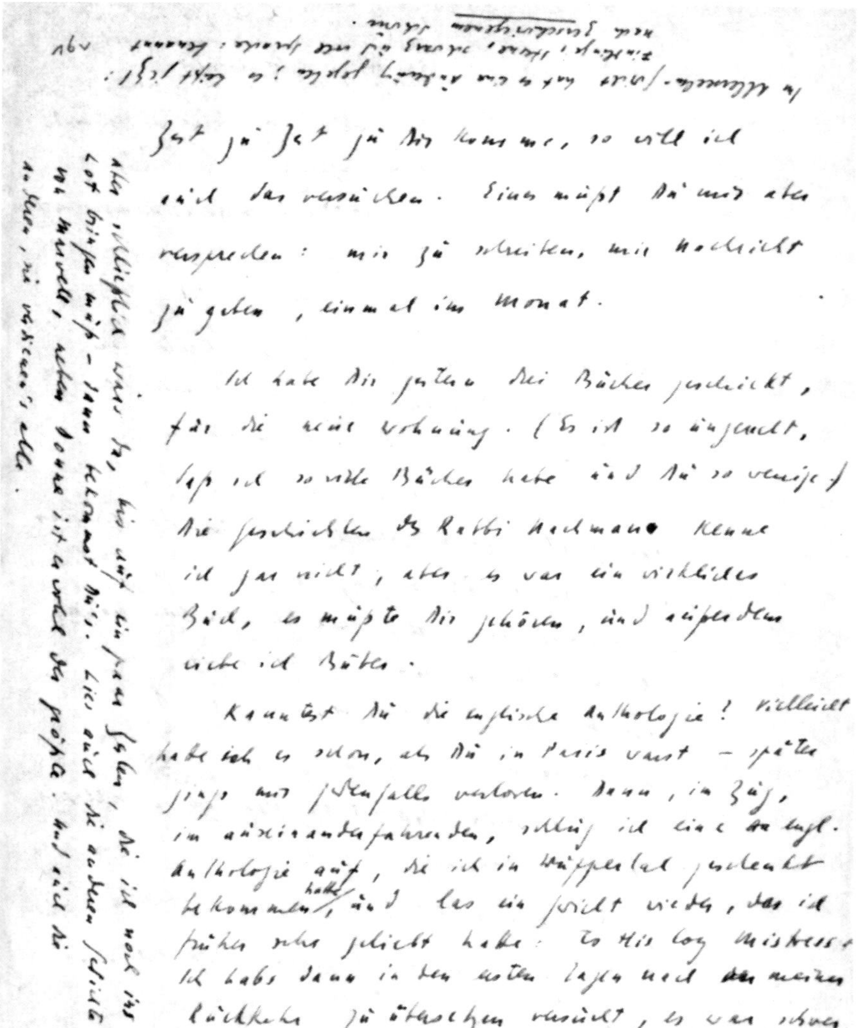

FIGURE 13 (*this and facing page*). Paul Celan, letter to Ingeborg Bachmann from 5 November 1957 (NO. 55, MAN/ANL).

Mittwoch

Paul, Lieber,

ich habe nur dieses zer-
knitterte Papier im Hotel,
alles andere ist in der Tram
vorgeblieben bei dem Lenchten.
Heute nachmittag habe ich
dort Deinen Brief abgeholt.
Nun ist mir unbehaglich
und schwer geworden, die
jetzt zu uns gehört. Warum
wollte ich böse sein? Nur
diesen Tram schreiben werde ich
noch, versteh, ich kann
nichts mehr von Belang hinzu-
fügen. (Und das schreiben an
andre macht mir mühe.)

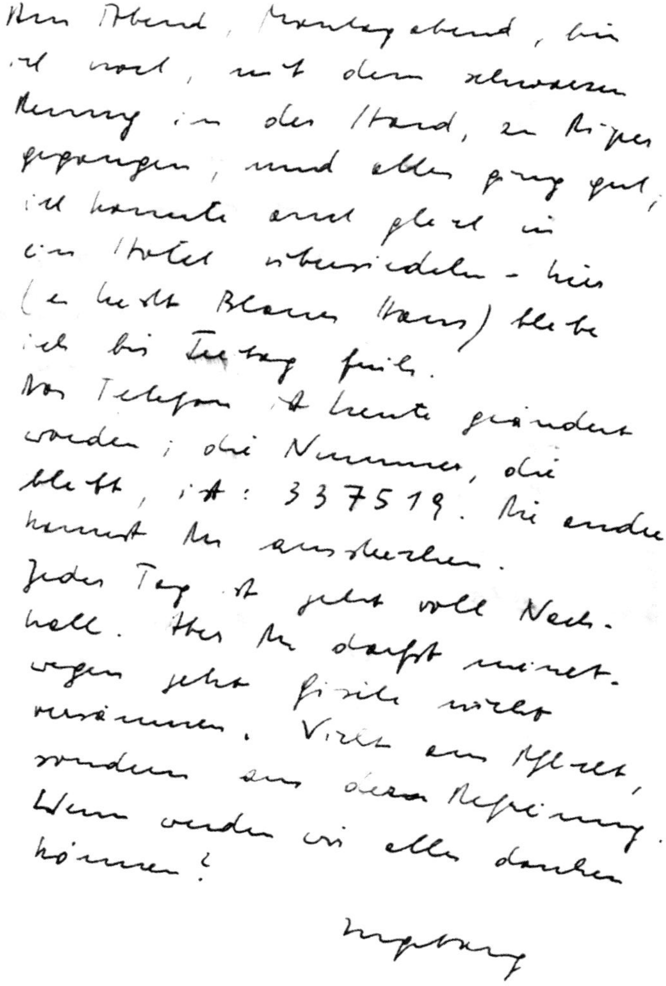
Am Abend, Montagabend, bin ich noch, mit dem schwarzen Kummer in der Hand, zu Piper gegangen, und alles ging gut, ich konnte auch gleich in ein Hotel übersiedeln – hier (es heißt Blaues Haus) bleibe ich bis Freitag früh.
Das Telefon ist heute geändert worden; die Nummer, die bleibt, ist: 337519. Die andere kannst Du ausstreichen.
Jeder Tag ist jetzt voll Nachhall. Aber Du darfst meinetwegen jetzt Gisèle nicht versäumen. Nicht am Abgrund, sondern an dieser Hoffnung. Wann werden wir alles danken können?

Ingeborg

FIGURE 14 (*this and facing page*). Ingeborg Bachmann, letter to Paul Celan from 11 December 1957 (no. 70, GLA).

FIGURE 15. Paul Celan to Ingeborg Bachmann, envelope for letter from 9 January 1957 (NO. 58, MAN/ANL).

FIGURE 16. Ingeborg Bachmann to Paul Celan, envelope for letter from 18 January 1958 (NO. 85, GLA).

Ich ann alles überstehen durdh Gleichmütigkeit, urch eigen gelehtich
Anfall önhtselimmsten Falö Es fiele mir nichtein, mich an jemand zu
wenden, um Hilfe, auch nih an Dich, we l ich mich stärker fühle.
ch belage mich nicht. Ich habe, ohne es zu wissen, gewusst,,
dass dis r weg , den ich einschlagen woll e, einsc lagen habe, nicht
mit Rosen einfass s in würde.
Du sag s, Maian vereide Dir Deine Uerbersetzungen.Lieber Paul, ich
as war vielleicht das einzige, das i h ein wenig angezweifelt habe,
ch meine nich Deine B richte, ondern ihre Auswikungeen, aber ich
glaube Dr Dir jetzt vollkommen, denn ich habe nun die B sarzgike ti
der professionellen Uebersetzer auch zu spüren bekommen, mit d ren
xxxkandxxxx Einkischüng ich auch nicht rechnete. an macht sich einen
Wtz daraus, ber meine ahgeblichen Fehler zu sprechen, Leute, die
was mich nicht kr ne wrde, behlechter italinis he können und
ancre, diees vielleicht besser könn n, abr jedehfalls Leute, die
kein Ahnung haben, wie ein Vedicht im Deutscen aussehen sollte.
Versteh t Du: ich glaube Dir, alles, alles. Nur glaube ich nicht,
dass sch der Klatsch, die Kritik, auf Dich beschrän en, denn
ich könnte benesogut des Gkäubens sein, dass sie si h auf mich be
schränken. Indich könnte Dir beweisen, wie Du irbeweisen kannst,
dass es so ist.
as ich nict kann: es Dir ganz beweisen, weil ich die anohymen und
andren Papirfetzen wegwerfen, weil ich laube, dass ich star er bin
als diese Fetzen,
und ich will, dass Du stärker bist, als diese Fetzen, ie nichts,
nichts besagen.
Abr das willst Du janicht wahrhaben, dass dies nih s besagt, Dunwillst,
dass es träker ist, Du willst Dich begraben lassen darunter.
Das ist Dein Unglückl das ich für starker halte als das Unglück, das
Dir widerfährt. Du willst das Opfer sein, aber es lieg an Dir, es
nicht zu sein, und ich muss denken an das Buch, das Szondisc ibe,
an das moto, das mich etroffen ht weil ich nicht anders könnte, als
an Dich denken. Gewiss, es wird, es kommt, es wirdjetzt von aussen
kommen, aber Du sanktionierst es. Und es ist die Frage ob du es sankti
r , es annimmst. A er das ist dann Deine Vesichte nd dass
wird nicht meine Gesihte sein, enn Du dich ü erwälitigen lässt
davon. Wenn Du eingeshts darauf. Du gehst daraufnein. as nehme
ich dir übel. Du gehst daraufnein, und gibst ihm dadu ch den Weg frei.
Dunwillsr der ein, das dran zu chanden wird, aber ic ann das nicht
guthissen, denn du kannst es ändern. Du willst, dass die Schuld Laben
an dir, xkxx und das werde ich nicht hindern können, dass es wilät.

Verstehst Du mih einmal, von e e aus: ich glaube niht, dass die Welt
sich ändern kann, aber wir können es und ich wünsche, dass Du es
kannst. Hier sette der Hebel an. Nicht der "Strassenfeger" kann es weg
yondern Du annst es, Du allein. Du wirst sage; ich verlange zuviel
von Dir für Dich. Das tue ich auch. (Aber ich verlange es auch von
mir für mich, darum wage ich es, Dir das zu sagen) Man kann nichts
anders verlangen. Ich werde es nicht ganz erfülle können und das
Du wirst es nich t ganz rfüllen könne, aber af dem Weg zu dieser
Erfüllung ird vieles wegfallen.

ich bin oft sehr bitter, wenn ich an Dich denke, und manchmal v rzeihe
ich mir nicht, dass ich Dich niht hasse, für dieses vedicht, diese
Mordbeschuldigung, die Du geschrieben hast. HtaDih je einkwnwxhc,
den du liebst , des Mordes beschuldigt, ei Unschuldiger? Ich hasse
Dich nicht, das ist das Wahnsinnige, jd wenn je etwas gerad und
gutnwerden soll: dann versuch auch hier anzufangen, mir zu antworten,
nic t kit Antwort, sondernmi keiner schriftlichen, sondern
im Gefül, in der at. Ich erwarte darauf, wie auf einige andre,
keine Antwot, keine Entschuldigung, weil keine Entschuldigun ausreich
und ich sie auch nict anhemenkönnte. ch erwarte, dass Du, mämi Dur
mir h lfst, Di selbst ehilfst, Du ir.

ch habe Dir gesagt, dass Du es ser leicht hast m t mir, aber
so wahr das ist, - es is auch war, dass Du es schwerer haben wirst
mir mir als mit irgen einem anderen. Ich bin glücklich, wenn
ich Du auf mich zkomst im Hoel du Louvre, wennn Du heiter und begreit
bist, ich vergesse alles und bin froh, dass Du heiter bist, dass
Du es sein kannst. ch de ke viel an Gisele, wenn es mir auh
nicht gegeben ist, das seh laut werden zu laasen, am wenigsten ihr
g enüber, ab r ich denke wiric an sie und bewundre sie für eine
rosse und Standhaftigkeit, die Du ichts hast. Das musst Du mir
nun verzeihen: aberich laube, dass i e eibstv rle gung, ihr
sc öner Solz und ih Diden vor mir mehr sind, s Dein lagen.
Du gnügst ihr in De nem Unglüc aber Dir würde sie nie in einem Unglück
genügen. Ich verlamge, dass ein ann genug at an der Bestätigung
durch mich, aber Du billgst ihr das nicht zu, we.che ngerechtigkeit.

FIGURE 17 (*this and facing page*). Ingeborg Bachmann, last two pages of a draft letter to Paul Celan, after 27 September 1961 (NO. 191, MAN/ANL).

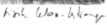

FIGURE 18 (*this and facing page*). Gisèle Celan-Lestrance, *Fin d'annee* 1971 II, I and III in the order shown here (Bachmann owned NO. 10 of each; see NO, 236. Property of Eric Celan; IBPE contains only etching II, here extreme left on facing page).

A Note on the Reproductions

The letters and other documents marked with the abbreviation ANL in the commentary section of the present edition are reproduced with kind permission from the Department of Manuscripts and Historical Prints at the Austrian National Library, Vienna. The rights for the documents featured as Figures 11, 13, 15 and 17 belong to the image archive at the Austrian National Library, Vienna, whom we thank for allowing their reproduction here.

Letters and other documents marked with the abbreviation GLA in the commentary section of the present edition are reproduced with kind permission from the Manuscript Department of the German Literature Archive, Marbach, which also granted permission for the reproduction of the documents featured as Figures 12, 14 and 16 in this volume.

Letters and other documents marked with the abbreviation MFA in the commentary section of the present edition are reproduced with kind permission from the Max Frisch Archive at the ETH Zurich.

For the rights to the remaining documents reproduced here, see the caption beneath each photograph.

We are grateful to the other authors (or present rights holders) of documents featured in the text and commentary for the permission to print these.

birthday book: A present for IB's 33rd birthday on 25 June 1959, noted in PCPC (see NO. 139).

137
Ingeborg Bachmann to Paul Celan, Uetikon am See, 5 August 1959

Uetikon am See, Haus Langenbaum
5 August 1959

My dear Paul,

there are so many things I want to reply to; I shall begin at the end. As things were going so badly in Rome, I left suddenly and went to Scuol, and then I saw that it was, and now Max and I are back in Uetikon.

I am glad the two of you still had the chance to meet again, but how I would like to have been there too! A great cold wave descended on the Engadin right after you left—it was autumnal, almost wintry when I arrived, with fresh snow lying on the mountain passes. But we may be going to Sils Maria for a few days when the weather improves, and then I will take the path you described in your last letter.

Botteghe Oscure: right at the start of my time in Rome, I accompanied Marie Luise von Kaschnitz to the editorial office; she also wanted to collect her fee. But the staff had changed; Eugene Walter was replaced months ago by a young Irishman, and all he could tell her was that he had the feeling there was no money. The Princess is in Paris, not Rome. I also saw Walter once; after some differences he left, or was made to leave by the Princess, but he told me that he wanted to give her a list of authors who have still not been paid. (I will write to him what the names are, as far as I know.) Paul, I know it is very awkward, for me too as I had asked Walter for a manuscript, but for now all we can do is be annoyed. I am sure there is nothing behind it, except that it probably became too much for her; she is very old, after all, and probably has bad advisers. (I have already explained everything to Enzensberger; I can tell Grass too, if he is still here or comes back.) The flight and the semester in Frankfurt are weighing very heavily on my mind.

I accepted both offers at a moment when I was not in my right mind and did not know what to do. Still, I am much less worried about the flying, and I do not quite share your reservations about it. You refer to the compromises we are all making; this was the part that struck me hardest, for I have hardly had this feeling about myself at all until now—for me, the compromise will begin with Frankfurt because I fear that I will be doing something I never wanted to do, and now I am looking for a way out. As it can hardly be reversed, I will try to face the danger I see by refraining from spreading my ideas about literary matters, by not talking 'about', so as to avoid augmenting the chatter with further chatter.

Please, Paul, tell me whether you think one is still allowed to say something despite great doubt, and from the position of having many doubts!

The air trip is a different matter; I see it as work that is strenuous and for which a certain amount of money is being paid, and I only have to write what I want to write. It may be a bad or unimportant job, but I am not abandoning or misrepresenting myself by taking it. I really only see a danger in the 'honourable' Frankfurt, for it is in such cases, where the suspicious elements are not so obvious, that one becomes entangled with them. The trip is probably foolish, but I am not afraid of doing anything stupid; afterwards, I will at least be able to tell Eric where there are really elephants and what the South Pacific looks like, and his father, shaking his head, will be lenient if I promise him never to go there again.

Paul, as the trip will end in October in London, I could return via Paris. I hope so. Then we could see each other soon after all.

Today Herr Neske called me about the contribution to the Heidegger festschrift, and I have to ask you something about that, as this is part of the compromise for me. Please, if you can, give me a brief answer—I do not know what to do. I wrote a critical dissertation on Heidegger years ago, and, though I do not place any value on that compulsory exercise, I have never changed my view of Heidegger. I still consider his political misconduct unacceptable, and I also see—as much now as I did then—where it left its mark on his work; but at the same time, because I truly know it, I realize the significance and quality of this work, which I shall never view in any way other than critically. On top of that, I would like to write the introduction to the German Wittgenstein edition when it is finally published—and if I do not end up doing so, it will be because I fear that my abilities are not sufficient; but it would be a sincere wish.

I have known for a long time that I am supposed to contribute to the festschrift, and I wanted to—I was pleased when I heard that Heidegger knows my poetry—but I have now acknowledged the hesitation I have been trying to suppress for months. (If I turn Neske down, I will <u>not</u> offer any explanation, for I do not want any superfluous chatter or personal offence; I simply want to do what I feel is right and ask you. And, above all, I do not want to make you confused on account of your acceptance, for there is no schematically correct course of action; that would rid us of all our vitality.)

I will write again soon. I am thinking of you a great deal.

Yours

Ingeborg

NOTES

GLA D 90.1.2831/9: tw. letter w/ hw. corrections to: '*M. Paul Celan/ 78, Rue de Longchamp/ <u>Paris 16ème</u>/ France*', Männedorf (*Zurich*), *8 August 1959*.

Rome: IB had tried to find an apartment for MF and herself in Rome. On 22 July 1959, she wrote to her parents from Naples: 'I am leaving Rome for Uetikon on Monday the 27th' (IBPE).

Scuol: Town in the Swiss Engadin (in German: Schuls); MF was staying there for treatment.

Sils Maria: See NO. 134n.

Kaschnitz/ Walser: Both were included in the latest issue of *Botteghe Oscure*, 23 (1959).

fee: See NO. 103.

The flight: See NO. 133.

semester in Frankfurt: The 'Frankfurter Vorlesungen'. The lecture 'Fragen und Scheinfragen' [Questions and False Questions] (25 November 1959) was followed by 'Über Gedichte' [On Poems] (9 December 1959, some parts dealing with PC), 'Das schreibende Ich' [The Writing Self] (concerning the date, see NO. 155n), 'Der Umgang mit Namen' [Dealing with Names] (10 February 1960) and 'Literatur als Utopie' [Literature as Utopia] (24 February1960).

Heidegger festschrift: *Martin Heidegger zum siebzigsten Geburtstag* [For Martin Heidegger on His Seventieth Birthday], Günther Neske ed. (Pfullingen: Neske, 1959), did not feature any contributions from IB or PC; IB's poem 'Anrufung des Grossen Bären' was, however, printed in full and extensively interpreted in the text by Walter Jens ('Marginalien zur modernen Literatur. Drei Interpretationen' [Marginalia on Modern Literature: Three Interpretations], pp. 225–31, esp. 229f.). PC and Heidegger had been in contact via the reciprocal sending of books since the late 1950s. Their first personal encounter in July 1967 is described in the critical poem 'Todtnauberg'; PC's engagement with the philosopher's works since the early 1950s is documented by the extensive reading traces in the LPC.

dissertation on Heidegger: IB's doctoral thesis 'Die kritische Aufnahme der Existentialphilosophie Martin Heideggers' [The Critical Reception of Martin Heidegger's Existential Philosophy] was directed against him, but ends, in keeping with Heidegger's thought, with an apotheosis of art and literature as the true expressive forms of existential experience. Heidegger had personally requested a poetic contribution to the festschrift from IB; IB also turned down other similar requests.

political misconduct: See NO. 138.

Wittgenstein edition: The first edition of Wittgenstein's *Tractatus logico-philosophicus* and *Philosophische Untersuchungen* [Philosophical Investigations] (*Schriften*, VOL. 1 [Frankfurt: Suhrkamp, 1960]) came about largely through IB's initiative. The wish expressed by Siegfried Unseld, head of Suhrkamp Verlag, for IB also to take over the editorial duties (12 June 1959, Suhrkamp Verlag archive, University of Frankfurt), was not fulfilled. PC, who owned a supplement to the volume, only seems to have become aware of the Austrian philosopher, who taught in Cambridge (England), in 1967 through Franz Wurm.

138
Paul Celan to Ingeborg Bachmann, Paris, 10 August 1959

Paris, on the tenth of August 1959.

It is not easy to answer your questions, but I shall try—right now.

About the Heidegger festschrift: Neske wrote to me a few days ago. The letter also includes a list; I am on it, without having been asked, i.e. without Neske, whom I told a year ago that I would also consider contributing if he first sent me the names of the other people involved, having kept his promise. So he did not, and I am on this list for certain (quite acceptable) reasons, and am now, as quickly as possible, supposed to send my poem . . . So this is the context, and this context also makes me think in other respects. I for my part will not send anything. But in that respect Neske made it easy for me, and surely not without reason. I also see that Martin Buber, of whom Neske said at the time that he had also promised to contribute, is not included. Those are the immediate facts; that leaves Heidegger. I am, as you know, surely the last person who would turn a blind eye to the Freiburg rectoral address and various other things; but I also think to myself, especially now, having garnered experiences with such patented anti-Nazis as Böll or Andersch, that someone who chokes on his errors, who does not pretend he never did any wrong, who does not conceal the guilt that clings to him, is better than someone who has settled so very comfortably and profitably into the persona of a man with a spotless past (was it, I must ask—and I have good reason—genuinely and in all its aspects spotless?), so comfortably that he can now—only 'privately', of course, not in public, for that, as we all know, is harmful to one's prestige— afford to indulge in the most shameful behaviour. In other words: I can tell myself that Heidegger has perhaps realized some of his errors; but I <u>see</u> how much vileness there is in someone like Andersch or Böll; I also <u>see</u> how 'on the one hand' Herr Schnabel writes a book about Anne Frank, and donates the fee for this book with the most visible generosity to some reparative cause, and 'on the other hand' that this same Herr Schnabel awards Herr von Rezzori a prize for his book, in which—against what kind of background!—he shows his ability to serve up that whole—'pre-Nazist', of course—anti-Semitism so charmingly and amusingly, *n'est-ce pas* (and then, after I have reprimanded him—but why do <u>I</u> have to be the one who steps in when the situation demands it?—presents himself as enormously offended by the 'form' in which I have done so).

This, my dear Ingeborg, is what I see, what I see <u>today</u>.

And now to your Frankfurt lectureship: I had, I have—and it would be wrong to keep it from you—genuine reservations. Aside from the fact that it shows the academic trade (among others) using poetry as a feather in its cap, so to speak—and, pardon me for saying so, that is simply part of German ostentation (now 'we' are just as distinguished as Oxford)—aside from the fact that, by turning one's mind to a poem (for there is a programme, and one part of that, by all accounts, is also a 'third' one), one demonstrates the 'performance' of that mind in the prettiest fashion—aside from all that (and various other things), I hardly think that 'poetics' is capable of helping the poem reach the place for which, under our dark skies, it has set out. But—and I am not saying this simply because you cannot go back on this now—<u>but</u>: try it nonetheless, do try it. Something that is perhaps not entirely clear to you yet, something small and invisible, a stuttering of the eyes over something supposedly all too obvious, should help you truly to <u>communicate</u> one or two things. (Marginal note: I am certainly in favour of the articulated.)

And then your flight, Ingeborg: please fly, if you cannot help yourself. But if you can, do not fly. Ultimately your 'freedom' to write about it in this way or that is simply a minor refinement of the advertising idea involved in your flight. For, the fact that you are flying, you of all people—<u>that</u>, Ingeborg, is enough for those people. (You call it work; please think of the added value, and consider that the poem you write will contribute to that.) And, Ingeborg, that little bit of 'having been there' . . . Those however-many hours of South Pacific and elephants . . . Would you not prefer for Eric to draw you an elephant that, if you are lucky, will bear a great resemblance to a field mouse? But (here too): in these times, people are flying—so why should you not fly too? Perhaps by flying you will gain something that I, who has only flown a kite a handful of times, cannot see, and will only see once you have made it visible? So I wish you all the best, in the air too!

Give Max Frisch my regards!

Yours, Paul

Are you coming to Wuppertal at the end of October?

NOTES

MAN/ANL folder 5, pp. 21–2: tw. letter w/hw. corrections, envelope missing.

a few days ago: In his letter of 29 July 1959 (PCE), Neske both requested that PC contribute a poem to the festschrift and informed him that Heidegger was occupying himself intensively with *Sprachgitter*, and would be especially pleased by a contribution from PC.

list: Not only PC was on the list, but so also were IB and a number of common friends, as well as certain persons whom PC viewed very critically (see NO. 140).

Freiburg rectoral address: It is unknown when and in what form IB and PC became acquainted with the precise wording of Heidegger's speech of 10 May 1033. In it, the philosopher had expressly welcomed the seizure of power with the words: 'We will ourselves. For the young and youngest strength of the people, already reaches beyond us, *has* by now *decided* the matter.' He also spoke of the 'splendour' and 'greatness' of 'this settting out' ('The Self-Assertion of the German University', in Martin Heidegger, *Philosophical and Political Writings*, Manfred Stassen ed. and Karstein Harries trans. [New York: Continuum, 2003], p. 11).

Böll/today.: On 3 April 1959, in his reply to a letter written by PC on 2 February 1958 (see NO. 112) containing Firges' account of the Bonn reading, Böll had stated that his full response would be contained in his next novel. After PC's bitter reproaches of 8 April 1959, Böll replied equally bitterly (see NO. 197). On 10 August 1959, in the fourteenth instalment of Böll's novel *Billard um Halbzehn* [Billiards at Half Past Nine], printed in advance in the *FAZ*, PC was able to read what Böll had presumably been referring to. The narrator recalls his uncle, who had dreamt of the fame 'which he hoped to achieve through successful verses; a dream, dreamt on walks through the moor for two years [. . .] what remained was a quarto notebook of verses and a black suit.' In the narrator's portrait of himself shortly after that passage, one can recognize PC as he appeared in photographs of the time: 'I was delicate, almost small, looked like something between a young rabbi and a bohemian, with black hair and black clothes, and the undefined air of a rural background.'

Andersch: PC had reservations about the first publisher of *Die gestundete Zeit* after he failed to respond directly to his long letter of 27 July 1956 concerning the Goll affair; he also considered Andersch's novel *Sansibar oder der letzte Grund* [Zanzibar or The Last Reason] latently anti-Semitic (to Hermann Lenz, 21 March 1959).

Schnabel: PC read about the author's decision to forgo his fee for the book *Spur eines Kindes* [The Footsteps of Anne Frank] in an article about the radio programme on which the book was based (*FAZ*, 11 March 1958). In a letter—beginning without any formal address—accidentally dated 1958 (8 April 1959), PC criticized him for being on the jury that had awarded Rezzori the Fontane Prize for his novel *Ein Hermelin in Tschernopol* [An Ermin in Chernopol] (*FAZ*, 26 March 1959). PC accused the Czernowitz-born novelist of writing about 'miasmas of the gutters in the Jewish courtyards' and, like Andersch, about 'beautiful almond-eyed Jewesses' (MSS 200.1n).

Oxford: PC is alluding to the article 'Poeta doctus' [Learned Poet] in *Die Welt*: 'In England, at the illustrious University of Oxford, there is a chair for poetry' (14 July 1959).

'*third*': The NDR, where Schnabel was employed, had had a culture programme ('Drittes Program', i.e. third programme) since 1956 that featured Rezzori's work on various occasions, for exmple in the series 'Idiotenführer durch die deutsche Gesellschaft' [An Idiot's Guide to German Society].

dark skies: See the 'Letter to Hans Bender' (18 May 1960).

flight: See NO. 133.

Wuppertal: See NO. 135n. This sentence was added by hand along with the date.

139
Ingeborg Bachmann to Paul Celan, Uetikon am See, 3 September 1959

Uetikon am See
3-9-59

Dear Paul,

I have cancelled the flight. It cost a great deal of effort to get out of the commitment once I had made it, and that has consumed the last few days. I did not want to write to you before that, not before being able to tell you that for certain. Now I am happier. That leaves Frankfurt . . .

I certainly understand what you write concerning Heidegger, and I continue to believe that the refusal should not be twisted into an affront, let alone a judgement.

'Valéry' arrived, my birthday book, I am so happy about it! But back then, in Paris, you were able to give me its partner books yourself. When will I see you again? In the winter, in Frankfurt? Will you send me the translation?

Things are quiet here, and going well; I am trying to work a little, but I always feel tired, exhausted by doubts, before I even begin.

I keep thinking again and again, but always in this language in which I no longer have any faith, in which I no longer want to express myself. Take care, dear Paul.

Ingeborg

NOTES

GLA D 90.1.2831/10: *hw. letter to 'M. Paul Celan/78, Rue de Longchamp/PARIS 16ème/France', [xx.xx.]1959.*

flight: See NO. 133.

Frankfurt: The 'Frankfurter Vorlesungen'.

'Valéry'/translation: Paul Valéry, *Poésies. Album de vers anciens [Poems: Album of Ancient Verses]—La Jeune Parque—Charmes [Charms]—Pièces diverses [Various Pieces]—Cantate du Narcisse [The Narcissus Cantata]—Amphion—Sémiramis* ([Paris: 1942]; LIB, also in LPC). Concerning PC's translation, 'Die junge Parze', see NO. 160.

back then, in Paris: Is IB referring to her stays in 1950/51 or her visit in the summer of 1958?

140
Paul Celan to Ingeborg Bachmann, Paris, 7 September 1959

on 7 September 1959.

Ingeborg, I am glad you are not flying.

Now that you have cancelled it for good, I can tell you that it was primarily the shocking nature of this news that made me find all the (secondary) arguments.

I am truly glad you are not flying.

Frankfurt: please do not cancel it, I am quite sure it will go well.

The Heidegger festschrift: I do not have the slightest doubt that Neske is a shady character. After my experiences with the recording, and after being placed on his list without consultation, I must conclude, among other things, that the festschrift, once it is printed, will include one or two names not mentioned before (Friedrich Georg Jünger is not exactly one of the most pleasant either . . .) and with which I must absolutely avoid being associated . . . So I merely told him that I hoped he, Neske, would notify me in time if he publishes another festschrift for Heidegger's 75th birthday . . .

(And God knows I am no 'shepherd of Being' . . .)

I am sending you the first third of 'Die junge Parze', Ingeborg. It is the corrected Rundschau version—the most readable text I have at the moment. Please return it to me once you have read it; I should have a fair copy of the whole things by early October—I am completely unable to think of it now—you will receive it then.

The Mandelstamm will soon be there, but I have already had such bad experiences with it that I am not expecting much from its existence as a book. (I am, incidentally, back in darkness in other respects too.)

I wonder, are you coming to Wuppertal? I have a few invitations to readings, one of them even in Vienna (!), a matinée at the Burgtheater; but I am tired of reading, all these letters are still unanswered; aside from that I have also accepted a position as German Assistant at the Ecole Normale, not least for the monthly salary it involves. I think I have to get through an extended period of silence.

All the best, Ingeborg!

Paul

Enclosed: hand-corrected make-up for the partial publication of his translation of Paul Valéry, 'La jeune Parque', in Die Neue Rundschau.

NOTES

MAN/ANL folder 5, pp. 23–4: hw. letter, envelope missing; concerning supplement, see NO. 142.

Frankfurt: The 'Frankfurter Vorlesungen'.

recording: See NO. 103. The bad experiences PC is thinking of relate to an allocation of authors' names that deviated from what had been agreed, as well as the yet unpaid fee (PC to Neske, 12 November/28 August 1959; PCE).

Friedrich Georg Jünger: The younger brother of Ernst Jünger (who was also on the list sent on 29 July 1959, see NO. 138) had close connections to various *Kampfbünde* (National Socialist groups) and the NSDAP; he influenced Heidegger, for example with the critique of technology he developed in the 1940s in opposition to the technologized National Socialist society.

75th birthday: No festschrift was published on said occasion. In addition to his suggestion, PC wrote to Neske: 'if only you had written to me in time, as you promised over a year ago! But you are only writing now, at the last minute, and my reserves of unpublished material have meanwhile shrunk to a minimum; I really have nothing that could form a contribnution to the Heidegger festschrift. And I cannot dash something off quickly, I truly cannot, for it would be anything but serious—and Heidegger demands seriousness and reflection' (28 August 1959, PCE).

'shepherd of Being': In his copy of *Wegmarken* [Pathmarks] (Frankfurt: Klostermann, 1967; LPC), PC marked the passage in 'Brief über den Humanismus' [Letter on Humanism] (1946) that reads 'Der Mensch ist der Hirt des Seins' [Man is the shepherd of Being] with a line in the margin.

'Die junge Parze': PC's translation of 'La jeune Parque'.

the corrected Rundschau version: Lines 1–173 of the translation 'Die junge Parze' were published in 1959 in *Die Neue Rundschau*, 3; the corrected make-up was sent to S. Fischer Verlag on 7 September 1959 (this and letter to IB noted in PCPC).

Mandelstamm [. . .] *bad experiences*: One reaction to PC's translations in *Die Neue Rundschau* (3, 1958, IBE without dedication) was the sending of an anti-Semitic magazine (to Hirsch, 22 April 1959). Concerning the book edition *Gedichte*, see NO. 154.

Wuppertal: See NO. 135.1n.

a matinée at the Burgtheater: Helmut Schwarz of the Burgtheater asked PC on 27 August 1959 whether he would be willing to come for a reading during the 1959/60 season. Made uneasy by the Goll affair, PC decided in late December 1960 not to participate in the event, which had meanwhile been planned as a joint reading with IB and Ilse Aichinger and postponed until the following season.

a position as German Assistant: PC held this position at the Parisian elite university École normale supérieure (rue d'Ulm) from 1 October 1959 until his death.

period of silence: PC wrote no poems of his own between 'Es war Erde in ihnen' (27 July 1959) and 'Zürich, Zum Storchen' [Zurich, the Storchen, i.e. the name of a hotel] (30 May 1960).

141
Paul Celan to Ingeborg Bachmann, Paris, 22 September 1959

22.9.59.

A request, Ingeborg: could you send me back 'Die junge Parze'? I see that I did not add the corrections to the MS.

How are you? Well, I hope; well.

Paul

NOTES

MAN/ANL folder 5, p. 25: hw. letter, envelope missing.
22.5.59: Letter noted in PCPC.

142
Ingeborg Bachmann to Paul Celan, Zurich, 28 September 1959

Kirchgasse 33
Zurich, 28-9-59

Paul,

forgive me for not replying sooner. I am moving to Zurich in a few days, into a small work apartment that became available by chance. Max will stay in Uetikon—so will I, but we never got any work done living so close together. It was a calm decision, it does not change anything.

I have made a few notes about 'Die junge Parze'; could I share them with you?

Page 3, line 16:

Der Geist—er ist so rein nicht, dass (would this word order not be better?)

Page 5, 3 lines from the bottom:

die Wange glüht, als flammt' drauf, etc. (apostrophe or not?, because else-where you also add one where there is a possibility of confusing it with the present form)

last page, 4th line

Mein Sinn . . . , als schlief' er—(here because one might suppose the imperfect otherwise.)

But that is all. The translation must be very difficult with so little room to manoeuvre. It is quite beautiful.

I will not be coming to Wuppertal (I do not think I received an invitation anyway).

I do not know what to say about your assistant position; it pains me that you have to do it, but perhaps it will at least be good during the expected period of silence, so that you have something to do. Tell me whether the work is bearable and not too much.

Take care, Paul.

Ingeborg

Could you write to me at the Kirchgasse address? I am moving there on 1 October; the house is old and is called 'Steinhaus'—it is the highest in the city, between the houses of Zwingli, Büchner and Gottfried Keller.

Enclosed: hand-corrected make-up for the partial publication of his translation of Paul Valéry, 'La jeune Parque', in Die Neue Rundschau.

NOTES

GLA D 90.1.2831/11: hw. express letter to: 'M. Paul Celan/78, Rue de Longchamp/PARIS 16ème/FRANCE', Zurich, 28 September 1959, from: 'Ingeborg Bachmann, Kirchgasse 33 Zürich', Paris, 29 September 1959: GLA D 90.1.490 (ass. supplement): 6-page corr. make-up, top right corners marked '-i-' by PC.

Kirchgasse 33 / Gottfried Keller: In October, IB moved into an apartment in the house that had been inhabited by the Swiss writer between 1861 and 1876.

notes: PC did not incorporate IB's suggested corrections.

er ist so rein nicht, dass: The spirit—it is not so pure that.

die Wange glüht, als flammt' drauf: The cheek glows as if it were flaming.

apostrophe or not?: Without the apostrophe, *flammt* is the third-person singular, present tense of *flammen* ('to flame'); the apostrophe would indicate that the full word is *flammte*, which is the subjunctive (or imperfect) and hence correct, form. [Trans.]

Mein Sinn . . . , als schlief ' er: My sense . . . as if it were sleeping.

here because one might suppose the imperfect otherwise: In this case, *schlief* is the third-person singular imperfect form of *schlafen* ('to sleep'), whereas *schliefe* is the subjunctive, and hence correct, form here. [Trans.]

Wuppertal: See NO. 135.1n. It is unclear whether IB was genuinely not invited.

assistant position: See NO. 140.

Zwingli: The Swiss reformer lived at Kirchgasse 13 from 1525.

Büchner: The house at Spiegelgasse 12, in which the German writer and revolutionary Georg Büchner lived from October 1836, is directly connected to Kirchgasse 33 by a side street.

143

Paul Celan to Ingeborg Bachmann, Paris, 17 October 1959

17.X.59.

Dear Ingeborg,

the review enclosed came this morning—please read it and tell me what you think.

Paul

NOTES

MAN/ANL folder 5, pp. 26–7: hw. letter to: 'Mademoiselle Ingeborg Bachmann/Zürich/ Kirchgasse 33/Suisse', Paris, [xx.xx.]1959, from: 'Celan, 78 r. Longchamp/Paris 16ᵉ'; MAN/ANL folder 14, p. 3 (ass. supplement): cpy w/hw. corrections and highlightings by PC.

review: PC obtained Blöcker's review of *Sprachgitter* through his Berlin acquaintance Edith Aron (letter of 14 October 1959, PCE). PC sent the text to Schroers the same day; on 23 October 1959, he made a note that he had not received a response to it from anyone yet (PCPC). PC wrote on 21 October 1959 in 'Wolfsbohne' [Wolfsbane]: 'Mutter, ich habe/Briefe geschrieben./Mutter, es kam keine Antwort./Mutter, es kam eine Antwort./Mutter, ich habe/Briefe geschrieben an—' [Mother, I/wrote letters./Mother, there was no answer./Mother, there was an answer./Mother, I/wrote letters to—'] (lines 39–44). For PC's response to the article, see NO. 201.1.

143.1
Supplement (Günter Blöcker, review of Sprachgitter)

POEMS AS GRAPHIC CONSTRUCTS

The title of the new poetry volume by Paul Celan is both uncommonly fitting and revealing. The thin filaments of these poems are indeed speech-grilles [Sprachgitter]. The only question is what one sees through these grilles. That question—as always with Celan—is difficult to answer, as his poetry only rarely faces an object. On the whole, its verbal filigrees develop like silk threads that seem to issue from the glands of language itself. Throughout the volume, Celan's wealth of metaphors is neither derived from reality nor serves it. In his work, the image as a reality that is better understood, more penetratingly examined and more purely felt remains the exception. His pictorial language feeds off itself. The reader witnesses something like a primal creation of images that are then joined to form structured language-masses. The decisive element is not the view but, rather, the combinations.

Even where Celan introduces nature, it is not a lyrical evocation in the manner of the nature poem. The carpet of thyme in 'Sommerbericht' does not have anything intoxicating about it; it is odourless—a word that can be applied to all of these poems. Celan's verses are for the most part graphic constructs. Nor does their musicality necessarily compensate for the lack of concrete sensuality. Certainly, the author likes to work with musical terms: the <u>much-praised</u> 'Todesfuge' from Mohn und Gedächtnis, *or, in the present volume, 'Engführung'. But these are more like <u>contrapuntal exercises</u> on the <u>manuscript paper</u> or on silent keys—music for the eye, visual* *scores that are not fully released as sound. Only rarely do the poems develop that sound far enough for it to contribute to some larger meaning.*

Celan approaches the German language with more freedom than most of his fellow poets. That may be due to his background; he is less inhibited and burdened by the communicational character of the language. Admittedly, however, this is precisely what often induces him to speak into a vacuum. It seems to us that his most convincing poems are those in which he does not abandon all connections to the reality located outside the combinatorial fervour of his intellect. Lines such as the beginning of the poem 'Nacht':

> *Kies und Geröll. Und ein Scherbenton, dünn,*
> *als Zuspruch der Stunde.*

> [Gravel and scree. And a shard-note, thin,
> as the hour's word of encouragement.]

It is especially effective how the intimidating night (the stumbling 'Kies und Geröll') is softened by noises, and the 'dünner Scherbenton' takes on the sonorous sound of assurance: the reference to 'der Zuspruch der Stunde', hinging entirely on the darkest of the vowels. Or how, in the poem 'Die Welt' [The World], bare tree shafts become flags at whose base man, abandoned, fights:

> */ Zwei Baumschäfte...............................den Fahnen./*

> [/Two tree shafts....................................the flags./]

These are true lyric metamorphoses that lie beyond any overly self-obsessed combinatorial techniques. One could imagine the author developing further in this direction, very much in the sense that the poet is a man who 'goes to language with his very being, aching from and searching for reality.'

Günter Blöcker, Der Tagesspiegel, *Berlin, 11.X.59.*

NOTES

poetry volume: Sprachgitter, referred to in the original version as a 'Lyrikband' rather than a 'Gedichtband'; in his immediately preceding work towards the lecture 'Von der Dunkelheit des Dichterischen' (see NO. 135.1n), PC had expressly distanced himself from the concept of the lyrical (MSS 245, 246, 253).

Two [. . .] *flags*: In the original version, lines 3–11 of 'Die Welt' are quoted without omissions, but without any reference to the missing first stanza; hence presumably the slashes.

searching for reality': Ending of the Bremen speech (GW III 186).

144
Ingeborg Bachmann to Paul Celan, Zurich, 9 November 1959

Kirchgasse 33
Zurich, Monday./9 November 1959/

Dear Paul,

I was in Germany briefly and came home with a heavy attack of flu and headaches that prevented me from replying immediately. And now something else is preventing me from replying as I have in the past, for everything is now overshadowed by my knowledge of the letter Max wrote you, by my fears and helplessness because of it. I could have prevented the letter from being sent, but I still think I did not have the right to do that, and so I simply have to endure these coming days in uncertainty.

I want to find my way back to the starting point and give you my answer as it would have been without any of this, but it almost eludes me—not because I lack independence, but because the first problem is engulfed by the new one.

Did Blöcker reply in any way, and if so, what did he say? I know that he can sometimes be insulting in the most haphazard and reckless way in his reviews; the same thing happened to me after my second volume of poems. Is there a different reason this time, is anti-Semitism the reason?—after your letter I thought so too, but I am not sure yet, hence my question about his response.—Let me start again somewhere else: Paul, I often worry that you do not see at all how much your poems are admired, how much of an impact they have, and that it is actually only because of your fame (allow me to use the word just this once, and do not dismiss it) that people will keep trying to detract from it in any way they can, finally culminating in attacks with no motive—as if something unusual were so unbearable and intolerable to them. I would like nothing more than to call you, because of all these things, and this time I am loath to pick up the telephone because one can only speak so briefly and I do not know what frame of mind I will find you in.

I will be in Frankfurt on 25 and 26 November, then again two weeks later, in December, for the readings.

If only we could see each other! If you never come to Frankfurt in the winter, I will try to go to Paris.

Dear Paul, too little of what has been going through my mind is in these words. I wish you could sense how to fill in the gaps until I see you again!

Yours

Ingeborg

NOTES

GLA D 90.1.2831/12: *hw. letter* (*hw. date in PC's handwriting*) *to*: '*M. Paul Celan/78, Rue de Longchamp/* <u>*PARIS 16ème*</u> */France*', *Zurich, 10 November 1959, at top left of envelope in PC's handwriting*: '*Paris*, <u>*12*</u>*.XI.59*'.

Germany: Participation in the Gruppe 47 conference at Schloss Elmau, near Mittenwald (23–25 October 1959).

the letter Max wrote you: PC characterized MF's response (see NO. 203) with the words 'Cowardice, mendacity, infamy' (12 November 1959, PCPC).

Blöcker: IB knew about PC's letter to Blöcker from MF (see NO. 201.1).

reviews [. . .] *second volume of poems*: Blöcker's collective review with underlinings (by IB?) in the section on *Anrufung des Grossen Bären* is contained in the IBPE: '<u>Has the author become worn out or careless on account of her success? She indulges in softness, lapsing into broad psalmody at times. The images do not always stand in the poetic space as powerfully and unassailably as in the past</u>. The ideogrammatic quality sometimes seems musically smoothed over: a slightly blurred Sibelius-like tone establishes itself. Some sections have been pulled apart into excessively loose language patterns, and the volume seems a little stretched. <u>Here and there one even finds self-quotations</u>.' ('Unter dem sapphischen Mond' [Under the Sapphic Moon], *Der Tagesspiegel*, 7 July 1957).

in Frankfurt on 25 and 26 November: Regarding the beginning of the poetics lectureship, see NO. 137.

to Paris: Concerning the planned meeting on the occasion of the third of the 'Frankfurter Vorlesungen', ultimately avoided by IB, see NO. 155.

145
Paul Celan to Ingeborg Bachmann, Paris, 12 November 1959

Paris, 12 November 1959.

I wrote to you on 17 October, Ingeborg—in a time of need. On 23 October, after I had still not received an answer, I wrote, equally in need, to Max Frisch. Then, as my need continued, I tried, several times, to reach you by telephone—in vain.

You had—I read it in the newspapers—gone to the meeting of Gruppe 47 and received much acclaim for a story entitled 'Alles'.

This morning your letter came, and this afternoon the letter from Max Frisch. You know, Ingeborg, what you wrote to me.

You also know what Max Frisch wrote to me.

You also know—or, rather, you used to know—what I was trying to say in 'Todesfuge'. You know—no, you used to know—so now I must remind you—that for me 'Todesfuge' is not least this: an epitaph and a grave. Whoever writes <u>those</u> things about 'Todesfuge', the things this Blöcker character wrote, is desecrating the graves.

My mother too has only <u>this</u> grave.

Max Frisch suspects me of vanity and ambition; he responds to the line I wrote in my need—yes, it was just one line: how much I (foolishly) thought I could take for granted!—with various eloquent remarks and assumptions about the problems of the 'writer', e.g. concerning 'the way we deal with literary criticism in general'.—No, here I must, though I assume that Max Frisch kept a copy of his letter—I too am now making a carbon copy . . .—quote one more sentence: 'For it seems to me that if there is even a hint of that (referring to the 'stirrings of vanity and hurt ambition') in your anger, the invocation of the death camps is impermissible and egregious.'—Thus writes Max Frisch.

You, Ingeborg, expect me to be content with my 'fame'.

As hard as it is for me, Ingeborg—and it is hard for me—I must now <u>ask</u> you not to write to me, not to call me, not to send me any books; not now, not in the months ahead—not for a long time. And <u>please</u>, both of you, do not force me to send back your letters!

Though a number of other things are becoming apparent to me, I will not make this letter any longer.

I have to think of my mother.

I have to think of Gisèle and the child.

I sincerely wish you all the best, Ingeborg! Farewell!

Paul

NOTES

MAN/ANL folder 5, pp. 28–9: tw. letter w/hw. corrections to: '*Mademoiselle Ingeborg Bachmann/<u>ZURICH</u>/Kirchgasse 33/<u>SUISSE</u>*', *Paris, 13 November 1959, from*: '*Paul Celan, 78 rue de Longchamp, Paris 16ᵉ*'; *GLA D 90.1.2820/1* (*two cpys*): *hw. corrections only in one of them.*

to Max Frisch/in my need: See NO. 201.

'*Alles*': See NO. 156. PC had been able to read in the *FAZ* what IB had read as 'proof of her great ability' (Hans Schwab-Felisch, 'Lyriker lesen Prosa' [Poets Read Prose], 29 October 1959).

from Max Frisch: See NO. 203.

mother/Gisèle and the child: Friederike Antschel was murdered in the winter of 1942/43 in a German concentration camp. PC evokes her and his son Eric in connection with Blöcker's review in *Wolfsbohne*: 'Unser/Kind/weiss es und schläft.//(Weit, in Michailowka, in/der Ukraine, wo/sie mir Vater und Mutter erschlugen' [Our/child/knows it and sleeps.//(Far away, in Mikhaylovka, in/the Ukraine, where/they struck my mother and father dead].

146

Paul Celan to Ingeborg Bachmann, Paris, 17 November 1959

17.XI.59

I am worried about you, Ingeborg—

But you have to understand: my cry for help—you do not hear it, you are not within your own heart (where I expect you to be), you are . . . in literature.

And Max Frisch, who is using this 'case'—which is such a scream!—as a source of literary inspiration . . .

So please, write to me, or send me—by telegram—your telephone number in the Kirchgasse.

(Please do <u>not</u> call: we have a guest: Rolf Schroers . . .)

Paul

NOTES

MAN/ANL folder 5, pp. 30–1: *hw. express letter to*: '*Mademoiselle Ingeborg Bachmann/ Zürich/ Kirchgasse 33/ Suisse*', *from*: '*Paul Celan, 78, rue de Longchamp/ Paris 16ᵉ*', *Paris, 17 November 1959 and Zurich, 18 November 1959.*

literature: Presumably a reference to the Gruppe 47 conference (see NO. 144n). On 1 October 1959, PC noted down information about the conference that he had received from Grass: 'Ingeborg did not say a word about the Blöcker business' (PCPC).

Max Frisch [. . .] literary inspiration: See NO. 203.

Schroers: Evidently since 13 November 1959 (PCPC).

147

Ingeborg Bachmann to Paul Celan, Zurich, 18 November 1959

Wednesday afternoon,

your express letter just came, Paul, thank God. I can breathe again. Yesterday, I tried to write to Gisèle in my desperation, now the letter is lying there unfinished; I do not want to distress her, but, rather, implore her—through you—to offer me some sisterly sentiment, one that can translate my helplessness for you, the conflict I am in,—as well as my lack of freedom in a letter that was bad, I know, that was unable to come to life.

The last few days here, since your letter—it was horrible, everything becoming unstable, close to breaking up, and now each of us has inflicted so many wounds on the other. But I cannot, I must not speak of that.

But I <u>must</u> speak about us. We cannot let it happen, we must not fail in finding the way back to each other again,—it would destroy me. You say I am not within myself but, rather, . . . in literature! No, do not be absurd—what strange directions your thoughts are taking. I am where I always am, but often despairing, collapsing under the different burdens; it is difficult for me to carry even one person who is isolated by self-destruction and illness. I have to learn to do more, I know, and I will.

I will listen to you, but please help me too by listening. I shall send the telegram with my number now, and pray that we will find the words.

Ingeborg

NOTES

GLA D 90.1.2831/13: *hw. express letter to*: '*M. Paul Celan/78, Rue de Longchamp/<u>PARIS 16ème</u>/FRANCE*', *Zurich, 18 November 1959 and Paris, 19 November 1959.*

MAN/ANL folder 17, pp. 1–4: 3 hw. drafts (not publ.)

Gisèle: See NO. 221.

letter that was bad: See NO. 144.

speak of that: That is, the relationship with MF.

148

Ingeborg Bachmann to Paul Celan, Zurich, 18 November 1959

342987   BUT NOT TONIGHT LET US FIND THE WORDS

INGEBORG

NOTE

GLA D 90.1.2831/14: telegram to: 'Paul Celan, 78 Rue de Longchamp Paris/16', Zurich 18 November [1959], 15^{13} and Paris, 1 November 1959, 16^{35}.

149

Ingeborg Bachmann with Klaus Demus to Paul Celan,
Zurich, 20–21 November 1959

Zurich, 20/21 November 1959

We send you our greetings Paul—
your closest, your most loyal friends.

Ingeborg   *Klaus*

NOTES

GLA D 90.1.2831/15: picture postcard (Zurich, St Peter's Church) to: 'Paul Celan/PARIS 16ème/78, Rue de Longchamp/France', Zurich, 21 November 1959.

Klaus: Demus was returning from a business trip to Luxembourg.

150

Ingeborg Bachmann to Paul Celan, Zurich, 23 November 1959

THE MUSIC IS FOR YOUR BIRTHDAY AND CONGRATULATIONS
I WISH YOU ALL THE BEST

INGEBORG

NOTES

*GLA D 90.1.2831/16: telegram to: 'Paul Celan, 78 Rue de Longchamp Paris/16', Zurich, 23
[November 1959], 01^{36} and Paris, 23 November 1959, 8^{10}.*

MUSIC: Evidently an unidentified record sent separately (see NO. 221).

BIRTHDAY: His 39th, on 23 November 1959.

151

Ingeborg Bachmann to Paul Celan, Zurich, 21 December 1959

Monday,
20-12-59

Dear Paul,

I have hesitated for so long now, and sent nothing but my birthday greetings. I was
hoping I would think of something, or be helped out by something, that I can say
to you to help all of us; for it is not only you and I who are affected, and I was
also hoping that Klaus would give you an idea of the difficulties here better than
I can in a letter. I saw Klaus for an hour last night; we were not able to speak much
amid the noise from the loudspeaker of a cafe between two trains, and it was only
afterwards that everything overwhelmed me again: questions, questions, and I feel
as if I were no better off than before, despite Klaus' great, kind efforts.—Paul,
that is why I still have to say a few things very directly, so that nothing will be
unclear or unresolved. The answers I could not think of on the telephone—you
remember? But before I come to that, I must tell you something else: first of all,
you did not deem the letter from Max worthy of any response, and the insult

through your hurtful rejection in the letter to me still exists for him, even now that you and I have found the words to save each other from this. This cannot apply to him, for his letter was the main cause—it even makes him feel worse, also towards me, because it looks as if I were only concerned about you, your neediness, our relationship. At the time, after your first letter and the trouble it caused between Max and me, when I had to fear for everything, I was only able to achieve one thing,—that we would keep silent about it (and that turned into more, a heavy silence between us). And recently, Hildesheimer told me while passing through that you found Max 'suspicious'; I was with him alone and did not mention anything to Max about it, but I was horrified by his account, and then I cannot comprehend what you expect from me, how this silent acceptance, this shaming, could be reconciled with the slightest expectation that a person we are living with is entitled to have of us. Sometimes I was so beside myself that I wanted to go away, to leave this place forever, and did not want to see you again because of it, and because I thought I could only keep both or lose both and now saw the impossibility of it all. But the possibility is there, it must be there, but one person cannot create it alone. I think you have to write to Max, in whatever way—but with the clarity that removes all misunderstandings. And I know what he cannot bear—to think that I must answer for what has gone on between the two of you.

Paul, I have an inkling of the terrible things you have been through, but I wonder whether you realize what has happened over here—I often doubt it. I was not even able to tell Klaus everything, it was simply not possible.

On top of that these burdens—Frankfurt, working day and night for weeks, two households with no one to help; the way everything has come together at once could not be worse, and I am sometimes amazed that I do not simply collapse. And it cannot go on like this; as soon as the term is over, we plan to go away, to the country, to Southern Switzerland or Upper Italy, for good—if we can only manage to get through everything before then.

And now Christmas. I am not going to Carinthia; I have to work for the whole time, and will not be celebrating.—This afternoon I wrote to Gisèle—you must never make things too difficult for her, you must both be happy, and there is Eric; I often think of him, and think that he is there too.

Ingeborg

NOTES

GLA D 90.1.2831/17: *hw. letter to*: '*M. Paul Celan/78, Rue de Longchamp/PARIS 16ème/ FRANCE*', Zurich, 22 [December] 1959.

Monday/This afternoon I wrote to Gisèle: Monday was 21 December 1959; perhaps the letter was begun around midnight, see the letter to GCL dated 20 December 1959 (NO. 222).

the difficulties here: The crisis between IB and MF.

Klaus [. . .] last night: Demus had stopped off briefly in Paris on 19 December 1959 during a business trip (PCPC).

letter from Max: See NO. 203.

hurtful rejection: See NO. 145.

your first letter: Does IB mean NO. 143?

Hildesheimer: As a member of Gruppe 47, the writer and painter, who took the position of reader at Piper after his return to Germany from exile in 1946, had been one of IB's closer literary acquaintances since 1953. For her and Henze, he quickly became one of the most important political interlocutors. A long-standing correspondence between Hildesheimer and IB, full of affectionate irony, demonstrates their affinity. For PC, this would have been the first written contact with him (to Hildesheimer, 23 December 1959). He visited the Celans in Paris in December 1959. In a letter to IB dated 'end of November', he informed her that he would visit her in Zurich (IBE).

these burdens—Frankfurt: The 'Frankfurter Vorlesungen'.

152
Ingeborg Bachmann to Paul Celan, Zurich, 28 December 1959

28-12-59

Dear Paul,

thank you again, you and Gisèle, for the call on Christmas Eve. I was unable to say much, and my French was a complete muddle, but it was good nonetheless. And now let us calm down, all of us, and let that conversation rest until we see each other again.

I will write from time to time, or send you a manuscript as soon as I have finished a piece for the book,—I have been wanting to show it to you for a long time, but I have not got any further with the corrections at the moment.

My thanks again—and pass them on to Gisèle too.

Ingeborg

NOTES

GLA D 90.1.2831/18: *hw. letter to*: '*M. Paul Celan/78, Rue de Longchamp/PARIS 16ème/ France*', *Zurich, 29 December 1959*.

book: *Das dreissigste Jahr*.

manuscript: See NO. 156.

153
Ingeborg Bachmann to Paul Celan, Zurich, 29 December 1959

Tuesday night

Dear Paul,

Rolf Schroers told me about the Bremen affair, and as I now had to call him, as I had no addresses and was uncertain about the correct form of 'address', I also found out that you are seriously worried because of it. Paul, please let me reassure you, even though I understand the thoughts it stirred up in you; for, unfortunately, it is unlikely that any of the prize-winners would be in a position to raise the money and give it back, and it is no help to anyone, I cannot see any point in it, if it is precisely this same senate that benefits from the demonstration. But, because of your thoughts, I had a different idea. I think the demonstration might be of some use like this: could we not try, you and I and the others, to get enough money together, as far as our respective situations allow, for a prize—that would support the jury's decision and teach the senate the most effective lesson. I am not sure, perhaps the idea is very foolish; tell me what you think! But, if anything is to be done, I would like it to be something that has a purpose.

I enclose a copy of my letter to the senate so that you know what I have written.

And do not worry too much!

Ingeborg

NOTES

GLA D 90.1.2831/19: *tw. letter w/hw. corrections to*: '*M. Paul Celan/78, Rue de Longchamp/Paris 16ème/France*', *Zurich, 30.(?) December 1959*; *supplement*: *cpy w/hw. corrections. Printed in*: Der Bremer Literaturpreis 1954–1987. Reden der Preisträger und andere Texte [*The Bremen Literature Prize 1954–1987: The Speeches of the Prizewinners and Other Texts*], *Wolfgang Emmerich ed.* (*Bremerhaven: Neuer Wirtschaftsverlag NW, 1988*), *p. 88.*

Schroers [. . .] *Bremen affair/Grass*: The veto of the Bremen Senate prevented the awarding of the Bremen Literature Prize to Grass. PC had expressly asked Schroers (on the jury as the previous prizewinner) to vote for Grass (3 December 1959, Nordrhein-Westfälisches Stattsarchiv, Münster). Schroers first informed PC by telephone; in his subsequent letter, he told PC about his parallel contact with other prizewinners, including IB (28 December 1959, PCE).

153.1

Supplement

Ingeborg Bachman
Kirchgasse 33/Zurich
29 December 1959

To the Senate of the Free Hanseatic City of Bremen
State Chancellery—Bremen

Dear Sirs,

allow me, as I had the honour of receiving the literature prize of the Free Hanseatic City of Bremen three years ago, to express my displeasure at your veto of the choice made by this year's jury. It is my view that the judgement of a respected jury including, as far as I know, Professor von Wiese and Dr Rudolf Hirsch, should not be disavowed, and that the choice cannot be annulled—otherwise every previously approved choice and every future one approved by you would be declared a sad, politic farce.

I therefore hope that the jury will stand by its decision and that you, Herr Senator, and you, dear gentleman of the senate, will take the path that is not closed to any of us—that of turning back after recognizing an error of such fundamental significance that it must inevitably affect and alarm me, and indeed every writer who has enjoyed this honour in the past.

Respectfully yours

NOTES

three years ago: See NO. 87n.

Wiese: The Bonn professor of German, a jury member, was in contact with PC concerning the dissertation of Firges (see NO. 112).

Hirsch: The writer and employee of S. Fischer Verlag (editorial director, 1954–63) had been in personal contact with PC since May 1952. An extensive correspondence testifies to their critical kinship.

Herr Senator: Presumably Eberhard Lutze, the Senator of Education at the time.

154
Paul Celan to Ingeborg Bachmann, Paris, 3 January 1960

on 3 January 1960.

All the best, Ingeborg!

I sent you the Mandelstamm yesterday, both of you.

I received a good letter from Hildesheimer. I responded to his words of clarification with bright words of my own; please do the same.

Yours, Paul

(I sent a letter telegram to the Bremen Senate on 30 Dec.)

NOTES

MAN/ANL folder 6, pp. 1–2: *hw. letter to*: '*Mademoiselle Ingeborg Bachmann/ Zürich/ Kirchgasse 33/ Suisse*', *from*: '*Paul Celan, 78 rue de Longchamp, Paris 16ᵉ*, [*Paris*], *3 January 1960*.

Mandelstamm: PC sent the volume *Gedichte* (Paul Celan trans. [Frankfurt: S. Fischer, 1959]), published in November, on 1 January 1960 (date and letter noted in PCPC). The LIB does not contain a dedicated copy of PC's translation, only one received as a gift from Klaus and Nani Demus.

Hildesheimer: See NO. 151; in a letter to Hildesheimer on 23 December 1959, PC denied using the word 'suspicious' [*suspekt*] with reference to MF's reaction to Blöcker's review. On 27 December 1959, Hildesheimer (copy sent to IB) explained the word as *his* interpretation of PC's statements and apologized for its use as 'too harsh'. PC replied on 2 January 1960 with an affirmation of friendship. PC wrote to Demus concerning the present letter, with the request *not* to pass it on to IB: 'I also spoke that "*bright*" word to Ingeborg and Max Frisch—in vain, Klaus, in vain . . . ' (25 January 1959).

Bremen Senate: See PC/HHL 232, as well as the picture in *Der Bremer Literaturpreis* (p. 88, see NO. 153n.).

155
Ingeborg Bachmann to Paul Celan, Zurich, 22 January 1960

22 January 1960

Paul,

Dr Hirsch will have told you how it went in Frankfurt; I almost decided to stay. But you were probably happier this way, otherwise you would have let me know.

Thank you for the Mandelstamm poems; the volume has turned out so beautifully, and is more important to me than the Char and Valéry translations. My favourite alongside the Block. But are you able to get back to your own work now?

I can barely catch my breath in Frankfurt; I search for a few spare hours so that I can finally make fair copies of what I have written in the last year.

With all my best wishes!

Ingeborg

(Everything is fine between Hildesheimer and me.)

One more thing: have you already, or finally, or still not received any payment from *Botteghe Oscure*? I suddenly received a letter from Rome asking about that.

NOTES

GLA D 90.1.2832/1: hw. letter to: 'M. Paul Celan/78, Rue de Longchamp/*PARIS 16ème*/ France', *Zurich, 23 January 1960 (originally inserted in* VOL. *2 of the French edition of Pindar,* Pythiques, *A. Puec trans.* [*third edition*; *Paris: Collection Budé, 1955*]*, p. 83*; BC IV, 73).

Frankfurt: For the third of the 'Frankfurter Vorlesungen'. Concerning his reading from 'Die junge Parze' in Frankfurt on 16 January 1960, PC wrote bitterly to Demus: 'Ingeborg had been there two days earlier, but could not stay any longer, even though she knew that I was expected . . .' (25 January 1960). PC had arrived in Frankfurt on 15 January 1960.

Char and Valéry translations/Block: 'Hypnos', 'Die junge Parze' and *Die Zwölf*.

your own work: Concerning PC's writing block, see NO. 140n.

written in the last year: The stories for *Das dreissigste Jahr*.

payment: See NO. 103.

156
Ingeborg Bachmann to Paul Celan, Zurich, 1 February 1960

1 February 1960

This is the first story. I cannot say anything about it, only hope . . .

Best wishes!

Yours

Ingeborg

Enclosed: the story 'Alles'.

NOTES

GLA D 90.1.2832/2: hw. letter to: '*M. Paul Celan/78, Rue de Longchamp/* <u>Paris 16ème</u> */ France*', *Zurich, 2 February 1960; supplement: 23 pp., hw. corr. cpy* (*printed in* Das dreissigste Jahr, *pp. 77–104*).

157

Ingeborg Bachmann to Paul Celan, Zurich, 19 February 1960

February 1960

Zurich

Dear Paul,

after all that has happened, I think there is no way for us to go on together. It is no longer possible for me.

It is very hard for me to say this.

I wish you all the best.

Ingeborg

NOTE

GLA D 90.1.2832/3: hw. letter to: '*M. Paul Celan/78, Rue de Longchamp/* <u>PARIS 16ème</u> */ FRANCE*', *Uetikon, 19 February 1960, in top left corner of envelope in PC's handwriting*: '*Bravo Blöcker! Bravo Bachmann!/20.2.60*'.

158

Hans Mayer with Ingeborg Bachmann (among others)
to Paul Celan, Leipzig, between 29 and 31 March 1960

(2.4.1960)

Dear Paul Celan, this card is just pretty and appropriate enough to convey our best wishes to you.
I hope we shall be able to welcome you, like the poets listed below, as a guest at our university.
Yours with warmest regards, Hans Mayer

With best wishes

Georg Maurer

Warmest regards! Yours, Peter Huchel

Ingeborg

Yours sincerely

Ernst Bloch   Werner Krauss

Inge Jens

Walter Jens.—   *Karola Bloch*

Werner Schubert   *Ingeburg Kretzschmar*

hmenzensberger   Stephan Hermlin

NOTES

GLA D 90.1.1661: hw. greetings (date in PC's handwriting, text and address in Hans Mayer's) on picture postcard (Messestadt Leipzig, Völkerschlachtdenkmal; creased and unstamped) to: 'Herrn Paul Celan / 78, rue de Longchamp / <u>Paris 16^e</u> / Frankreich', envelope missing.

Leipzig: IB took part in a poetry symposium in Leipzig chaired by Mayer (29–31 March 1960). Mayer, Jens, Huchel and Enzensberger had participated in the 1957 Wuppertal conference (see NO. 44). No accompanying letter from Mayer or any of the other signatories could be identified.

Mayer: PC had seen the German-Jewish literary scholar, who was still teaching in Leipzig at the time, at a seminar on Büchner at the ENS in February.

Maurer: PC knew the name of the Transylvanian-born poet, who lived in the GDR, from an anonymous letter sent by Claire Goll in 1956, in which an alleged statement from a speech by Maurer was used to support PC's supposed dependence on Yvan Goll (see GA 198f.); Maurer later denied having used the formulation 'master plagiarist' [*Meisterplagiator*] (GA 198, see NO. 179).

Ernst Bloch: IB's early engagement with the German-Jewish philosopher, still teaching in Leipzig at the time, is apparent in her concept of utopia; see the fifth of the 'Frankfurter Vorlesungen', 'Literatur als Utopie'. PC's interest is demonstrated by reading traces and poems in *Die Niemandsrose* (see CAE 678–682, 688 and 692).

Krauss: The German Romance scholar, a committed opponent of the Hitler regime, was professor in Leipzig. PC was not in contact with him.

Karola Bloch: The Polish-German architect and publicist was married to the philosopher Ernst Bloch.

Schubert: Assistant of Hans Mayer.

Kretzschmar: At the time, managing secretary of the PEN Centre East and West (i.e. the branch in the GDR).

Inge Jens: German scholar of English and German, married to Walter Jens.

Hermlin: The German-Jewish writer returned to Germany from emigration (Palestine, France, Switzerland) in 1945 and lived in East Berlin from 1947. He had no personal contact with PC.

159
Paul Celan to Ingeborg Bachmann, Paris, 19 May 1960

/Poincaré 39-63/

Paris, on 19 May 1960.

I am writing to you, Ingeborg.

Do you remember what I said to you when I saw you last, two years ago, in Paris, in the taxi, before you left?

I remember, Ingeborg.

'Do not get into adventures, Ingeborg'—that is what I said to you.

You <u>did</u> get into adventures,—the fact that you do not even know it is . . . proof of that.

You believe every word from those who are more than happy to slander me; you do not even ask me. For you, everything that has been fabricated about me seems like evidence. As for me, you do not want to perceive me, to acknowledge me or ask me.

Ingeborg, where are you?—Someone like Blöcker comes along, a grave desecrator, I write to you in my desperation, and you cannot spare a word for me, not even a syllable, but go to literary conferences. (And when the subject is some literature prize, you write on 'Tuesday night'.)

And one day—I will not list all the things again for you—I receive a letter in which, 'after all that has happened', you terminate our friendship . . .

Are you not ashamed, Ingeborg?

I am writing to you, Ingeborg.

I am also writing to you because I must tell you that I am going to Zurich on the 24th to see Nelly Sachs.

I know you will meet her at the airport. I would have liked to accompany you there—now I had to tell Nelly Sachs that this possibility has been taken away from me.

If you think it possible nonetheless, then tell Nelly Sachs at once, and please also tell me. I am sure Nelly Sachs will be <u>happy</u> about it.

And if you want us to talk, please tell me that too.

You were not in my good books these last few months, Ingeborg—if you can be yourself for one moment now, you will understand the why and wherefore.

And—<u>please</u>—do not ask <u>others</u> for advice before replying or not replying to me—<u>ask yourself</u>.

    Paul

NOTES

MAN/ANL folder 6, p. 3: *tw. letter w/hw. corrections, envelope missing; GLA D 90.1.2820/2 (cpy)*: *hw. corrections incomplete.*

/Poincaré 39-63/if you want us to talk: IB telegraphed GCL on 24 April 1960 (see NO. 223), and this was followed by a telephone conversation; on 21 May 1960, PC had twice tried to call her, but without success (PCPC).

I am writing to you: PC noted down that he had kept a copy.

before you left: See NO. 103.

evidence: In early May, in an article entitled 'Unbekanntes über Paul Celan' [Unknown Facts about Paul Celan], Claire Goll published claims that PC had plagiarized Yvan Goll's late works in German; appearing directly before PC was awarded the Büchner Prize (press report on 19 May 1960), these accusations set off an extensive press campaign (Goll affair); in fact, Claire Goll had herself plagiarized PC (see NO. 179). It is unclear what PC is specifically referring to; IB had almost certainly not read the publication yet.

Blöcker/'Tuesday night': See NOS 144 and 153.

'after all that has happened': See NO. 157.

24th [. . .] Sachs: Coming from Zurich, the poet accepted the Droste Prize in Meersburg on 29 May 1960; PC, in fact, arrived in Zurich on 25 May 1960. He knew from Sachs' letter of 6 May 1960 that IB and others wanted to collect her from the airport. It is unclear whether PC did actually write to Sachs (with or without reference to IB) that he could not come to the airport, as one letter was destroyed at his request (PC/Sachs 40f.).

160
Paul Celan to Ingeborg Bachmann,
dedication in Paul Valéry, Die junge Parze, *Paris, 30 May 1960*

For Ingeborg,
on 30 May 1960.

Paul

NOTES

LIB: *hw. dedication (p. [1]) of Paul Valéry*, Die junge Parze, *Paul Celan trans. (Wiesbaden: Insel-Verlag, 1960), envelope missing.*

30 May 1960: Sending noted in PCPC; the translation had already been published in March.

161

Ingeborg Bachmann to Paul Celan, Zurich, 7 (?) June 1960

Dear Paul,

thank you for 'Die Junge Parze'. It is a joy to see it printed so beautifully—and a modest reward for the unrewardable, wonderful work you have done.

I hope you all returned home in good spirits and are living without disturbances. Nelly Sachs is coming to Paris on Monday the 13th at 4:15 p.m., with the aeroplane that departs from Zurich at 3:05. You know that she is only going there on your account. I was very happy and confident during the days she remained here; I felt in good hands. She has a great heart.

Take care—

yours

Ingeborg

NOTES

GLA D 90.1.2832/5: *hw. letter to*: 'M. Paul Celan/78, Rue de Longchamp/<u>PARIS 16ème</u>/FRANCE', *Zurich, 7 (?) June 1960.*

returned home: From Zurich. There were several meetings between PC and IB on the occasion of the Droste Prize ceremony, some of them including GCL and MF (see NOS 224 and 225).

disturbances: IB had almost certainly been told about the renewed accusations of plagiarism (see NO. 159n), and knew how much the reappearance of the Goll affair, brewing since 1953, troubled PC.

the 13th: Sachs then stayed in Paris until 17 June 1960.

remained here: PC left Zurich on 28 May 1960, and Sachs probably travelled from Zurich to Ascona on 2 June 1960.

162
Ingeborg Bachmann to Paul Celan, Uetikon am See, 10 July 1960

Uetikon am See
Haus zum Langenbaum
10-7-1960

Thank you, dear Paul, for the splendid book! My birthday was enjoyable, but one does not learn to get older without a certain shudder, because so many boundaries are drawn.

You may already be out in the country. I wish you all a very good time!

Ingeborg

NOTES

GLA D 90.1.2832/6: *hw. letter to*: '*M. Paul Celan/78, Rue de Longchamp/PARIS 16ème/FRANCE*', *Uetikon, 11 July 1960*.

book: Guillaume Apollinaire, *Œuvres Poétiques* [Poetical Works], Marcel Adéma and Michel Décaudin eds (Paris: Bibliothèque de la Pléiade, 1959; LIB), sent on 22 June 1960, along with 'happy returns' (not found, PCPC).

Birthday: Her 34th, on 25 June 1960.

country: PC went to Brittany on holiday with his family (10–24 July 1960).

163

Ingeborg Bachmann to Paul Celan, Zurich, 28 August 1960

28-8-60

Dear Paul,

my half-finished letters are in part already out of date. The last two weeks with family, worries and trips because of Bobbie, then your alarming news as well—it was a great deal. I already told you on the telephone that I have not had any news from Stockholm, but forgot to say that I received, with some delay, an early card from Nelly Sachs containing a different address: c/o Fräulein Hella APPELTOFFT, HJALMAR SÖDERBERGSVÄGEN 16ᶜ, STOCKHOLM, but it is possible, or even very likely, that this address is not valid anymore. I do not know what else to do. We will now be going away on Wednesday morning— please, if you have any news for me, write so that the letter reaches me around <u>14</u> September in <u>Madrid, poste restante</u>! And from 10 October I will be back in Uetikon.

As for the response written by Klaus: Paul, I must tell you, and must unfortunately write it to Klaus too, that I do not consider it good; in this form, I think it would only do further harm. I cannot think of any better suggestions than to ask Dr Hirsch to take care of the formulation. The facts are lost in this manuscript and fail to have the necessary impact, and the tone also strikes me as misjudged.

I have not heard from Marie Luise von Kaschnitz, or Dr Hirsch, but I would like to know what they think about it.

Take care of yourselves, you, Gisèle, Eric—I wish you a good end to your summer, and Max sends many regards!

Yours

Ingeborg

NOTES

GLA D 90.1.2832/7: hw. letter to: 'M. Paul Celan/78, Rue de Longchamp/<u>PARIS 16ᵉᵐᵉ</u>/ FRANCE', Zurich, 28 August 1960.

half-finished letters/telephone/Stockholm: IB told PC on 25 August 1960 of two letters (drafts not found) which she promised to send. The subject matter of the conversation was, first, IB's criticism of the tone of the 'Entgegnung' [Response]; and second, the dramatic deterioration of Sachs' condition: PC learned on 9 August 1960 (PCPC) that she had been admitted to a psychiatric ward. They had already spoken about Sachs and her illness on 11 August 1960 (PCPC).

family: M. Bachmann, who had already retired from teaching, took a position at a Swiss boarding school in 1960; O. Bachmann followed him later on.

Bobbie: IB learned of her longstanding friend Elisabeth Liebl's severe illness in March 1960; she died on 25 May 1961.

APPELTOFFT: Stockholm friend of Nelly Sachs; there is also a letter from Sachs to PC with this as the sender's name (PC/Sachs 126).

Wednesday/Madrid: In September 1960, IB and MF went on a trip to Spain that also led them to Morocco. Wednesday was 31 August 1960.

response written by Klaus: PC, Hirsch and Demus had agreed on responding to Claire Goll's accusations (see NO. 159n) in this form in May 1960; Demus had written the text *together with* PC (see MSS 886). IB only signed the statement in late September.

it would only do further harm: IB is referring to a typescript signed only by Demus (*MAN/ANL folder 14, pp. 5–8*). She spoke more plainly to Demus: 'I think that the response, because of its formulations, is unhelpful, even disastrous; it would only harm Paul' (28 August 1960, PCE). It may have been after learning about that letter that PC wrote about the present one: 'False and cowardly letter from Ingeborg' (30 August 1960, PCPC).

manuscript/Kaschnitz: Demus had sent Kaschnitz a copy of the text for countersigning on 12 August 1960; she agreed, with reservations about particular choices of words, on 16 August 1960.

164

Ingeborg Bachmann and Max Frisch to
Gisèle Celan-Lestrange and Paul Celan, Madrid, 11 September 1960

Madrid, 11-9-60

Dear Gisèle, dear Paul,

we came here too soon because the South and the warmth are beckoning us, will continue the journey tomorrow and send you our greetings!

Ingeborg

If only one could experience as many things as one experiences on such a trip!

Cordially yours, Frisch

NOTE

GLA D 90.1.2834/1: airmail picture postcard (Goya, 'El Pelele' [The Doll]) to: 'M. et Mme Paul CELAN/78, Rue de Longchamp/PARIS 16ème/FRANCIA', Madrid, 11 September 1960.

165

Paul Celan to Ingeborg Bachmann,
dedication in offprint of 'Gespräch im Gebirg', Paris, 29 October 1960

For Ingeborg,

Paul

Paris, on 29 October 1960.

NOTES

LIB: *hw. dedication on the cover sheet of 'Gespräch im Gebirg', offprint from* Die Neue Rundschau, *1 (1960), pp. 199–202.*

29 October 1960: The offprint was probably given to IB in person on the afternoon of 30 October 1960, when PC met with IB, MF and Unseld at Hôtel du Louvre (PCPC). The issue had appeared in August. PC wrote to Demus about the meeting: 'Three days ago I met Ingeborg and Max Frisch and asked them to forgive me' (1–2 November 1960).

166
Paul Celan to Ingeborg Bachmann, Paris, 17 November 1960

17.XI.60.

My dear Ingeborg,

are you, are the two of you still in Zurich? I am going there on the 25th, as I have to speak to Dr Weber.

The infamy returned in *Die Welt* of 11.11. in a form that could scarcely be surpassed. Also in *Christ und Welt* (Christ und . . .)

You see, Ingeborg: I knew that even the Büchner Prize would not stop   these machinations . . . How good it is that your response will be printed—I thank you with all my heart for putting your name to it. I hope you are both well, urbi et orbi.

Yours

Paul

NOTES

MAN/ANL folder 6, pp. 4–5: hw. letter on correspondence card made from handmade paper to: '*Mademoiselle Ingeborg Bachmann/Haus zum Langenbaum, Seestrasse/ Uetikon bei Zürich/ Suisse/ Faire suivre s.v.p./ Bitte nachsenden!*', *Paris, 17 November 1960, from*: '*Paul Celan, 78 rue de Longchamp,/Paris 16ᵉ*'; *the letter may also have contained a supplement connected to a correspondence card made from handmade paper marked 'Ingeborg*'.

Zurich [. . .] *Weber*: From 25 to 27 November 1960, PC was in Zurich to discuss the Goll affair (see NO. 159n); he spoke with IB on all three days and with Weber on 26 November 1960. These were the last personal encounters between IB and PC. PC knew of IB's and MF's plan to move to Rome (see 'urbi et orbi') from a meeting in Paris on 30 October 1960 (see NO. 165n).

'*Die Welt*'/'*Christ und Welt*': Under the title 'Umstrittener Ausflug in die Vergangenheit' [Controversial Excursion to the Past], the doctoral student Rainer Kabel (writing as Rainer K. Abel) took up the accusations first published by Claire Goll in *Baubudenpoet* (see NO. 179). The goal of the article was to prevent the awarding of the Büchner Prize to PC, but it only appeared on 11 November 1960. On 27 October 1960, in an article in *Christ und Welt*—'Jeder ist Orpheus' [Everyone Is Orpheus]—Kabel had written more cautiously, not mentioning theft or including 'Todesfuge' in his charges. A typewritten note by IB concerning both articles with the publishing address of *Christ und Welt* suggests that she was planning to write a reader's letter (*MAN/ANL folder 14, p. 4*).

infamy: PC consistently used this word [*Infamie*] when referring to the Goll affair.

your response: The text, signed by Kaschnitz, Demus and IB, appeared on 2 November 1960, *Die Neue Rundschau*, 3.

urbi et orbi: 'to the city [i.e. Rome] and to the world', the name of an Apostolic Blessing used in the most important of papal addresses. [Trans.]

167

Ingeborg Bachmann to Paul Celan, Uetikon am See, 18 November 1960

18-11-60

Dear, dear Paul,

I will be here on the 25th—so we shall see each other! It makes me so happy that I can be glad I found you again on that rainy day in Paris. We will also find the counsel and the way to get rid of this *Welt*. I will be seeing Dr Weber next week; we shall speak about it, and he will also show me the articles. I hear Szondi wrote a very good response in one newspaper.

I was only in Rome for a few days, to make the start easier for Max and set up the necessary things. Now I have to stay here for the next 4 weeks, lock myself away and work; I can only do that here, and it is the only way. Please let me know when you are coming so that I can pick you up. Not by telephone, as I have turned it off! And where do you plan to stay? I would like to say you can come here, but I cannot, as this apartment house is so Swiss.

I will be at the station—

Yours

Ingeborg

GLA D 90.1.2832/8: *hw. letter to*: '*M. Paul Celan/78, Rue de Longchamp/<u>PARIS 16ème</u>/ FRANCE*', *Uetikon, 18 November 1960*.

rainy day in Paris: Presumably 30 October 1960 (see NO. 165n).

Szondi: The article in question is 'Anleihe oder Verleumdung? Zu einer Auseinandersetzung über Paul Celan' [Loan Or Slander? On a Discussion about Paul Celan] in the NZZ (18 November 1960, foreign edition on 19 November 1960). PC had been in personal contact with the Swiss literary scholar of Hungarian-Jewish origin since April 1959.

168
Ingeborg Bachmann to Paul Celan, Uetikon am see, 23 November 1960

I WISH YOU ALL THE VERY BEST ON YOUR BIRTHDAY THE PARCEL IS WAITING HERE

YOURS INGEBORG

GLA D 90.1.2832/9: *telegram to*: '*Paul Celan, Rue de Longchamp Paris/16*', *Uetikon, 23 November [1960], 13⁰⁵ and Paris, 23 November 1960, 14¹⁵*.

BIRTHDAY: His 40th, on 23 November 1960.

PARCEL: See NO. 170.

169
Paul Celan to Ingeborg Bachmann, Paris, 24 November 1960

Am in Zurich tomorrow three 49 until Sunday evening

Please book room Urban or nearby

Yours gratefully Paul

NOTES

MAN/ANL folder 6, p. 6: telegram to: 'Ingeborg Bachmann, Haus Langenbaum Seestrasse Uetikon am See bei Zürich', Paris, 24 November [1960], 10¹³ and Uetikon, [24] November 1960, 11⁰⁵.

Urban: PC did not stay at Hotel Urban (see writing paper of NO. 224) during his visit to Zurich (see NO. 166), as he often had in the past, but at Hotel Neues Schloss, Stockerstrasse 17.

170
Ingeborg Bachmann to Paul Celan,
dedication on a loose sheet in Gertrude Stein, Drei Leben, *Uetikon am See (?),*
between 25 and 27 November 1960

Dear Paul

for your birthday

on several November days

Yours

Ingeborg

NOTES

GLA D 90.1.3606: hw. dedication on correspondence card, originally in Gertrude Stein, Drei Leben *[Three Lives], Marlis Pörtner trans., with an afterword by Marie-Anne Stiebel (Zurich: Die Arche, 1960, LPC); there seems to have originally been a photograph on the back.*

birthday/November days: The card was delivered personally during PC's stay in Zurich, possible together with the book (see NO. 168).

Gertrude Stein, 'Drei Leben': In this book (original edition: *Three Lives* [New York: Grafton Press, 1909), the American writer describes the suffering of three female figures. Aside from a ribbon (pp. 84f.), PC's copy does not show any reading traces (also in LIB).

171
Paul Celan to Ingeborg Bachmann, Paris, 2 December 1960

Something has to happen I cannot wait any longer please call

P.

NOTES

GLA D 90.1.3291: telegram, here edited according to a hw. diary note from PC dated 2 December 1960, with the addition '2^{30} telegram to Ingeborg'; the telegram text is in quotation marks, followed by a dash (original telegram not found).

any longer: The letter sent by PC after his return to Zurich, for which an envelope postmarked 29 December 1960 has survived (*MAN/ANL folder 6, p. 8*), and to which he here expects a response, was not found. See also NO. 226.

172
Ingeborg Bachmann to Paul Celan, Uetikon am see, 3 December 1960

TRIED IN VAIN TO CALL YOU SECRET NUMBER NOT REVEALED PLEASE CALL ME AROUND 10:00 IN MORNING OR SEND ME YOUR NUMBER BY TELEGRAM

YOURS INGEBORG

NOTES

GLA D 90.1.2832/10: telegram to: '*Paul Celan, 78 Rue de Longchamp Paris/16E*', *Uetikon*, *3 December* [*1960*], *00³⁰ and Paris, 3* [*December 1960*], *6⁵⁵*.

SECRET NUMBER: A measure to ward off unwanted calls, primarily in connection with the Goll affair.

173

Ingeborg Bachmann to Paul Celan, Uetikon am see, 3 December 1960

Saturday night

Paul,

I have already written to Gisèle about the most important things. Then tonight I spoke to Hirschfeld, who will write the letter to the publisher.

Something will happen, but it will still take days and more days before it takes effect, please, you understand that. Paul, dear, you must work and not keep thinking about it, it is devastating you, and we cannot allow that.

I send you many many ardent, good thoughts!

Yours

Ingeborg

NOTES

GLA D 90.1.2832/32/11: hw. letter to: '*M. Paul Celan/78, Rue de Longchamp/PARIS 16ᵉᵐᵉ/FRANCE*', *Uetikon, 5 December 1960*.

to Gisèle: See NO. 227.

Hirschfeld: The German-Jewish director was dramatic adviser at the Zurich Schauspielhaus.

the publisher: Presumably Axel Springer, publisher of *Die Welt* (named in letter from Hirschfeld to PC on 19 December 1960, PCE) and a reader's letter to the paper from Enzensberger, already written on 11 November 1960, the day Kabel's article appeared (see NO. 166n), but still unpublished; it was only printed on 16

December 1960 (alongside an article by Dietrich Schaefer commissioned by Claire Goll).

174
Ingeborg Bachmann to Paul Celan, Zurich, 5 December 1960

5-11-60

Dear Paul,

Dr Weber has the flu, so our meeting is being postponed for another week. I have obtained the documents, the most important ones, for Kurt Hirschfeld, so that he can send them to the editor. He will write. Nothing has appeared in *Die Tat* yet, but there may be a delay—or I bought different copies. On Wednesday morning I have to go to Frankfurt for three days. I will write again after that!

Fond regards.

Ingeborg

NOTES

GLA D 90.1.2832/12: hw. letter to: '*M. Paul Celan/78, Rue de Longchamp/PARIS 16ème/ FRANCE*', Männedorf (*Zurich*), 5 December 1960.

5-11-60: See postmark!

documents: Hirschfeld wrote to PC on 19 December 1960 that IB had not yet given him all the material promised (PCE).

'*Tat*': Mohler's article 'Zu einer Kampagne. Ein notwendiges Wort' [Regarding a Campaign: Some Necessary Words] only appeared on 17 December 1960 in the daily Zurich paper (see NO. 226).

Frankfurt: IB attended a performance of Henze's opera *Der Prinz von Homburg*, where she met with Adorno and Kaschnitz.

175

Ingeborg Bachmann to Paul Celan, Rome, Christmas 1960

Paul,

may the good things stay good and the others turn out well!

Ingeborg

Christmas 1960

NOTE

GLA D 90.1.2832/13: hw. greeting on card in unmarked envelope (perhaps accompanying a present).

176

*Ingeborg Bachmann and Max Frisch
to Gisèle Celan-Lestrange and Paul Celan, Rome, 24 December 1960*

MERRY CHRISTMAS FROM

INGEBORG AND MAX FRISCH

NOTE

GLA D 90.1.2834/2: telegram to: 'M. et Mme Paul Celan, bei Wüst Les Fougères Montana Wallis', Rome, 24 December [1960], 14^{15} and Montana-Vermala, 24 December 1960, 17^{00}.

177

Paul Celan to Ingeborg Bachmann and Max Frisch, Montana, 27 December 1960

Montana, on 27 December 1960.

Dear Ingeborg, dear Max Frisch!

Our Christmas wishes have been en route for days: I had sent the telegram first to '152, Via Giulia', then '125', and finally, as that house number also proved incorrect, to the old address in Uetikon. Please forgive the delay. (In the haste of our departure, I left the Rome address, which I had noted down by the telephone, on my desk.)

Once again, here too: glad and bright wishes to you both!

I am already going back the day after tomorrow, via Zurich./One more thing, for your information: Leonhardt sent me, along with Christmas greetings, the article by Abel; his formulation was that the matter has to be 'got through', and he would like it best, he wrote, if I could answer myself . . .

These messengers are everywhere: yesterday I met a man here, in Montana, who visited me in Paris years ago: Enrique Beck. He asked me if I had read what had been written about me in the last issue of *Kultur* (December) . . ./

My best wishes and regards!

Paul

NOTES

GLA D 90.1.2822/1: hw. letter (cpy, original not found).

Montana: The Celan family spent their winter holidays from 15 December 1960 until 4 January 1961 in the Swiss Wallis.

telegram: Not found.

Via Giulia: IB and MF had lived in Rome since December; the correct house number is 102.

telephone: Telephone conversations on 12 and 13 December 1960, as well as a further call that was unsuccessful despite prior arrangement on 14 December 1960, all of them probably in connection with a planned further response from IB to the Goll affair (see NO. 166n). On 13 December 1960, PC noted: '13^{00} called Ingeborg (about whether she could change something in the response . . .)' (PCPC).

Zurich: PC met Szondi there on 30 December 1960.

Leonhardt [. . .] *answer*: The publication of an article by Kabel for *Die Zeit* ('Es gollt in Celans Lyrik. Wird Paul Celan zu Recht des Plagiats bezichtigt?' [The Sound of Goll in Paul Celan's Poetry: Are the Accusations of Plagiarism Justified?], GA 292–301) was prevented by, among others, IB, who pointed the weekly newspaper's features editor to Szondi's arguments (see NO. 167) (15 December 1960, *MAN/ANL folder 13, pp. 4–5*). PC received the proofs of Kabel's text from Leonhardt with a note that he had asked IB and MF in vain to write an opposing article, and the request for PC to react himself (19 December 1960, PCE; article also in IBE, *MAN/ANL folder 14, pp. 10–11*).

Beck: PC had probably known García Lorca's translator, who had left Germany in 1933 and was living in Basel since July 1957.

Kultur: An article concerning the Goll affair by Reinhard Döhl ('Deutsche Herausge-bersitten. Einige notwendige Angaben zur Ausgabe der "Dichtungen" von Yvan Goll' [German Editorial Customs: Some Necessary Observations Concerning the Edition of Yvan Goll's *Dichtungen*], pp. 6f.) only appeared in the Munich magazine in December 1961. Regarding the actual publication, see NO. 179.

178

Ingeborg Bachmann to Paul Celan, Rome, 3 January 1961

3 January 1961

Dear Paul, thank you both for the telegram and thank you for your letter! By some postal miracle, the issues of *Commerce* all arrived here just in time for it—if it had come when you sent it—but sadly the post cannot always work miracles.—I enclose a letter I wrote you a few days ago, as there are a few things in it that you should know; first, I did not want to send it, to avoid disturbing your holiday. I had a look in *Kultur*, but there is nothing in there. I expect Dr Weber was able to give you some advice in Zurich concerning Leonhardt.

The statement from the past winners of the Büchner Prize should be coming out soon.

Wait until spring before you come to Rome, for the winter is not enjoyable; one shivers all day, and I am constantly feeling sick or half-sick.

All the best, dear Paul!

Yours

Ingeborg

NOTES

GLA D 90.1.2833/1: hw. letter; D. *90.1.2832/14 (ass. supplement)*: tw. letter w/hw. corrections; envelope for letter to: '*M. Paul Celan/bei Frau Wüst/Les Fougères/Montana/Wallis/Svizzera*' (*folded, not stamped*), envelope missing.

3 January 1961: Letter received on 9 January 1961 (PCPC).

Commerce: International literature quarterly, edited by Paul Valéry, Léon-Paul Fargue and Valéry Larbaud in Paris between 1924 and 1932 and financed by Caetani. It published contributions from important authors of European modernity, including Ungaretti (whom IB translated) and Michaux (whom PC translated).

Dr Weber [Zurich]: Probably only on the telephone, on 24 December 1960 (PCPC).

statement [. . .] Büchner Prize: MF, who had won the prize in 1958 (see NO. 205), had signed a statement with K. Edschmid, G. Eich, E. Kreuder, K. Krolow and F. Usinger, testifying to PC's 'human and literary incorruptibility' (GA 325); it was circulated through the German press as a DPA (Deutsche Presse-Agentur) announcement. GCL noted: 'Text by the "Büchner Prize Winners"—insignificant, attacking nothing, unbelievably bad. Shameful—Krolow and Max Frisch did not have to exert or commit themselves too greatly to grant Paul his integrity' (13 January 1961, PCPC/GCL). See NO. 209.

178.1
Supplement

Dear Paul,

I have now received a short message from Leonhardt, to whom I had written after he prevented the publication of Abel's article; he writes that he sent you the article (and that was one of the things I wanted to prevent, that you should ever set eyes on it!), as I evidently did not give him sufficient guidelines for what he should do from a 'journalistic' perspective! You already know that Dr Weber considers it pointless and unwise for me, or someone chosen by me, to respond, as there is nothing to respond—it is Abel who has to rectify things. Leonhardt's main concern is obviously something 'journalistic and interesting' for his paper, and that is the last thing one should give him.

Abel himself has also written to me now, reproaching me for some of the formulations in the text of the 'Response' in the *Neue Rundschau*. It would certainly be appropriate not to reply, but I will probably do so nonetheless; for he is still young, and perhaps a word or two can help him realize that he has done you wrong.

I just need a little time, as I still have to get us set up; starting here is not easy. I hope Montana is good and doing you both good.

I am terribly depressed.

Yours

Ingeborg

Via Giulia 102
Rome 23-12-60

NOTES

message: Not found.

Abel [. . .] *rectify/written/reply*: Kabel was the only person among those involved who apologized in an article by Eckart Klessmann published in *Christ und Welt* (9 June 1961). IB does not appear to have replied to his letter (not found) (see NO. 180).

179

Paul Celan to Ingeborg Bachmann, Paris, 9 January 1961

Paris, on 9 January 1961.

My dear Ingeborg,

your two letters just arrived—I shall answer them both right away, in all brevity and haste, as I have to go to the Rue d'Ulm.

You are familiar with Abel's first essay in *Die Welt*; it is based on vile slander—he 'asks' whether I rob the dying—and on 'quotations' and dates falsified for that purpose. Even <u>after</u> the 'Response' and the essay by Peter Szondi, this is still continuing—see *Die Zeit* and its proofs—undisturbed, i.e. even more infamously.

If Abel is writing to you, Ingeborg, it is a <u>provocation</u>. Please do not react! Not under any circumstances, Ingeborg!

Maurer, as I learned the day before yesterday, denied using the words put in his mouth by C. G., namely 'master plagiarist', in *Die Welt* of 31.12.

Ingeborg, do not forget: the so-called literary remains are—<u>demonstrably</u>—a construction. After G.'s death, there were <u>a</u> <u>few</u> poems written in German. The dates given by C. G. in 1951, 1956 and 1960, as well as a comparison of the two 'versions' of her foreword to *Traumkraut* written in 1951 and 1960, show clearly enough how and why she retouched these.

Three cycles I had translated were published by C. G. under her name after she 'reworked' them—this is also demonstrable. (Luchterhand Verlag is fully aware of all this.)

Once again, Ingeborg: Abel is acting mala fide. Do not let yourself be provoked!

Along with these lines I enclose, for you and Max Frisch, a photocopy of 'Baubudenpoet': so that you can see <u>what</u> is being achieved and <u>how</u> . . .

All the best!

Yours, Paul

I have already written to you that it was not *Kultur* but *Panorama* . . .

Enclosed: *photocopy of the article 'Unbekanntes über Paul Celan'* [*Unknown Facts About Paul Celan*] *by Claire Goll.*

NOTES

MAN/ANL folder 6, pp. 10–11: *tw. express letter w/hw. corrections to*: '*Ingeborg Bachmann/* <u>*Roma*</u>/*Via Giulia 102/*<u>*Italie*</u>', *Paris, 9 January 1961, from*: '*Paul Celan, 78 rue de Longchamp/Paris 16ᵉ*', *Rome, 11 January 1961*; *GLA D 90.1.2820/3* (*two cpys*): *hw. corrections only complete in one of the copies, one further correction missing in original*; *MAN/ANL folder 14, pp. 1–2* (*ass. supplement*): *photocopy from* Baubudenpoet, *5* (*March/April 1960*), *pp. 115f., with hw. highlighting and additions by PC.*

rue d'Ulm: See NO. 140n.

Abel's/Szondi: The articles (see NOS 166–7) were not found in the IBE. PC probably expected IB to enclose a copy of Kabel's letter (9 January 1961, PCPC/GCL).

Die Zeit: See NO. 177n.

Maurer: Under the title 'Meisterplagiator?' (*Die Welt*, 31 December 1960, see NO. 158n).

literary remains/aware of all this: Claire Goll had reworked the German poems and fragments left by Yvan Goll in the style of PC's *Der Sand aus den Urnen* and augmented them with German translations of his posthumous French poems, as well as material of her own; she also used PC's unpublished Goll translations ('Malaiische Liebeslieder' [Malayan Love Song], 'Pariser Georgika' [Parisian Georgics], 'Iphetonga Elegie' [Iphetonga Elegy] and 'Aschenmasken' [Ash Masks]) for translations of her own. The dating of posthumous poems in the subsesquent volumes (Traumkraut' [Dream Herb; 1951], 'Pariser Georgika' [1956], 'Dichtungen' [Poems; 1960]), published by Luchterhand from 1956, show a successive backdating to *before* 1948. PC had already informed the publisher of the manipulations in 1956.

'*Baubudenpoet*': See NO. 159n. (PCE: issue in three original copies, as well as photocopies and manual duplicates of the article). On the photocopy, PC marked the following passage with a double line: 'His sad legend, which he was able to relate so tragically, had shaken us: his parents murdered by the Nazis, no homeland, a great, misunderstood poet, as he incessantly repeated . . .'; he also corrected the innacurately quoted texts of poems and the exaggerately high university position of Richard Exner, both typical of Claire Goll's manipulative strategy of argumentation. The American Germanist had drawn her attention to similarities between Goll's and PC's poems in 1953.

Kultur: See NO. 177.

Panorama: The letter from PC containing a reference to the anonymous article 'Plagiat' [Plagiarist] in the Munich magazine *Panorama* (12 [1960], p. 7; PCE), which speaks of the 'amazing resemblances' between PC and Goll and cites the press with the words 'influence', 'dependence' and 'master plagiarism'.

180

Ingeborg Bachmann to Paul Celan, Uetikon am see, 20 January 1961

Uetikon am See
20-1-1961

Dear Paul,

thank you for the letter! Regarding *Panorama*: clearly the only right thing to do would be for Fischer Verlag to send them *Die Neue Rundschau* with an accompanying letter, so that the editors are put in the picture and rectify the matter.

So I will not write to Abel. I did begin drafting a letter, but that really does mean letting down one's guard in a fatal manner, and one is so uncertain that there is any goodwill on the other side—in fact, everything suggests otherwise. But how one would like to presume a good will and let oneself be tempted . . .

I shall still be here in Switzerland for a while, until the start of February; then I will not have any address until 20 March, as I have to go on a trip (readings). And at the end of March I will be back in Rome. And then you will hopefully come soon.

Yours, Ingeborg

NOTES

GLA D 90.1.2833/2: *tw. letter w/hw. corrections, envelope missing.*

20—1—1961: The letter probably only arrived on 24 January 1961, and was summarized by GCL as follows: 'Three lines from <u>Ingeborg</u>, not saying anything much, but meaning: I am in Zurich, alone, you can call me, and finally: I hope you will come to Rome soon' (PCPC/GCL).

Fischer Verlag/'Die Neue Rundschau': Regarding the 'Entgegnung', see NO. 163.

drafting a letter: No draft found.

readings: On 21 February 1961 and other days, IB read 'Undine geht' and various poems in the main hall of the University of Tübingen (previously planned for the substantially smaller lecture theatre NO. 9).

181
Ingeborg Bachmann to Paul Celan, Zurich, 27 January 1961

27-1-61

Dear Paul,

I enclose an article that appeared in the student magazine NOTIZEN!

Fond regards.

Ingeborg

Enclosed: original copy of the article 'Die Hetze gegen Paul Celan' [The Agitation Against Paul Celan] by Jürgen P. Wallmann.

NOTES

GLA D 90.1.2833/3: hw. letter to: 'M. *Paul Celan/78, Rue de Longchamp/Paris 16ème/ FRANCE', Männedorf (Zurich), 27 January 1961*; *supplement: original article from* Notizen, *31 (February 1961), p. 8.*

27-1-61: GCL noted on 28 January 1961 about this letter: '½ line' (PCPC/GCL).

NOTIZEN: PC had already received the article from the author (with a letter of 22 January 1961, PCE); the issue also included IB's 'Geh, Gedanke' [Go, Thought] and 'Die grosse Fracht' [The Great Freight].

182

Ingeborg Bachmann to Paul Celan, Uetikon am See, 28 January 1961

28-1-61

Dear Paul,

I have found out that further articles have been published in your defence, one by Szondi in the *Neue Deutsche Hefte* and one, referring to the *Neue Rundschau*, in *Das Schönste*. I did not receive them, unfortunately, so I cannot send them to you. The fact that Maurer in the East took back his malicious claim is very important, and will have an effect. Be in good spirits—you should be.

Yours

Ingeborg

NOTES

GLA D 90.1.2833/4: hw. letter to: 'M. Paul Celan/78, rue de Longchamp/<u>PARIS 16ème</u>/ FRANCE', *Uetikon, 29 January 1961.*

Szondi: 'Zu einer Auseinandersetzung über Paul Celan' [Concerning a Debate over Paul Celan] (*Neue Deutsche Hefte,* January 1961, pp. 949f.); Szondi sent PC an offprint on 11 January 1961.

Neue Rundschau: That is, the 'Entgegnung'.

Das Schönste: Karl Krolow, 'Deutsch mit französischem Schliff. Die lyrische Sprache des Dichters und Übersetzers Paul Celan' [German with a French Touch: The Lyric Language of the Poet and Translator Paul Celan] (*Das Schönste,* February 1961, pp. 42f., PCE).

Maurer: See NO. 179.

183

Ingeborg Bachmann and Max Frisch to Paul Celan, Rome, 25 April 1961

ARE WORRIED UETIKON APARTMENT IS AT YOUR DISPOSAL KEY

WITH GUENTHART IN SAME HOUSE
INGEBORG AND MAX FRISCH

NOTE

GLA D 90.1.2834/3: telegram to: 'Paul Celan, rue de Longchamp 78 Paris', Rome, 25. [April 1961], 02³⁰ and Paris, 25 April 1961, 8²⁰.

184

Paul Celan to Ingeborg Bachmann and Max Frisch, Paris, 25 April 1961

78, RUE DE LONGCHAMP. XVIᵉ

Dear Ingeborg, dear Max Frisch,

thank you, thank you from both of us for your telegram.

Go away? We cannot. Being here and staying here: we felt this was the only option, especially on Sunday night. (That has nothing to do with any prognoses.)

Thank you again for the telegram

Best wishes

Paul

Paris, on 25 April 1961.

NOTES

MAN/ANL folder 6, p. 12: hw. letter on paper with printed letterhead (here in italics), envelope missing; GLA D 90.1.2822/2: tw. copy (hw. note 'hdgeschrieben') with small variations.

Being here and staying here: See the letterhead with the Paris address, a unique appearance in this correspondence.

Sunday night: A concrete occasion for these thoughts on 23/24 April 1961 may have been the publication of Reinhard Döhl's study 'Geschichte und Kritik eines Angriffs. Zu den Behauptungen gegen Paul Celan' [History and Critique of an

Attack: Concerning the Claims against Paul Celan] in the *Jahrbuch 1960* of the Deutsche Akademie für Sprache und Dichtung [German Academy of Language and Literature] (Darmstadt, 1961, pp. 101–32), which PC rightly considered careless and harmful; it was this that made PC turn down a membership in the Academy and consider returning his Büchner Prize. The volume had been sent to members on 22 April 1961.

185
Paul Celan to Ingeborg Bachmann and Max Frisch, Paris, 2 May 1961, not sent

Paris, on 2 May 1961.

Dear Ingeborg, dear Max Frisch,

a few days ago I wrote to Marie Luise Kaschnitz—I hope she showed you my letter.

What Kasack—he is not the first conspirator in this business—has cooked up with that Nazi Martini surely cannot leave you cold.

Best wishes

NOTES

GLA D 90.1.2823: *tw. letter; the text on the back is not part of the letter*: '*In memory of Georg Büchner, I have taken the liberty of rejecting this membership telegraphed by the godfather of the aforementioned "study"*' (*ts.*).

Kaschnitz / Kasack / Martini: PC assumed that Kaschnitz, as his eulogist for the Büchner Prize, would want to know why he had turned down the membership in the Deutsche Akademie für Sprache und Dichtung offered in a telegram from its president Hermann Kasack on 24 April 1961 (PC to Kaschnitz, 27 April 1961, PCE). Kasack, the initiator of the study in the Academy's yearbook, had originally asked the Stuttgart Professor of German Studies Fritz Martini—a former member of the NSDAP and the SA—for support; Martini passed the task on to his assistant Döhl.

186

Ingeborg Bachmann to Paul Celan, Rome, 31 May 1961

VIA de NOTARIS 1 F
ROMA
31-5-61

Dear Paul,

thank you for your letter. Now, thank God, the worst has been prevented; and I understand why you and Gisèle have made your decision, but you should still always remember that you have the option, that we are there for you!

We were away for a while, in Greece, and had trouble finding an apartment before and after that, but now we have resolved it: we are in the process of moving, and the new address is on the first page.

I received a Claire Goll letter from Fischer Verlag, with a note saying you know about it. I think the only possible way to respond to it is <u>not</u> to respond. Or do you think one should? The only reason I have not thrown it in the bin yet is that I would like to know whether you consider it important. Nothing else was to be expected—new malicious lies, as she is running out of old ones.

———

I read the Büchner Prize speech again, with great pleasure, and now all the Yesenin poems too. How beautiful they are, and found by you. You will have to be patient for a little longer with my Ungaretti attempts, which I will soon be able to send you. A page and another page . . .

Will you come to Rome—? the new apartment also has a guestroom waiting for you. (We have rented for two years.)

Take care, my dear Paul, give Gisèle my best, and many regards from Max.

With many, often worried thoughts—

Yours

Ingeborg

NOTES

GLA D 90.1.2833/5: *hw. airmail letter to*: '*M. Paul Celan/78, rue de Longchamp/<u>PARIS</u> <u>16ème</u>/FRANCE*', Rome, 2 June 1961.

VIA de NOTARIS 1 F: The long, sought-after apartment, north of the Villa Borghese.

Greece: For MF's 50th birthday.

Fischer Verlag: Publisher, *Neue Rundschau*, where the 'Entgegnung' had appeared.

letter from Claire Goll: Demus received the same letter (see GA 608f.).

Büchner Prize speech: The speech, given in Darmstadt on 22 October 1960, appeared in the same Academy yearbook as Döhl's essay (see NO. 184n, pp. 74–88) under the title 'Der Meridian'. The first edition of the speech, published by Fischer in January 1961, is not in the LIB.

all the Yesenin poems: Sergej Jessenin, *Gedichte*, Paul Celan comp. and trans. (Frankfurt: S. Fischer, 1961) (not in LIB), was published in March; PC had enclosed individual Yesenin poems with letters (see NOS 90 and 101).

Ungharetti attempts: Regarding the book edition, see NO. 188; IB did not send any loose pages. PC may, however, have known some translations from Enzensberger's anthology *Museum der modernen Poesie*, in which he was included (Frankfurt: Suhrkamp, 1960; LPC), as well as a publication in the *NZZ* (3 December 1960, see NO. 68n, there also Supervielle translations by PC).

Gisèle: GCL noted concerning this letter: 'Letter from Ingeborg, insipid and false (she and Enzensberger no doubt on the way to Zurich for the "Poetry Soirée" at the Schauspielhaus)' (5 June 1961, PCPC/GCL; letter noted in PCPC).

187
Ingeborg Bachmann to Paul Celan,
dedication in Das dreissigste Jahr, Rome, 4 June 1961

For Paul—
    Ingeborg
    Rome 4-6-61

NOTE

GLA LPC: hw. dedication on the flyleaf of Giuseppe Ungaretti, Gedichte *(Italian and German),*
  Ingeborg Bachmann trans. and afterword (Frankfurt: Suhrkamp, 1961 = Bibliothek Suhrkamp
  70), envelope missing. A page from Die Welt der Literatur *with a review of the volume by*
  Ingeborg Brandt from 30 November 1961 was originally inserted between pp. 30 and 31
  ('Tramonto'/'Sonnenuntergang' [Sunset]) (BC II, no number, between 780 and 781).

188

Ingeborg Bachmann to Paul Celan,
dedication in Giuseppe Ungaretti, Gedichte, *Rome (?), summer 1961*

For Paul—
  Ingeborg
  Summer 1961

189

Paul Celan to Ingeborg Bachmann, Paris, 11 September 1961, not sent

Dear Ingeborg,

I am not well at all, especially after the provocation in *Vorwärts* (which will almost
certainly not be the last). I have been thinking—and perhaps it is not an entirely
egotistical thought—that a conversation with you and Max Frisch could help,
could make things clearer and brighter.

And so I would like to ask you and Max Frisch for such a conversation.

Unfortunately I cannot come to you—so please come here, some time,
tomorrow or the day after, but let me know now.

I sincerely wish you both all the best!

                                                                    Paul

11.9.61.

NOTES

GLA D 90.1.2821: *hw. letter.*

provocation in Vorwärts: Concerning the publications by Rolf Schroers and Felix Mondstrahl in the SPD magazine *Vorwärts*, see longer letter draft to MF (NO. 207).

190

Paul Celan to Ingeborg Bachmann, Paris, 27 September 1961

78, rue de Longchamp
(Poi 39-63)
         27.9.61.

My dear Ingeborg,

I have not written for a long time, and missed congratulating you on your birthday, and also thanking you for your books.—Let me do so now.

All my very best, Ingeborg!

I am thinking to myself—and will also tell Max Frisch now—that what has come between us can only be a misunderstanding; one that is difficult to untangle, perhaps, but no more than <u>that</u>.

So let us try to clear it up together. I <u>believe</u> in <u>dialogue</u>, Ingeborg. Yes, let us speak to each other—and I would ask Max Frisch the same.

Fond regards!

Paul

NOTES

MAN/ANL folder 6, p. 13: *hw. letter, envelope missing; GLA D 90.1.2820/4 (carbon copy).*

books: *Das dreissigste Jahr* and Ungaretti's *Gedichte* (see NOS 187 and 188).

Frisch: See NO. 210.

191
Ingeborg Bachmann to Paul Celan, Zurich, after 27 September 1961, not sent

Dear Paul,

we spoke on the telephone a few minutes ago—but let me try to answer your letter first. I am not sure if what has come between us is based on misunderstandings or something requiring clarification. I see it differently: sudden silences, an absence of the most basic reactions, something that makes me helpless because I can only make assumptions and these inevitably lead nowhere; and then I hear from you again, like now, hear how bad you are feeling and remain just as helpless as I was during the silence, and do not know how I can find the way out, how I can ever feel lively and alive with you again. Sometimes the reasons are very clear to me, incidents from the terrible time last year that I do not understand to this day, and which I try to forget because I do not want them to be true—because I wish you had not done, said and written those things. Now too, I was shocked again when you said on the telephone that you have to be pardoned for something; I do not know what you meant by that, but I am already scared again—not so much because something could embitter me again as because I sense how much it takes away my courage for friendship, for one involving more than sympathy and the hope that your whole situation could change for the better. These feelings are not enough for me, nor can they be enough for you.

Dear Paul, perhaps this is, once again, not the right time to say a number of things that are difficult to say; but there is no right time, otherwise I would have had to bring myself to do it before. I truly think that the greater misfortune lies within you. The awful things that come from outside—and you do not need to assure me they are true, for I know about most of them—may poison your life, but you can get through it, you have to get through it. Now it can only depend on you to deal with it in the right way, for you can see that all the declarations and all the advocacy, as right as they may have been, have not diminished that misfortune within you. When I hear you speak, it seems as if everything is the same as it was a year ago, as if the efforts of so many people meant nothing to you, as if only the other things, the dirt, the scorn, and the stupidity meant anything. And you are losing friends, because people feel that it means less to you, and that the objections they make where it seems necessary do not mean anything either. Objections can easily seem worse than agreement, but they can sometimes be more useful—even if only to help one realize better than the others where the error lies. But enough of the others.

Of all the many injustices and injuries I have experienced so far, the ones you inflicted have always been the worst—not least because I cannot respond to them with contempt or indifference, because I cannot protect myself against them, because my feelings for you always remain too strong and make me defenceless. Of course, you are primarily concerned with other things now, with your needs; but for me, if they are to be addressed, the primary concern must be our relationship, so that the other things can become open to discussion. You say you do not want to lose us, and I translate that for myself into not wanting to lose *me*, as this superficial relationship with Max—without me, you would probably never have become acquainted—or under different conditions that would probably have had a better chance than the ones created through me—so let us be honest: to lose each other. And then I ask myself: who am I for you, after so many years? A phantom, or a reality that is no longer like a phantom? Because for me, a great deal has happened and I want to be the person I am, today, and do you even see who I am today? That is precisely what I do not know, and that makes me despair. For a while, after we met again in Wuppertal, I believed in this 'today'; I affirmed you and you affirmed me in a new life, that is how it seemed to me. I accepted you, not only together with Gisèle but also with new developments, new hardships and new chances for happiness that came for you after the time we shared.

You once asked me what I thought of the review by Blöcker. Now you congratulate me on my book, or books, and I am not sure whether you see my own Blöcker review in there, and all the other reviews—or do you think that a line against you counts for more than thirty against me? Do you really think so? And do you really think that a paper which has been agitating against me since its inception, e.g. *Forum*, is suddenly justified because it deigns to come to your defence? Dear, I never complain to anyone about those malicious words, but they occur to me when the very people capable of writing them suddenly invoke you. You must not misunderstand me.

I can endure everything through indifference, through an occasional fit at worst. It would never occur to me to turn to someone else for help, not even you, because I feel stronger.

I am not complaining. I knew, without knowing it, that this path I wanted to follow, and did follow, would not be paved with roses.

You say people are ruining your translation work. Dear Paul, that was perhaps the one thing I questioned slightly—not your reports, but their effects—but now I believe you completely, for I have also tasted the spitefulness of professional translators, whose interference I too had not expected. People are making a pastime of discussing my alleged mistakes, people whose Italian is worse (which would not offend me) as well as some who could perhaps do it better—but, at any rate, people who have no idea how a poem should read in German. Do you understand: I believe you, I believe everything, every word. But I do not believe that the gossip and criticism apply to you alone, for it would be just as easy for me to believe that they only apply to me. And I could prove it to you, just as you can prove it to me.

What I cannot do is this: prove it to you beyond all doubt, as I throw away the anonymous scraps of paper and all the others, because I think I am stronger than all those scraps, and because I want you to be stronger than those scraps, which mean nothing, nothing at all.

But you do not want to see that, to see that this means nothing, you want it to be stronger, you want to let it bury you.

That is your misfortune, the one that I consider stronger than the misfortune being inflicted upon you. You want to be the victim, but it is up to you not to be, and it makes me think of the book Szondi wrote, of the motto that so affected me because I could not help thinking of you. Of course it is coming, and will continue to come, from outside, but you sanction it. And the question is whether you sanction it, whether you accept it. But then that is your affair, and it will not be mine if you let it overwhelm you. If you react to it. You do react to it. That is what I hold against you. You react to it, and by doing so you clear a way for it. You want to be the one who is wrecked by it, but I cannot endorse that—for you can change it. You want them to have your ruin on their conscience, and I will not be able to stop you from wanting that. Just understand me for once [illegible]: I do not think the world can change, but we can, and I wish you could. That is where you have to start. It is not the 'road sweeper' who can sweep it away but you, you alone. You will say that I am asking too much of you for yourself. And I am. (But I also ask it of myself for myself, that is why I dare to tell you the same.) That is the only way to ask for anything. I will not be able to fulfil it entirely and you will not be able to fulfil it entirely, but many things will fall by the wayside on the path to that fulfilment.

I am often very bitter when I think of you, and sometimes I cannot forgive myself for not hating you, for that poem you wrote, accusing me of murder. Has someone you love ever accused you of murder, when you were innocent? The insane thing is that I do not hate you; but if you ever want anything to be worked out and made good again, then try to start here, by answering me—not in a reply, not in writing, but in your heart and your actions. I am waiting for that, like various other things: no answer, no apology, for no apology could ever be enough and I could not accept it in any case. I ask that you, by helping me, help yourself—that you help yourself.

I said you would have a very easy time with me, but as true as that might be—you will also have a harder time with me than with anyone else. I am happy when you approach me at Hôtel du Louvre, when you are in good spirits and free; I forget everything and am glad that you are in good spirits, that you can be. I think of Gisèle a great deal, even if it is not my place to say too much about it, least of all to her—but I truly think of her, and admire her for a greatness and steadfastness that you do not have. Now you must forgive me, but I think that her self-denial, her beautiful pride and her forbearance mean more to me than your complaining.

She is content with you in your misfortune, but you would never be content with her if she were befallen by misfortune. I expect a man to be content with my affirmation, but you do not grant her that—what injustice.

NOTES

MAN/ANL folder 10, pp. 10–11: tw., partly unclear letter draft with numerous spelling errors. [See Figure 17.]

how bad you are feeling: PC's serious mental problems should be viewed in connection with the Goll affair.

last year: Regarding the difficulties caused by Blöcker's review, see NOS 143 and 147.

all the declarations and all the advocacy: IB is most likely thinking of the 'Entgegnung' signed by her and others and of the statement by the Büchner Prize winners (see NO. 178), but perhaps also those by Szondi (see NOS 167 and 182), Schroers (see NO. 207), Enzensberger (see NO. 173n), Mohler (see NO. 174n) and Maurer (see NO. 179), the study by Döhl (see NO. 184n), as well as the text by Wieland Schmid published in Austria ('Literarischer Rufmord. Zum Streit um Paul Celan und Iwan Goll' [Literary Defamation: The Dispute over Paul Celan and Iwan Goll], in *Wort in der Zeit*, 2 (Graz, 1961, pp. 4–6) and the article in *Forum* mentioned below.

Wuppertal: See NO. 44.

review by Blöcker: See NO. 143.

book, or books: *Das dreissigste Jahr* and Ungaretti's *Gedichte*.

Blöcker review: In the September issue of *Merkur*, Blöcker gave a negative summary of IB's development by playing off her poetry against *Der Prinz von Homburg* and *Das dreissigste Jahr* ('Nur die Bilder bleiben' [Only the Images Remain], pp. 883–6).

Forum/defence: A statement on the Goll affair signed by nine other Austrian authors, including common acquaintances such as Doderer and Dor, written by Franz Theodor Csokor and Friedrich Torberg ('In Sachen Paul Celan' [Concerning Paul Celan], in *Forum*, Vienna, January 1961, p. 23). Regarding Weigel's attacks against IB in the journal, see NO. 122.

ruining your translation work: There were critical reviews of PC's 'Die junge Parze' by Karl August Horst ('In Ketten tanzen' [Dancing in Chains], *FAZ*, 9 April 1960) and Peter Gan; the latter was prevented from appearing in *Merkur* through the intervention of others, but PC was familiar with it (now in *Celan wiederlesen* [Rereading Celan], Lyrik Kabinett München ed. [Munich, 1998], pp. 85–96). For reviews of Yesenin's *Gedichte*, see Karl Dedecius, 'Slawische Lyrik. Übersetzt—übertragen—nachgedichtet' [Slavic Poetry: Translated—Transferred—Freely Adapted] (*Osteuropa*, March 1961, pp. 165–78), Horst Bienek, 'Der Dandy aus Rjasan' [The Dandy from Ryazan] (*FAZ*, 20 May 1961) and Günther Busch, 'Zecher am Tisch der Geschichte' [A Reveller at the Table of History] (*SZ*, 3–4 June 1961).

spitefulness [. . .] *mistakes*: Three reviews of Ungaretti's *Gedichte* had already been published in national newspapers. In *Christ und Welt*, the translation work was not mentioned at all (K-nn, 'Die eigene schöne Biographie' [One's Own Nice

Biography], 28 July 1961); in the *FAZ*, it was praised highly (Horst Bienek, 'Archipoeta der Moderne', 19 August 1961); only Günther Busch criticized 'mannerisms' in *SZ* ('Ungarettis lyrische Kurzschrift' [Ungaretti's Poetic Shorthand], 26–27 August 1961).

Szondi [. . .] *motto*: Szondi placed two French mottos at the start of his *Versuch über das Tragische* [Essay on the Tragic] (Frankfurt: Suhrkamp, 1961) 'Si tu nous fais du mal, il nous vient de nous-mêmes' [If you hurt us, it comes from ourselves] by Agrippa d'Aubigné and 'En me cuidant aiser, moi-même je me nuits' [By thinking I am making it easy for myself, I harm myself] by Jean de Sponde.

that poem you wrote, accusing me of murder: IB is assuming that the following passage from PC's 'Wolfsbohne' refers to her: 'Gestern/kam einer von ihnen und/tötete dich/zum andern Mal in/meinem Gedicht' [Yesterday/one of them came and/killed you/a further time in/my poem' (lines 21–5, not found in IBE). But 'one of them' is undoubtedly Günter Blöcker and his comments on 'Todesfuge' (see NOS 143 and 145).

Hôtel du Louvre: See NO. 165n.

192
Ingeborg Bachmann to Paul Celan, Basel, 24 October 1961

24-10-61

My dear Paul

every, or almost every evening I have tried to continue my long letter. Now I cannot send it, because it tries to do too many things. I would rather bring it with me to Paris, and fill it out in conversation and let you fill it out. To make something clearer that concerns no one but you and me. I do not see the misunderstandings you presume; I just thought, when no further news came, that my books had displeased you.—

I cannot give you a date yet at the moment. I will not be able to come before 5 or 7 November, i.e. before Max's work at the theatre is finished. And I can only go to Paris alone, for Max is very worn out, and will be even more worn out afterwards, and an immediate return to Rome is necessary for him in every respect.

I hope very much that you are feeling better, I wish you a recovery so very much, and will tell you next week when I can come!

Many regards to Gisèle.

Ingeborg

NOTES

GLA D 90.1.2833/6: hw. letter to: 'Paul *Celan/78, Rue de Longchamp/PARIS 16ème/ FRANCE*', *Basel, 26 October 1961.*

to Paris: IB and PC did not meet in the autumn of 1961.

my books: *Das dreissigste Jahr* (see NO. 187) and the translation Ungaretti, *Gedichte* (see NO. 188).

Max's work at the theatre: The rehearsals for the performance of *Andorra* (see NO. 212) at the Zurich Schauspielhaus on 2 November 1962.

193
Ingeborg Bachmann to Paul Celan, Rome, 5 December 1961

5-12-61
Via de Notaris 1 F
Roma

Dear, dear Paul,

I probably wanted to write every day, but our return journey, and in my case a further trip in between, did not leave me time for anything. If I could at least write a letter in an hour or an evening like other people—but it has long been like an illness; I cannot write, I am already crippled when I write the date or put the paper in the typewriter.

I wish you could finally feel better, that you could be protected by better health—or rather, that a new composure and calm could restore you to full health again.

It often seems to me that you do know how much is down to you, and that you could take hold of yourself from that point of self-recognition.

Our lessons are becoming ever more difficult. May we learn them.

Give my regards to Gisèle, and you or both of you come when you can!

Fond regards and best wishes.

> Yours
>
> Ingeborg

NOTES

GLA D 90.1.2833/7: hw. letter, envelope missing.

return journey [. . .] *trip in between*: In November, IB travelled directly from Zurich to Berlin to receive, in combination with a reading, the German Critics' Literature Prize for *Das dreissigste Jahr* [*see Figure 9*].

restore you to full health: See NO. 191.

Our lessons [. . .] *learn them*: GCL noted the two sentences down with reference to IB's letter, underlining 'Our' (11 December 1961, PCPC/GCL).

194
Ingeborg Bachmann and Max Frisch
to Gisèle Celan-Lestrange and Paul Celan, Rome, December 1961

December 1961

Dear Gisèle, dear Paul,

we wish you a lovely Christmas and a good, a better time ahead!

Ingeborg   Max Frisch

NOTE

GLA D 90.1.2834/4: hw. greeting, presumably to accompany a gift (NO. 212?), envelope missing.

195

Paul Celan to Ingeborg Bachmann, Paris, 21 September 1963

78, rue de Longchamp   Paris,
21 September 1963

Dear Ingeborg,

when I read in the newspaper that you had been to Russia, I greatly envied you for that trip, especially the stay in Petersburg. But shortly afterwards, in late August, I heard from Klaus Wagenbach in Frankfurt that this was not actually true, that you were very unwell and had only just returned from hospital.—I wanted to call you when I found out, but you did not have a telephone yet.

Now I am writing to you, just a few lines, to ask you likewise for a few lines. Please let me know how you are feeling.

I have a few less than pleasant years behind me—'behind me', as they say.

I have a new volume of poems coming out in the next few weeks—a variety of things have been woven into it, and in some of them I have taken a rather 'inartistic' path, as was essentially bound to happen. The document of a crisis, if you like—but what would poetry be if it were not that too, and radically so?

So please, write me a few lines.

I wish you all the best, Ingeborg

Yours

Paul

NOTES

MAN/ANL folder 7, pp. 1–2: hw. airmail letter to: '*Mademoiselle Ingeborg Bachmann/ Berlin-Grunewald/ Königsallee 35/ Berlin—Secteur Occidental*', *Paris, 21 September 1963, from*: '*Paul Celan, 78 rue de Longchamp, Paris 16ᵉ*'.

Russia/Petersburg: In an article about the appearance of the Soviet author Ilya Ehrenburg at a writers' congress in Leningrad (!) in August—'Nicht auf Kafka schiessen' [Don't Shoot at Kafka], published on 21 August 1963—*Der Spiegel* named Enzensberger, Hans Werner Richter and IB as German (!) participants;

the *FAZ* had already reported on the congress on 12 August 1963 without mentioning IB.

late August [. . .] *Wagenbach*: PC was in Germany for a reading at the end of August (Tübingen, 25 August 1963); it is not known when or where he met with the Kafka specialist and publishing reader at S. Fischer.

hospital: IB was treated at the Martin-Luther-Krankenhaus in Berlin during July and August 1963. Following her separation from MF in autumn 1962, she had fallen into a severe mental and physical crisis.

no telephone: IB had been in Berlin on the invitation of the Ford Foundation since the spring of 1963, first in a guest apartment at the Akademie der Künste, Hanseatenweg 10, then from 1 June 1963 in an apartment of her own at Königsallee 35.

a few less than pleasant years: As a result of the Goll affair, among other things, PC was also treated at a psychiatric clinic for the first time in late 1962 and early 1963.

new volume of poems [. . .] *woven into it*: *Die Niemandsrose* was published in late October (Frankfurt: S. Fischer, 1963; LIB without dedication). PC wrote to his publisher Gottfried Bermann Fischer: 'Bitter, yes, that is what these poems are. But the (truly) bitter already holds the no longer and the more than bitter—does it not?' (4 December 1962, GBF 633).

'inartistic' path: See the opposition of 'art' and 'literature' [*Dichtung*] posited at the start of the Büchner Prize speech 'Der Meridian'.

196

Paul Celan to Ingeborg Bachmann, Frankfurt am Main, 30 July 1967

Dear Ingeborg,

three days ago, on the way from Freiburg, Dr Unseld told me about the Akhmatova affair; then I bought *Der Spiegel*.

Let me thank you warmly for recommending me to Piper to translate the Russian poetess, whose poems I have known for a long time. Mandelstamm was one of her most faithful admirers.

Perhaps you could write me a few lines. If you do, then please at this address: P. C. Ecole Normale Supérieure, 45, rue d'Ulm, Paris 5e.

All the best!

Yours

Paul

Frankfurt, on 30 July 67

NOTES

MAN/ANL folder 7, pp. 3–4: airmail letter to: '*Fräulein Ingeborg Bachmann/Via Bocca di Leone 60/<u>Roma</u>/<u>Italien</u>*', *Frankfurt, 30 July 1967, from*: '*Paul Celan dzt. Frankfurt am Main,/Suhrkamp Verlag, Grüneburgweg 69*', *Rome, 2 August 1967.*

Unseld: Head of Suhrkamp Verlag, to which PC had changed in late 1966.

Freiburg: At his reading at the University of Freiburg (24 July 1967), PC also met Martin Heidegger.

Akhmatova affair [. . .] '*Der Spiegel*': IB had recommended PC to her publisher as an 'ideal translator' of the Russian poet Anna Akhmatova; she left Piper when they instead chose Hans Baumann, author of the NS song 'Es zittern die morschen Knochen' [The Brittle Bones Tremble] (*Der Spiegel*, 24 July 1967, pp. 95f.). IB wrote to Piper Verlag on 18 March 1967: 'I am acting on the letters and the events relating to the Akhmatova translation. I am leaving' (IBE). *Malina* was published by Suhrkamp. The PCE does not include any Akhmatova translations.

address: PC was still formally a patient at the Psychiatric University Clinic in Paris at the end of his compulsory admission, but was already teaching again.

PAUL CELAN—MAX FRISCH
CORRESPONDENCE

Paul Celan to Max Frisch, Paris 14 April 1959

78, rue de Longchamp
Paris, 14 April 1959.

Dear Max Frisch,

I called yesterday, without notice, in the hope that you would—as once before (though I did not realize at the time)—be on the telephone: I wanted to ask for your advice, for a conversation, in Zurich, in Basel, wanted to ask you what to do—for something has to be done!—in the face of this increasingly rampant mendacity, baseness and Hitlerism. For I had received a letter a few hours beforehand from Heinrich Böll, a letter that proved to me once more how much spitefulness still lies in the hearts of those whom, gullibly enough—but who, if one is to preserve one's faith in humanity, would give up their 'gullibility'?—I had taken for one of those who 'matter'.

But one only needs to show them <u>what</u> they are <u>actually</u> doing and actually are, and—they immediately revert to their true nature. Now I have also had this experience (by no means a new one) with Böll. Not that I was unprepared for it; but God knows I had not expected it to turn out like <u>that</u>, so blatant in its infamy.

And so I called you, to ask you and Ingeborg if I could come to Zurich with all these questions and feelings of helplessness—with which you have long been familiar, in <u>every</u> guise!—roughly one week from now. Please, tell me if this time would suit you; I could—really—come later (and keep living with my questions until then, and beyond), perhaps in May, on the way to Austria (where we plan to spend our summer) or in June.

Please excuse the hasty and erratic character of these lines, and allow me to send you my warmest regards

Yours, Paul Celan

NOTES

MA VIII/Celan, Paul: hw. letter to: 'Monsieur Max Frisch/Haus zum Langenbaum/<u>Uetikon</u> <u>bei Zürich</u>/Seestrasse/<u>Suisse</u>', *from:* 'Paul Celan, 78 rue de Longchamp, Paris 16^e', Paris, 14 April 1959.

14 April: Letter noted in PCPC.

as once before: Unknown.

Hitlerism: The original word *Hitlerei* is slightly looser than 'Hitlerism', referring not so much to a precise ideology or cult as a mindset and potentially an activity. 'Hitlery' would perhaps be more appropriate in tone (in the manner of 'thuggery'), but 'Hitlerism' was chosen because it is a reasonably established term. [Trans.]

Böll: See NO. 138.

Austria: See NO. 135.1n.

198

Max Frisch to Paul Celan, Uetikon am see, 16 April 1959

Dear Paul Celan,

your letter just arrived. Before that I had taken a letter from Inge to the post office. Come soon! You must excuse me if this letter does not sound very spontaneous; I wrote you a spontaneous one yesterday, but her majesty found a passing sentence, a trifle, a bit of chatter concerning the VW that is meant to collect you and bring you here inappropriate, while I do not like to disinfect such letters, the spontaneous kind. So we quarrelled!—I also tried to say in that letter, which I crumpled up, that I am sincerely looking forward to meeting you, that I have wanted to do so for quite some time, and that I am nervous about it, as I know a great deal about you through Inge and at the same time very little—not nervous because of Inge, but because of your work, which I admire, to the extent that I can find a way into it; and nervous because I have not yet found a way into all of it. I think

Uetikon would be better than Basel, where one always meets people coming and going between restaurants; there is a pleasant hotel near here, just two hundred paces from this apartment, where you could spend the night, and here we would have peace and quiet, and could also take some trips here or there. Do not make your stay too short! One has to use the chance to make one's thoughts clearer by repeating a conversation when one has slept on it. Could you stay for a few days? Believe me, I am looking forward to it.

Yours in anticipation and with warm regards

Max Frisch

NOTES

GLA D 90.1.1487/1: tw. letter w/one hw. correction, envelope missing.

from Inge: NO. 127.

spontaneous: Draft not found.

199

Paul Celan to Max Frisch, Paris, 18 April 1959

on 15 April 1959.

Dear Max Frisch,

your letter arrived, as did the letter from Ingeborg: many thanks!

It turns out I will not be able to come next week after all, only the one after that, for I have just been reminded of a duty I do not know how to evade, namely a <u>nephew's duty</u>: I promised months ago to visit an old aunt in London for Jewish Easter, and now, though I by no means recall ever escaping from Egypt, I will celebrate it in England with my relatives—who, even if they no longer eat unleavened bread, honour the occasion (or simply do not have to go to work).

So we are going to London in the middle of next week, and then I could come to Zurich on 28 or 29 April—hopefully not at an inconvenient time.

Warmest regards

Yours, Paul Celan

NOTES

MFA VIII/ Celan, Paul: hw. letter, envelope missing.

15 April 1959: PC is thanking MF for the letters of 14 (NO. 127) and 16 April 1959 (NO. 198); the reason for his error in the date is unclear (see NO. 128).

nephew's duty [. . .] *aunt*: Regarding the visit to Berta Antschel, see NO. 128.

200

Max Frisch to Paul Celan, Schuls, 20 July 1959

Schuls, 20.VII.

Dear Paul Celan!

My doctors here and in Zurich forbid me to flee to Sils-Maria, unfortunately, and predict the direst of consequences if I do. So I shall yield to them, and Rome is further away than I thought.—I was, I am, glad to have met you, Paul Celan. Perhaps I shall (secretly) go to Lake Sils again on Wednesday. I missed the chance to say goodbye to your wife; give your wife my regards.

Yours, Max Frisch

NOTES

GLA D 90.1.1487/2: hw. letter, envelope missing.

Schuls/ doctors: See NOS 131 and 132.

Sils-Maria [. . .] *Lake Sils*: Regarding the meeting between MF and PC on 19 and 22 July 1959 near Sils-Baselgia, see NOS 135 and 136.

201

Paul Celan to Max Frisch, Paris, 23 October 1959

23.X.59.

Dear Max Frisch,

Hitlerism, Hitlerism, Hitlerism. The peaked caps.

Correspondence

Please take a look at what Herr Blöcker, the leading figure in the new generation of critics by the grace of Herr Rychner, and author—alas—of essays on Kafka and Bachmann, has written.

All the best!

Yours, Paul Celan

NOTES

MFA VIII/ Celan, Paul: hw. letter in very large writing (MFL 201); supplement: tw. cpy (MSS 188); further supplement (unpublished): tw. cpy (text identical to the article, Berliner Tagesspiegel, *11 October 1959, see NO. 143.1); envelope missing.*

Rychner: The features editor at the Zurich daily newspaper *Die Tat* was one of the first in Western Europe to publish poems by PC in 1948. The connection between him and Blöcker is unclear.

essays on Kafka and Bachmann: Blöcker's essay collection *Die neuen Wirklichkeiten* (Berlin: Argon, 1957) contains a chapter entitled 'Franz Kafka' (pp. 297–306). Blöcker had reported on IB's new publications from the start, most recently *Der gute Gott von Manhattan* ('Ein vorbildliches Hörspiel. Der besorgte Bombenleger lässt Liebende in die Luft fliegen' [An Exemplary Radio Play: The Concerned Bomber Blows Lovers to Kingdom Come], *Die Zeit*, 17 October 1958).

201.1
Supplement

Paul Celan
78, rue de Longchamp (16ᵉ)
Paris, 23 October 1959.
(Registered letter)

To the reviews editors of DER TAGESSPIEGEL, Berlin

As, things being the way they once again are in Germany, I cannot count on any of your hopefully numerous readers to say what needs to be said about the review of my poems printed in your issue of 11 October this year (reviewer: Günter Blöcker), I shall do so myself: that may, like my greater freedom with the German language—my native language—be due to my background.

I am writing you this letter: <u>I</u> <u>am</u> <u>less</u> <u>inhibited</u> <u>and</u> <u>burdened</u> <u>by</u> <u>the</u> <u>commu-nicational</u> <u>character</u> <u>of</u> <u>the</u> <u>language</u> <u>than</u> <u>others;</u> <u>I</u> <u>am</u> <u>speaking</u> <u>into</u> <u>a</u> <u>vacuum.</u>

The poem 'Todesfuge', whose reckless author I must term myself today, is indeed <u>a</u> <u>graphic</u> <u>construct</u> <u>whose</u> <u>sound</u> <u>is</u> <u>not</u> <u>developed</u> <u>far</u> <u>enough</u> <u>for</u> <u>it</u> <u>to</u> <u>con-tribute</u> <u>to</u> <u>some</u> <u>larger</u> <u>meaning.</u> <u>The</u> <u>decisive</u> <u>element</u> <u>here</u> <u>is</u> <u>not</u> <u>the</u> <u>view</u> <u>but,</u> <u>rather,</u> <u>the</u> <u>combinations.</u>

Auschwitz, Treblinka, Theresienstadt, Mauthausen, the murders, the gassings: where the poem recalls those things, it consists of <u>contrapuntal</u> <u>exercises</u> <u>on</u> <u>the</u> <u>manuscript</u> <u>paper.</u>

It was indeed high time to <u>reveal</u> this person who—<u>perhaps</u> <u>due to</u> <u>his</u> <u>back-ground</u>—writes German poems while not dispensing entirely with memory. Such reliable turns of phrase as 'the combinatorial fervour of his intellect', 'odourless', etc. were quite especially suited to this purpose. Certain authors, incidentally—<u>perhaps</u> <u>due to</u> <u>their</u> <u>background</u>—even <u>reveal</u> themselves one fine day; then a brief reference to the finished self-revelation is sufficient, and one can continue to write about Kafka unchallenged.

But, you will object, the reviewer does not mean anything other than the birthplace of the author of those <u>graphic</u> <u>constructs</u> when he uses such words as 'background'. I must agree: Blöcker's <u>realities</u>, not least the friendly advice at the end of his review, unambiguously demonstrate this view. So this letter, you will now say in conclusion, has nothing to do with the review. Here too I must agree: indeed. Nothing. Not the slightest bit. <u>I</u> <u>am speaking</u> <u>into</u> <u>a</u> <u>vacuum.</u>

(Paul Celan)

P.S. Everything I have emphasized by underlining in this letter was penned by your employee Blöcker.

Also enclosed: *copy of the article 'Gedichte als graphische Gebilde'* [*Poems as Graphic Constructs*] *by Günter Blöcker.*

202

Max Frisch to Paul Celan, Uetikon am see, 3 November 1959, not sent

Uetikon, 3.11.59
not sent

Dear Paul Celan!

This is the fourth attempt to write a letter that is supposed to answer yours, so it has little chance of turning out well. Please bear with me! The first was warmer, but one cannot duplicate warmth. Are we friends? I have no idea how far you can take me seriously, how far you can see me outside of your own circle. Our brief encounter in Sils: I was glad to see your face and hear your voice after your name, long been known as that of a poet, had become a name in my own life through Ingeborg. What I do know is this: you give me credit for not being an anti-Semite. But that does not give me much leeway—do you understand what I mean? I fear slightly that you are reducing me to the role of a reliable anti-Nazi. Or an unreliable one, if I do not react to the Blöcker review in the way you expect. Will you be willing to pursue a friendship if I do not agree with you? I live with a wound that was certainly not inflicted by you, nor by Hitler, but with a wound too. Sensitized to a pathological degree, I very easily feel betrayed, given up, mocked, rejected, abandoned. Implied criticisms poison me, negligence is enough to torment me, and often—all to often—it takes all my strength to avoid being hurt by my mere imagination, to avoid converting my intellect into brilliant self-righteousness as a defensive measure. Why am I telling you this?! The one who turns to me with a wound, like you, must know that he is coming to someone wounded; towards you too, dear Paul Celan, I feel constrained by the need to be acknowledged, and too much inclined to agree with you. But I do not agree with your stance in this matter. I often read your poems during the summer, already in hospital; then again and again afterwards, as I have difficulties with some of them. Then I always think it is my doing if the communication does not succeed; I feel incompetent and say nothing. What Herr Blöcker, whom I do not know, writes about them is not my opinion, though I at least take it as an attempt to form one. And many opinions are permitted, after all. I do not consider his text good, and it is not without dubious formulations. I must concede that. You are not, however, concerned with the critic allowing himself a negative opinion but with symptoms of a political nature. You are, unfortunately, probably right in this respect. Does the friend's response you are expecting from myself and others consist in agreeing with you, persuaded by the incisiveness of your reply? I know you too little, dear Paul Celan; I do not, for example, know how you would react to criticism of your poetic work in a case where the possibility of anti-Semitism were out of the question. By no means am I trying to equate you with myself; I do not know whether it is true of you, but I know how glad I sometimes am to learn that a critic who does not praise me is a shady character, politically or otherwise. Most of the time they are, unfortunately. As the suspicion of being rebuked or misunderstood out of anti-Semitism is not applicable in my case, what explanation should I seek? I have to deal with myself, always a laborious and tiresome task; here, I have found that being utterly torn to pieces affects me less than those implied criticisms between the lines of a positive response that show me where the critic sees my momentary weakness or limits at all. Usually, it is not so difficult to use his own contradictions against him, but what do I gain from that? My acumen becomes the accomplice of my self-righteousness, that is all. Once one has reached a certain age, a time when one has already defined oneself through a number of achievements, one suffers less on account of a failure than because of the increasingly clear limits of one's entire possibilities; and I could even imagine someone whose possibilities are great and unusual suffering through this—that is to say, even someone like you. In this context, the reference to the death camps disturbs me. It forces me to believe that your outrage over Blöcker's review is completely free of all other emotions that such a review can trigger in an author. I want to believe it. You are forcing me to do so. For if, with reference to this review, there were the slightest hint of injured vanity in your response, then it seems to me that naming the death camps would be impermissible and egregious. Do not misunderstand me, dear Paul Celan: I do not doubt your horror at symptoms of Hitlerism, which also horrify me, and if your exclamation HITLERISM, HITLERISM, HITLERISM, THE PEAKED CAPS! had not ensued in the context of a literary review that may also irk you in other ways, I would have addressed the political problem. But here I cannot, for the political agreement you rightly expect from me would only conceal the disagreement between us through silence. That is why I am not comfortable with it. You force me to write a letter that may cause you to write me off like Böll and many others, almost everyone, or to a silence that would mean the end of a friendship before it had even begun. Perhaps you do not need any friendship, but it is the only thing I have to offer.

With warm regards

Yours

NOTES

MFA VIII/Celan, Paul: tw. letter draft w/hw. corrections and one hw. addition (MFL 200–202)

not sent: Added by hand.

fourth attempt: No further drafts were found. See the final letter, NO. 203 (notes on sections retained can be found there).

poems: *Sprachgitter*.

hospital: See NO. 132.

Böll: See NO. 197.

203

Max Frisch to Paul Celan, Uetikon am See, 6 November 1959

Uetikon, 6.11.59

Dear Paul Celan!

I have already written you four letters, long ones, then a fifth, short one—they are all no good. But I cannot leave you without an answer. What on earth shall I write? The political agreement you can expect from me would only conceal the other things that struck me in your short letter, your personal problem, which it is not my place to speak about, especially as you do not present it to me as that but as a political, objective one. It is truly difficult for me, believe me, and my letter to you has preoccupied me for days; I have devoted entire mornings and entire evenings to it. You give me credit for not being an anti-Semite. Do you understand what I mean if I say that this does not give me much leeway? I have no idea with what else you credit me. In my experience, relationships between people cannot work when one goes about them in the way that you and I would be if I simply agreed with you; and I am worried by the prospect of being reduced to a reliable anti-Nazi. Your letter, dear Paul Celan, does not ask me—your letter gives me a chance to prove myself if I react to the review by Blöcker in the same way as you. That is what bothers me. After so many failed letters, I simply wanted to write: you are right, you are right. I wanted to resign. How difficult it is for me, dear Paul Celan, to resign. Our encounter in Sils: I was so glad to see your face and hear your voice after your name, long been known as that of a poet, had become a name in the most intimate part of my life through Ingeborg. I was afraid of you, and now I am afraid once again. Are you, I wonder, willing to embark on a friendship? Even if I do not agree with you? I could assure you that symptoms of Hitlerism also horrify me, as well as point out that the new threats, as we know, will scarcely be recognizable in overt similarities to the Hitlerism of old. But if we intend to think in political terms, I think we should avoid all cases that could mingle with the problem of how we are to deal with literary criticism in general. I do not know whether it is true of you, but I know how glad I sometimes am to learn that a critic who offends my ambition is a shady character politically. And what hurts me the most, for example, is not being utterly torn to pieces but, rather, those implied criticisms between the lines of a positive response which show me that the critic (however miserably he might express himself) has sensed my momentary weakness or limits. Once one has reached a certain age, a time when one has already defined oneself through a number of achievements, one suffers less on account of a failure than because of the increasingly clear limits of one's entire possibilities; and I could even imagine someone whose possibilities are great and unusual suffering through this—that is to say, even someone like you. Do not be angry, dear Paul Celan, how hurtful it is to be publicly misunderstood even if the suspicion of anti-Semitism is not applicable. You write: HITLERISM, HITLERISM, HITLERISM, THE PEAKED CAPS! I do not consider Blöcker's review good; and it is not without dubious formulations, I will concede that—if I can also tell you my other thoughts. I do not consider your response good either, even if it is a masterpiece of linguistic acumen. It forces me to honour you (and I do so of my own accord), and to believe without reservations that you, dear Paul Celan, are completely free of the feelings that affect me and others, stirrings of vanity and injured ambition. For if there is the slightest hint of that in your anger, it seems to me that naming the death camps would be impermissible and egregious. Whom am I telling this! If you make a political phenomenon out of a review like Blöcker's, I think you are partly right, but also partly wrong, and the one problem blurs the other. It is not easy for me to send off a letter that may cause you to give up on me, or lead to a silence that would mean the end of a friendship before it had even begun. Perhaps you do not need what I think of as friendship, perhaps you do not want it, but it is the only thing I have to offer.

Yours most sincerely
Max Frisch

NOTES

GLA D 90.1.1487/3: tw. letter w/hw. corrections, envelope missing (*MFL 203f.*); *MFA VIII/Celan*: cpy.

6.11.59: Regarding the difficulties between IB and MF in connection with the letter and its assessment, see NOS 144 and 147.

anti-Nazi: MF here reacts very similarly to Böll—whom MF mentions at the end of his first draft of this letter—in the Firges affair (NO. 197).

Sils: See NOS 135 and 136.

friendship: PC takes this up in NO. 207.

HITLERISM [. . .] *PEAKED CAPS*: See NO. 201.

your response: See NO. 201.1.

204
Max Frisch to Paul Celan, dedication in Glossen zu Don Juan,
Uetikon am See (?), *end of 1959*

For

Paul Celan

at the end of a
confused year

Max Frisch
1959

NOTES

GLA LPC: hw. dedication on the flyleaf of Glossen zu Don Juan [Glosses on Don Juan], *illustrations by Walter Jonas, Zurich [1959]; NO. 217 of 250 numbered copies, signed on the back by Max Frisch and Walter Jonas, envelope missing.*

Glossen zu Don Juan: Separately published afterword to MF's *Don Juan oder die Liebe zur Geometrie* [Don Juan, or The Love of Geometry] (Frankfurt: Suhrkamp, 1953).

end of a confused year: It seems that PC thanked MF for the book in a telephone conversation on 23 December 1959 (PCPC). In addition to his infection with hepatitis and the conflicts, partly caused by PC, in his relationship with IB, 1959 also saw MF's divorce from Trudy Frisch von Meyenburg; they had been separated since 1954.

205

Max Frisch to Paul Celan, dedication in offprint of the acceptance speech for the Büchner Prize ('Emigranten'), Uetikon am See, 27 May 1960

For Paul Celan
in Uetikon,
27.V.60
sincerely   MF.

NOTES

GLA LPC: hw. on offprint of 'Emigranten. Rede zur Verleihung des Georg-Büchner-Preises 1958', pp. 49–66 (no location).

'*Emigranten*': This is the first printing of the speech in *Schauspielhaus Zürich 1938/39–1958/59. Beiträge zum zwanzigjährigen Bestehen der Neuen Schauspiel AG,* [Texts on the Twenteith Anniversary of the Foundation of the Neue Schauspiel AG] Kurt Hirschfeld and Peter Löffler eds (Zurich, 1958).

27.V.60: As PC still recalled in early 1962 (PCPC), MF gave him the copy at a meeting in Uetikon while PC was staying in Zurich on account of Nelly Sachs (see NO. 161n). At this point PC already knew that he had been chosen for the 1960 Büchner Prize.

206
Paul Celan to Max Frisch, Paris, 29 May 1960

Dear Max Frisch,

I would like to thank you again for the conversation at your home in Uetikon.

There was a great deal, I know, that could not be put into words, that could not be pinned down. But perhaps <u>that</u> was precisely what we both gained: that very sharp emergence of contours that we owe to the realm of psychology—it is undoubtedly one of the inescapable things in life—has another side, I believe— the distances, the spaces, the way things stand in time, all of that is eliminated. (In our conversation it was not.)

I truly think there is something 'interfering' here, interfering—in one way or another—with all of us; I mean what I referred to in our conversation as the 'objectively demonic' element—without really doing it justice with this formulation. 'Coincidence' would perhaps be another auxiliary term for it, in the sense that it coincides and has coincided with us; a word such as 'fate' may also lend a 'helping hand' from time to time. I daresay we come into contact with all this when we write.

Best wishes

Yours

Paul Celan

Paris, on 29 May 1960.

NOTES

MFA VIII/Celan, Paul: hw. letter (partial print MFB 236) to: 'Monsieur Max Frisch/Haus zum Langenbaum/ <u>Uetikon bei Zürich</u>/Seestrasse/Suisse', Paris, 29 May [1960], from 'Paul Celan, 78 rue de Longchamp, Paris 16e; on the back, in MF's handwriting: 'Pariserzug [zigzag line above it] 275010 // (17/15/16/18 Juillet/<u>Serreau</u>'; GLA D 90.1.780/1: tw. copy w/ hw. corrections, marked '<u>Abschrift</u>' [copy] in top left corner.

<u>*Serreau*</u>: Notes for a meeting with the director of the Théâtre Lutèce in Paris, in connection with the Paris premiere of *Biedermann und die Brandstifter* in the same year.

'<u>*Abschrift*</u>': Letter and copy noted in PCPC.

the way things stand in time/'fate': In sketches for 'Der Meridian', which he began around this time, PC referred to the poem as 'schicksalhaft bestimmte Sprache' [fatefully determined language] and postulated that it 'stands into time' (TCA/M NOS 340 and 17).

has coincided with us: Though this sentence has been rendered with a play on words, the original features a slightly different one. The word for 'coincidence' is *Zufall*, and its closest relative is the word *zufallen*, meaning (among other things) 'to devolve upon', 'to fall to'. Celan first speaks of *Zufall*, then refers to 'das uns Zugefallene und Zufallende' [what has devolved and does devolve upon us], elaborating in Heideggerian fashion on the meaning of the first word. [Trans.]

contact: See the Whitman quotation in NO. 135.1.

207
Paul Celan to Max Frisch, Trébabu par Le Conquet, late July/early August (?) 1961, aborted draft

Dear Max Frisch,

These lines are meant warmly—please do not take them in any other way.

It cannot have escaped your notice which phase this whole business instigated against me has entered with the Schroers-Mondstrahl publication. It cannot have escaped your notice what is being achieved by this, and what has indeed already been achieved with the help of various extremely friendly witnesses. You know that it amounts to my incapacitation, and it also—I am a writer, after all—has material aspects.

You also know that I cannot refute all of this any more than I can refute the charlatan/villain/thief motif repeated and parodied in various ways. This whole business defies all evidence; my own efforts—God knows there have been enough of them—have amply demonstrated this.

The forgeries are of the most blatant crudeness—but are gladly tolerated and supported. As are the slanderous claims. One of most devious aspects is a certain kind of defence. And all manner of double-dealing—orchestrated (though here too, many people have been in the picture for a long time) from the most unbelievable place and with the most unbelievable tools and methods.

Let me say it very briefly here: there was, and is, presumably from the start, an agent provocateur involved, and I—but also you and Ingeborg—have been fooled by him on various occasions.

Dear Max Frisch! When the Blöcker article stirred me up—that too was already a demonstrable part of this—you offered me your friendship. There was a misunderstanding between us then—I did my best to resolve it. I cannot believe that you would deny me that friendship now. I want to ask you to talk it over with me, and I want to ask you to come to Paris: because you will not believe what I want to tell you until I have shown you. It is a great deal, Max Frisch, a very great deal.

Ingeborg was right when she felt that the 'Response' was disastrous, that it had the wrong 'tone'. But the one setting the tone was, in more ways than one, Rudolf Hirsch.

But

NOTES

GLA D 90.1.781/2: *tw. letter draft.*

Trébabu par Le Conquet: PC's holiday address at the western tip of Brittany (early July until 5 September 1961).

Schroers-Mondstrahl publication [. . .] *forgeries*: In 'Literaturskandal' (*Vorwärts*, 28 June 1961),

Schroers had hinted at a breakdown on PC's part. Felix Mondstrahl, who had encouraged Claire Goll to publish her accusations in *Baubudenpoet* (see NO. 179), subsequently denied the claim that PC is 'not an epigone and epigangster [*Epigone und Epigauner*] in any of his poems' ('Eine sehr merkwürdige Sache' [A Very Peculiar Business], *Vorwärts*, 19 July 1961); to support this he cited a comparison of passages by Celan and Goll from *Baubudenpoet*. PC had replied to the slanderous accusations a few months previously with 'Eine Gauner und Ganovenweise' [A Rogue's and Robber's Tune]. Regarding the forgeries, see NO. 179n.

most unbelievable place [. . .] *provocateur/Hirsch*: PC broke off contact with the director of S. Fischer Verlag in July 1961; no reason is known for his suspicions.

Blöcker article: See NOS 143.1 and 201.1.

friendship: See NOS 202 and 203.

It is a great deal: PC left behind an entire suitcase of material concerning the Goll affair.

'Response': See NO. 163.

208
Paul Celan to Max Frisch, Trébabu par Le Conquet, 22 August 1961, not sent

Kermorvan, Trébabu par Le Conquet (Finistère), on 22.8.1961.

Dear Max Frisch,

it cannot have escaped your notice which phase this whole business instigated against me has now entered, and what it inevitably means for a writer to see his name and pen also discredited in this fashion.

But that has only made it clearer why this whole legacy fraud—how crude it is—and the slanderous claims it involves have been tolerated and supported for so long. What has also become clear is the interplay between the 'one side' and the 'other side'; the *Vorwärts* 'controversy', whose alliterative superlatives are no coincidence, also provides insight into this.

For me, this has the advantage (. . .) that I now know the identity of the true orchestrator—based in the most unbelievable place—of this entire matter.

I am thinking to myself that they must have succeeded in pulling the wool over your and Ingeborg's eyes: that was one of the methods used by these people from the very start—and there are more than a few of them, Max Frisch!—namely sowing discord between my friends and myself with all manner of distortions and provocations.

And I am, finally, thinking to myself that if you were to set eyes on what I have before my eyes (and ears) here, you would take a stand as the very thing that has ultimately been targeted here: as a person.

Give my best to Ingeborg!

Best wishes

Yours

NOTES

GLA D 90.1.781/1: *tw. letter draft, one cpy preserved.*

legacy fraud: See NO. 179.

alliterative superlatives: See Schroers' comment on the magazine *Baubudenpoet* in his *Vorwärts* article: 'in der allerlei *Ge*schwätziges und *Ge*sinnungshaftes sich genialisch aufblähte; dazu musste die Diskriminierung des echten *Ge*nies gehören' [in which all manner of chatter and opinion brilliantly inflated itself; this inevitably included discrimination against true genius' (see NO. 207; emphasis added).

209

Paul Celan to Max Frisch, Paris, 23 September 1961, not sent

Paris, on 23 September 1961.

Dear Max Frisch,

I warmly request a chance to talk things over with you and Ingeborg.

I cannot believe that you do not see where all these <u>provocations*)</u>—Schroers is just one of many—are coming from. I cannot believe that you do not see what and who is at work here—and why.

You know what it means for a writer to read and here <u>such</u> things as those being written and spread about me. (And the willing 'witnesses' they find for <u>that</u> purpose!)

And you also know that I can no more refute all that than I could any of the previous things: none of these characters are concerned with the truth. And hence, against all evidence, this entire bottomless infamy.

I cannot imagine that you are observing these things indifferently. (As for me, I have finally understood the interplay between the 'one side' and the 'other side'—as well as the 'Jewish' participation . . .)

There are many lies around us, Max Frisch. And many lies have come between us. I ask you and Ingeborg most sincerely: please, let us clarify all this and do away with it. And let us do so together.

I would like to come to you—I must ask you to come to Paris.

And, at the same time, I ask you to maintain the utmost discretion.

Best wishes

Paul Celan

Dear Max Frisch! Please, try to understand why I could not thank you for the joint statement by the winners of the Büchner Prize: instead of exposing the character assassination and literary forgery, the victim of the assassination is praised for his 'incorruptibility' . . . I am no Robespierre, Max Frisch! I am a human being like you and everyone else. No more, no less.

And this—terrible—business with the tribute to Nelly Sachs. How can I be expected to publish something alongside the Goll witness and <u>co-forger</u> Pinthus?!

---

*) We <u>have</u>—you, Ingeborg and I—been provoked, Max Frisch. In the most diverse, perverse ways . . .

NOTES

GLA D 90.1.781/3: hw. letter, one hw. cpy preserved.

Schroers: See NO. 207.

infamy: See NO. 166.

'Jewish' participation: PC was thinking not only of Claire Goll herself but also of R. Hirsch (see NO. 207).

joint statement by the winners of the Büchner Prize: See NO. 178.

tribute to Nelly Sachs: On 5 June 1961, PC had told Enzensberger, the initiator of the festschrift for Sachs' 70th birthday, that he would not contribute, because he did not want to stand alongside authors such as Kasack who had contributed to the Goll affair. On 27 September 1961, however, he offered his dedicatory poem 'Zürich, Zum Storchen' (*Nelly Sachs zu Ehren. Gedichte—Prosa—Beiträge* [Frankfurt: Suhrkamp, 1961], p. 32); see NO. 211. MF did not contibute, while IB is present with her poem 'Ihr Worte' [You Words] (pp. 9f.).

Pinthus: On the suggestion of Claire Goll, Kurt Pinthus wrote the following in the new edition of his anthology *Menschheitsdämmerung* (Reinbek: Rowohlt, 1959), first published in 1920: '[. . .] there is much Trakling, Benning and Golling' (p. 15). The bibliography for Yvan Goll, supplied by Claire Goll, includes several titles that do not appear in any published edition. Pinthus did not ultimately write anything for the tribute.

210
Paul Celan to Max Frisch, Paris, 27 September 1961

78, rue de Longchamp
Paris, on 27.9.61

Dear Max Frisch,

I often ask myself why so much silence has come between us.

It can only be due to misunderstandings—grave ones, certainly, but ones that a conversation can, I believe, do away with.

Let us try to clear all this up, once and for all!

I read in the newspaper that you are going to Cologne in the autumn—that would not be so far for me. Or will you be visiting Paris in the foreseeable future?

I am writing to Ingeborg at the same time—with the same intention, in the same hope.

Best wishes

Yours, Paul Celan

NOTES

GLA D 90.1.780/2: *only preserved as hw. cpy, document missing in MFA.*

Cologne: PC had read on 24 May 1961 in *Die Welt* that MF was to be dramatic adviser at Städtische Bühnen Köln (PCPC/GCL).

to Ingeborg: See NO. 190.

211
Paul Celan to Max Frisch, Paris, 10 October 1961

10.10.61.

Dear Max Frisch,

I heard from Dr Unseld, who called earlier—I sent something just in time to participate in the Nelly Sachs tribute—that you are in Zurich. Dr Unseld also mentioned a letter that you, he seemed to recall, wrote a number of months ago—that letter never reached me, dear Max Frisch! I myself wrote to you and Ingeborg at your Rome address some ten days ago.

Hopefully we will soon have an opportunity for a lengthy conversation!

Best wishes, Paul Celan

NOTES

GLA D 90.1.780/3: *only preserved as hw. cpy, document missing in MFA.*

Unseld [. . .] *Nelly Sachs tribute*: See NO. 209.

conversation: On 12 October 1961, PC noted: 'Called Frisch the day before yesterday, told him I needed his friendship. . .' (PCPC, see NOS 202 and 203). PC and MF did not meet again in 1961, but saw each other occasionally, for example on 18 April 1964 in Rome and on 19 September 1967 in Zurich (PCPC).

212
Max Frisch to Paul Celan, dedication in Andorra, *Rome (?), December 1961*

For
Paul Celan

sincerely
Max Frisch
XII. 1961

NOTES

GLA LPC: hw. dedication on the flyleaf of Andorra *(Frankfurt: Suhrkamp, 1961). Insert at back: Friedrich Torberg, 'Ein furchtbares Missverständnis. Notizen zur Zürcher Uraufführung des Schauspiels "Andorra" von Max Frisch' [A Terrible Misunderstanding: Notes on the Premiere of Max Frisch's Play* Andorra *in Zurich], double page from* Forum, *December 1961, pp. 455f.; envelope missing.*

Andorra/XII. 1961: The book (a gift accompanying NO. 194?) was published in the autumn of 1961 (premiere on 2 November 1961); PC received it on 3 January 1962 (DPC). In an aphorism, PC alludes to *Andorra* as 'a play about turning Jewish [*Verjuden*] (MSS 37). GCL noted for PC: 'The protagonist should have been a real Jew, not a non-Jew playing the Jew', and 'Read "Andorra", a crudely allegorical play, spiced up with a few sexual naturalisms. Judaism is dragged down to the level of the petty bourgeoisie, furnished for the occasion with a touch of guilty conscience from a para-religious perspective. That will be a joy for the Germans, for their Stalinist-Gomulkist intellectuals, left Catholics and pan-Germanic reunifiers' (26 December 1961 and 6 January 1962, PCPC/GCL). In the margin of the newspaper report 'Notizen von den Proben. Dramaturgisches zu "Andorra"' [Notes from the Rehearsals: Dramaturgical Thoughts on *Andorra*] (*NZZ*, 10 March 1962), PC wrote 'bastard and <u>anti-</u>

Semite' and 'see the passage on Theresienstadt in his diary, see his letter re. Blöcker [NO. 203]'. PC had already noted regarding his visit to Zurich in May 1960 that 'something is wrong' with MF's 'attitude to the Jewish' (PCPC).

Ingeborg Bachmann—Gisèle Celan-Lestrange
Correspondence

213

Gisèle Celan-Lestrange to Ingeborg Bachmann, Paris, before Christmas 1957 (?)

My dear Ingeborg,

allow me to wish you a good Christmas from the bottom of my heart!

    Gisèle Celan

NOTES

MAN/ANL folder 9, p. 14: hw. letter, envelope missing.

All letters in the correspondence between Ingeborg Bachmann and Gisèle Celan-Lestrange were written in French. [Trans.]

before Christmas: GCL knew since mid-October 1957 that PC had resumed his love affair with IB after their encounter in Wuppertal (see NO. 44).

214

Ingeborg Bachmann to Gisèle Celan-Lestrange, Munich, before 24 December 1957

I thank you with all my heart—dear Gisèle!

    Ingeborg

NOTE

GCLE: hw. letter to: 'Mme Gisèle Celan/78, rue de Longchamp/PARIS 16ème' [no stamps].

Needle marks on envelope and card, i.e. sent with flowers; envelope contains leaves and petals of red roses. The ensemble was inserted in GCL's diary.

215

Gisèle Celan-Lestrange to Ingeborg Bachmann, Paris, 29 December 1957

78 rue de Longchamp
             Paris 16ᵉ

29 December 1957

My dear Ingeborg,

your roses reached me on the evening of the 24th, so pretty, so pretty! I was very touched to receive them from you, and I wish I could have written you a long letter, but I am unable to; please excuse me.

Thank you very much for these roses, I keep them close to me, they come to me from you, they were so pretty!

Gisèle

NOTE

MAN/ANL folder 9, pp. 1–2: hw. letter to: 'Mademoiselle Ingeborg Bachmann/München 13/ Franz-Josephstrasse 9a/(Allemagne)', Paris, 29 December 1957, from: 'Made P. Celan/ 78rue de Longchamp/Paris 16ᵉ'.

216

Gisèle Celan-Lestrange to Ingeborg Bachmann, Paris, 23 January 1958

78 rue de Longchamp
             Paris 16ᵉ

23 January 1958.

My dear Ingeborg,

I read your poems for the first time tonight, and read for a very long time. They shook me to the core. They helped me understand many things, and I am ashamed that I could have reacted as I did when Paul went back to you. From tonight, I think I know you a little better. I understand how much you had to suffer these past six years. I wept, Ingeborg, over many of your poems. I understood and I was ashamed of myself. The world has truly been so unjust to you. How much everything is amiss!

I suffered, as you know, when I felt Paul drifting away from me, so far . . . when he returned from Cologne in October, but you have suffered so much more. So much more.

I would like to give you my hand, Ingeborg.

Gisèle

NOTES

MAN/ANL folder 9, pp. 3–4: hw. letter to: 'Mademoiselle Ingeborg Bachmann/<u>München</u> <u>13</u>/Franz-Josephstrasse 9a/(Allemagne)', *stamp torn off.*

23 January 1958: GCL's diary entry of the same day shows her difficulties in accepting PC's attitude (see PC/GCL II 92/3); he had left for Germany—to see IB, among others—that day (see NO. 86).

I read your poems: On GCL's reading of *Die gestundete Zeit* (NO. 42) and *Anrufung des Grossen Bären* (NO. 114n), see her diary entries from January (PC/GCL II 92/3).

217

Ingeborg Bachmann to Gisèle Celan-Lestrange, dedications in Die gestundete Zeit *and* Anrufung des Grossen Bären, *Munich, 10 March 1958*

For Gisèle.

Ingeborg

Munich, March 1958

For Gisèle

under the shadows: the roses.

> Ingeborg
>
> Munich, 10 March 1958

NOTES

GLA LPC: *hw. dedications on the flyleaves of* Die gestundete Zeit. Gedichte, *second edition* (*Munich*: *Piper, 1957*), *and* Anrufung des Grossen Bären. Gedichte (*Munich*: *Piper, 1956*).

Anrufung des Grossen Bären: Numerous reading traces left by GCL, especially in the poem 'Curriculum vitae'; several markings in the table of contents could also be PC's (by the poems 'Erklär mir, Liebe' [Explain to Me, Love] and 'Tage in Weiss' [Days in White]). GCL, most likely with PC's help, took down around 20 rough translations of poems from the volume, dated May and August 1958, in a notebook (GCLE).

under the shadows: *the roses.*: Allusion to IB's 'Schatten Rosen Schatten' [Shadows Roses Shadows].

218

Gisèle Celan-Lestrange to Ingeborg Bachmann, Paris, 5 April 1958

> 78 rue de Longchamp
> > Paris 16ᵉ

5 April 1958.

My dear Ingeborg,

I have long been meaning to thank you for your books; forgive me for not doing so until now.

I think very often of you, and very often of your poems.

Gisèle

NOTES

MAN/ANL folder 9, pp. 5–6: hw. letter to: 'Mademoiselle Ingeborg Bachmann/<u>München 13</u>/Franz-Josephstrasse 9a/(Allemagne)', Paris, 10 April 1958.

livres: Die gestundete Zeit and *Anrufung des Grossen Bären*.

219

Gisèle Celan-Lestrange to Ingeborg Bachmann, Rochefort-en-Yvelines, 30 July 1958

Le Moulin
Rochefort-en-Yvelines
    (Seine-et-Oise)

30 July 1958.

My dear Ingeborg,

thank you for letter, which was <u>so</u> kind!

It was truly a great pleasure to make your acquaintance, and I thank you for coming to visit us in Paris.

I would like to wish you a good summer, a great deal of sunshine and very good work, and also something very tender for your heart. May I wish you that?

Before returning to work in Paris, we—Paul, Eric, the big ball and I—have come out to the country for two weeks. Paul fishes for pike, Eric chases butterflies, and I watch the two of them.

Like you, we were very troubled by the events in the Middle East; we so wished there could be a little more peace in the world. But can one really hope for that?

I often think of you, I hope we shall see each other again soon and that you will keep in touch. There are so few friends around us!

Gisèle

You do not know how much I admire you for speaking such good French. It is a true joy to me that you speak my language so well.

NOTES

MAN/ANL folder 9, pp. 7–8: hw. airmail letter to: 'Mademoiselle Ingeborg Bachmann/Via Generale Parisi 6/<u>NAPLES</u>/(Italie)', Paris, [xx] July 1958, Naples, 6 August 1958.

Le Moulin: An old water-mill, about 50 km south-west of Paris, owned by GCL's sister Monique Gessain (see NOS 101 and 102).

letter: Not found.

visit us in Paris: See NO. 104.

Middle East: On 14 July 1958, the monarchy was deposed in Iraq, the royal family murdered and the country declared a republic. Because of the danger of a destabilization of the whole region, America sent troops to Lebanon and Great Britain sent soldiers to Jordan.

220

Gisèle Celan-Lestrange to Ingeborg Bachmann, Wald im Pinzgau, 13 June 1959

Hotel Walderwirt
WALD IM PINZGAU
(Salzburg)
Austria

13 June 1959.

My dear Ingeborg,

Just a little note to tell you that we think of you a great deal. We were very sad to hear that Max Frisch is still unwell. We hope you will soon have better news for us, and that you will both have good holidays, full of sunshine and good work.

I send you, with all my heart, my best wishes—with all my heart

Gisèle

NOTES

MAN/ANL folder 9, p. 10: *hw. letter, envelope missing.*
WALD: See NO. 135.1n.
Frisch is still unwell: Regarding MF's illness, see NOS 131, 132 and 200.

221

Ingeborg Bachmann to Gisèle Celan-Lestrange, Zurich,
17 (?) November 1959, aborted draft

Kirchgasse 33
Zurich/Switzerland

My dear Gisèle,

I am coming to you in my despair after Paul's letter, and I do not even know what to ask of you. I understand him so well, yet at the same time it seems too awful because my letter was bad, written in such a state of confusion, one that you are perhaps better able to understand, and now it is tearing me apart even more. I do not know how to live in such a state, rejected, because I no longer knew how to act without disavowing Max and without losing Paul's trust—even worse, I no longer know what he expects of me

I could explain the reasons, the context, which also stem from an injury; but this is not the time, least of all the time for Paul. I would like to tell you, Gisèle, that I cannot bear this distance and this banishment—do you think that I deserve it, I do not know where all this is leading me . . . except that if you are still hesitating, Gisèle, do not reply, if you cannot, but give me a word of hope some time, so that all my mistakes   Your place is with Paul, and I cannot but think it better for him to be sure of you than of me, in such paralysis when I am visible to Paul again, as I hoped I forever would be, and perhaps I will forever be without importance to Paul.

All I ask of you, if it is possible for you, is to give him a little parcel that I will send in the next few days for his birthday.

NOTES

NOTES

MAN/ANL folder 18, pp. 2–3, heavily corrected letter draft.

17 (?) November 1959: See NO. 147. A further, considerably shorter draft of this letter, written on 15 November 1959, has also survived (*MAN/ANL folder 18, p. 1*); it is followed there by the draft of a letter to Klaus Demus: 'Unfortunately can only come to Frankfurt on the 15th, impossible before then/letters to you and Nani on the way to Vienna—Would Zurich trip to Zurich not be possible?/Yours, Inge/Kirchgasse 33, Zurich'.

Paul's letter: See NO. 145.

my letter: See NO. 144.

without disavowing Max: See NO. 151.

little parcel: See NO. 150.

222
Ingeborg Bachmann to Gisèle Celan-Lestrange, Zurich, 20 December 1959

Kirchgasse 33
Zurich, 20-12-59

My dear Gisèle,

you probably know that I wanted to send you a letter, asking for your help, when I was so desperate last month. But ultimately I want too much to spare you from having to bear more than Paul's pain and worries, and I know that this already demands all your great and beautiful strength. So there is little left for me to say— but I still have more faith in your strength and your presence than in any number of words and letters. No friendship could ever be enough to help Paul in this misfortune and to save him from all distrust, wherever it exists without any reason; what can, however, is this presence and everything you give him, your inexhaustible and courageous love.—Gisèle, I am sorry once again that we did not meet in the summer, and I often think that many things might not have become so difficult if we could have spoken. I am becoming more and more afraid of letters because they look upon us so rigidly, when all one is after is the living word— and even living disagreement.

In a few days Eric will be waiting for Father Christmas. But we, who do not wait for him and not even for the slightest miracle . . . we must wait for it, each one of us for the other, and this is what makes me live in patient expectation that everything will work out.

I wish you a peaceful, enjoyable time, with all my heart—and I wish you happiness!

Ingeborg

NOTES

GCLE: *hw. letter to*: '*Mme Paul Celan/78, Rue de Longchamp/<u>PARIS 16ème</u>/FRANCE*', *Zurich, 22. December 1959.*

you probably know: See NO. 147.

we did not meet: See NO. 132.

223

Ingeborg Bachmann to Gisèle Celan-Lestrange, Uetikon am See, 24 December 1960

ONLY JUST RETURNED TO ZURICH PLEASE SEND PAUL'S ADDRESS IN ZURICH BY TELEGRAM OR ASK HIM TO CALL 342987 TONIGHT OR TOMORROW MORNING

INGEBORG

NOTES

GLA D 90.1.2832/4: *telegram to*: '*Madame Paul Celan, 78 rue de Longchamp Paris*', *Uetikon am See, 24 May 1960, 16³⁰, Paris, 24 May 1960, 17³⁰.*

RETURNED: IB was coming from the premiere of Henze's *Der Prinz von Homburg*, for which she had written the libretto, at the Hamburg State Opera (22 May 1960). The telegram (noted in PCPC) is a reaction to NO. 159 regarding the meeting with Nelly Sachs; IB evidently assumed that PC was already in Zurich.

224

Gisèle Celan-Lestrange to Ingeborg Bachmann, Zurich, 26 May 1960

Thursday evening

My dear Ingeborg,

I was glad we had a chance to talk a little with you tonight, and I hope that we will have the chance to see each other more often in future. I also wanted to tell you that I too do not always know how to help Paul. His life and his fate are very hard; he is very unhappy and it is not easy for me to be for him what I should be, what I would like to be.

I know you have many difficulties, and I sincerely wish that you will find a true way to bring you a little happiness; my greatest hope, tonight, in this moment when you are with Paul, is that he can understand you and you can understand him. I wish you that with all my heart.

Eric is sleeping next door, he is happy, he is full of trust. He knows many things and he knows nothing—I want to ensure that he is very happy for as long as possible, but I also know it cannot last forever. It is very difficult to raise a child in such a wicked, badly made world. How can I protect him? How can I help him? For the moment it is still easy; he belongs to us completely, but children do not belong to us for long. He is a great blessing to us, this son, but also a great worry at every moment. He is Paul's son; he is similar to him, and I think he will understand him.

We will meet again soon, I hope, please think of me as a friend, I am your friend—

Gisèle

NOTES

MAN/ANL folder 9, p. 9: hw. letter (letterhead: Urban Hotel Garni Zürich, Stadelhoferstr. 41), envelope missing.

very unhappy: About, among other things, the renewed charges of plagiarism (see NO. 159n) and the experiences with Firges and Blöcker (see NOS 112 and 143).

with Paul: See NO. 161n. PC made the following comment on his meeting with IB that evening: 'Ingeborg (Kirchgasse).—The conversation was shapeless, and could thus only result in even more unhappiness' (PCPC).

225

Ingeborg Bachmann to Gisèle Celan-Lestrange, Zurich, 24 June 1960

24-6-60
Zurich, Kirchgasse 33

My dear Gisèle,

your letter was so touching! Thank you so much. I hope your thoughts that evening helped all of us. Since your departure, and that of Nelly Sachs, I have been working incessantly—I am almost unaware of time passing in this humid, hot summer. I will be leaving here on 15 July to return to Uetikon am See. We will stay there until September, in spite of our original plans (to go to Spain), because I can no longer see an end to this book. And Max has to go to Scuol again in a few days to repeat his treatment.

The circus in Zurich gave me this handkerchief for Eric; the clowns use the same ones.—If I can get hold of some picture frames for you—write to me! I would be happy to give you this little bit of help.

I wish you all the very best, a restful and easier summer after such a hard year! I am your friend—

Ingeborg

NOTES

GCLE: hw. letter to: '*Mme Paul CELAN/78, rue de Longchamp/PARIS 16ème/FRANCE*', Zurich [*stamps torn off*] from '[*I*]ngeborg Bachmann, Kirchgasse 33/Zurich'.

Nelly Sachs: See NO. 161.

I have been working: On *Das dreissigste Jahr*, especially 'Unter Mördern und Irren' [Among Murderers and Madmen].

Spain: See NO. 163.

Scuol: See NO. 137.

circus in Zurich: In May 1960, PC, GCL and Eric had gone with IB to see Zirkus Knie in Zurich; the small handkerchief, almost certainly bought in the circus, was decorated with clowns.

226

Gisèle Celan-Lestrange to Ingeborg Bachmann, Paris, 2 December 1960

78 rue de Longchamp
Paris 16ᵉ

2 December 1960

My dear Ingeborg,

a week has passed since Paul went to Zurich; he went there with a light heart in the hope of encountering responses that were human and true, and he was not disappointed—he saw you and also Weber. He had found courage and hope again.

A week has passed! . . . And nothing has happened. Ingeborg, Paul is desperate, Paul is very tired, Paul is not well. He has lost all courage. It is absolutely vital for the truth about this business to become known. I beg you, do everything you can to make that happen. Help people understand that this whole business is shameful and that no one has the right to sit there and do nothing.

This has been going for seven years, and it is getting late for Paul, very late. It is not a matter of words or consolations now, but time for action: people have to write something in the papers denouncing the lies, the slander—but they must do it quickly, Ingeborg, they must do it at once. It is their duty to do so, in the name of the truth and in the name of poetry, which is the same thing—it is vital to resist, to be outraged, not to let it continue. Let me repeat, Ingeborg: Paul cannot go on like this. He waits for every letter, every newspaper, his head is filled with all this. There is no room for anything else—how could it be otherwise, after seven years?

Since his return from Zurich, when he was truly full of hope again, full of courage, determined to work and almost happy, not a single line has reached him. A few lines in the *NZZ* referring to the 'Response' in the *Rundschau*: that is all, it is very meagre, it is very, very little, and it would be awful if that were all that came. There was also a telephone call from Armin Mohler, a former Nazi, who intends to publish something on his behalf in Rychner's journal, assuming it has not already happened; you will understand that this is no great source of joy to us, and that we were hoping for other voices than his. Armin Mohler, the former Nazi, coming to Paul's defence: understand, Ingeborg, how hurtful that is.

Kasack: Paul called him after returning from Zurich, he wants 'Der Sand aus den Urnen' . . . yes, of course, but nonetheless, does one really need to see proof? Is it not possible to be outraged by those who slander Paul's name, to react immediately when people attack his 'Todesfuge', to denounce the infamies she is spreading about him? Can one only write about one's indignation if one possesses his first volume? It is all terrible. In front of Paul, people are outraged and listen to him, but, as soon as he is gone, everything collapses as if it did not concern them.

Ingeborg, you have met with Weber, you have perhaps spoken again to the director of the Burgtheater, you have written to Max Frisch about the matter. I beg you: do it, do it very quickly and keep Paul informed.

Please, call him. Help people to take action. If only you knew how alone Paul is, how unhappy, how completely annihilated by what is happening to him.

I beg you, do everything in your power to make something positive happen as quickly as possible. Do not leave him in the dark.

On Sunday Frau Fischer is coming to Paris, we were supposed to see her at the house of friends. But . . . as incredible as it sounds, friends of C. G. are also invited—that is what things have come to. Even with his own publisher, he does not know whom he will meet. He cancelled yesterday.

That is the situation, Ingeborg, it is very bad. Allow me to tell you once again: it is vital to act, to act very quickly—do not let Paul down, keep him informed. You can help him. Please, do so. Do so immediately. Not with words or consolations, for they are no use to him. Facts, gestures, focused and courageous actions—in the name of truth, in the name of poetry, in the name of Paul, I beg you.

Please view this letter as very personal, and do not speak to anyone about what I have said regarding Paul's condition.

We are quite desperate, let me tell you—you, who understand.

Gisèle

NOTES

MAN/ANL folder 9, pp. 11–13: hw. express letter to: '*Mademoiselle Ingeborg Bachmann/Haus zum Langenbaum/Seestrasse/Uetikon bei Zürich/(Suisse)*', Paris, 2 December 1960.

went to Zurich [. . .] *and also Weber*. See NO. 166.

help people to understand: See NOS 166n and 177n.

for seven years: This formulation, an allusion to the 'Entgegnung', refers to the period between the first accusation presented by Claire Goll in a circular (1953, GA 187–198) and her article in *Baubudenpoet* at the height of the affair (1960, see NO. 179).

write something in the papers: Regarding later texts in Celan's defence, see NO. 191n.

NZZ: In the note 'Blick in die Zeitschriften' [A Look at the Magazines] of 1 December 1960, signed 'jc', the 'Entgegnung' in *Die Neue Rundschau* is mentioned as a text 'that takes a clear stand against the attacks directed at Paul Celan'.

Mohler: See NO. 174n. The right-wing conservative Swiss publicist, who had deserted from the Swiss army in 1942 with the aim of joining the Waffen-SS, had already corresponded with PC in 1951 as Ernst Jünger's secretary, and met him in person in the mid-1950s as a correspondent for various German and Swiss newspapers.

Kasack [. . .] *proof*: PC noted the call on 29 November 1960 (PCPC). *Der Sand aus den Urnen*, written before PC's arrival in Paris, contained most of the poems incriminated by Claire Goll (see NO. 179n).

Todesfuge: See NO. 166n.

Burgtheater: The man in question was, in fact, Kurt Hirschfeld, director of the Zurich Schauspielhaus (see NO. 173).

call him: IB only seems to have done so on 12 December 1960 (see NO. 177).

Mme Fischer: PC was supposed to meet the co-owner of S. Fischer Verlag at the home of the French Germanist Pierre Bertaux on 4 December 1960 (PCPC); it could not be ascertained which friends of Claire Goll were also invited.

227
Ingeborg Bachmann to Gisèle Celan-Lestrange, Uetikon am See, 3 December 1960

3-11-60

My dear Gisèle,

I just now received your letter. I understand your distress, but please do not despair, not at this moment! After Paul's departure, on Monday, I sent Max Frisch a letter—taking into account the irregular Italian mail, I am not expecting a reply before next week. On the same day I met Herr Weber; he was in a great hurry, and I only managed to ask him for the article by Szondi, some copies—which arrived yesterday owing to a postal error (Kirchgasse!). I will finally see Weber next Monday (or the next day) to speak to him properly. I made a copy yesterday, so that I can inform people better, and I sent it to Herr Leonhardt (*Die Zeit*). I so hope he will do something, and I hope I found the right words to convince him, to make him understand the necessity and the urgency. Tomorrow I will go to meet the director of the Schauspielhaus, who is returning from a trip tonight; he had also gone away, before Paul.

Gisèle, believe me, I am doing everything I can, I am truly making an effort! I do not think of anything else. Nonetheless, we have to be patient; an infamy that has already lasted 7 years cannot be stopped in a week. You will reassure Paul. I was very happy during the two days Paul spent here, and I too have regained some confidence after this horrible, unwholesome year. Dear Gisèle,

Ingeborg

I leave for Rome around the 14th, I will call before then!

NOTES

GCLE: *hw. express letter to*: '*Mme Paul CELAN/78, rue de Longchamp/PARIS 16ème/ FRANCE*', *Uetikon am See, 5 December 1960, from*: '*Ingeborg Bachmann/Uetikon am See, Suisse*', *Paris, 6 December 1960*.

3-11-60: See postmark!

Paul's departure, on Monday: PC had left Zurich on Sunday, 27 November 1960 (see NO. 166n).

the article by Szondi: See NO. 167.

postal error (Kirchgasse!): See NO. 225.

director of the Schauspielhaus: Hirschfeld.

228

Ingeborg Bachmann to Gisèle Celan-Lestrange, before Christmas 1960 (?)

My dear Ingeborg,

with all my heart—

and may you, Paul and Eric have a happy evening!

Ingeborg

NOTE

GCLE: hw. letter, envelope missing. Card with two needle marks along the upper edge, i.e. sent with flowers.

229

Ingeborg Bachmann to Gisèle Celan-Lestrange, dedication in Das dreissigste Jahr, *Rome, 4 June 1961*

Dear Gisèle, for you—

Ingeborg
Rome, 4-6-61

NOTES

GCLE: hw. dedication on the flyleaf of Das dreissigste Jahr (*Munich: Piper, 1961*); *envelope missing.*

Rome, 4-6-61: See NO. 187.

230

Gisèle Celan-Lestrange to Ingeborg Bachmann, Paris, 10 May 1970

78 rue de Longchamp
Paris 16ᵉ
10 May 1970

My dear Ingeborg,

I do not know if this letter will reach you. I daresay you have heard the terrible news. I wanted to write to you nonetheless.

On Thursday 16 April, my son Eric, who was having lunch with Paul as he usually did, realized that he was in a very bad state again. I called him myself the next day, and up until Sunday 19 April; friends who had tried to reach him or who had seen him could only confirm that he was having a crisis again.

In the night of Sunday 19 April he left his home, never to return.

I spent two weeks looking for him everywhere, and had no hope of finding him alive. It was on the first of May that the police found him, almost two weeks after his terrible deed. I did not find out until 4 May—

Paul threw himself into the Seine. He chose the most anonymous, lonely death.

What else can I say, Ingeborg. I was not able to help him as I would have wanted.

Eric will be fifteen next month.

Fondest regards

Gisèle Celan

NOTES

MAN/ANL folder 9, pp. 15 and 17: hw. letter to: 'Mademoiselle Ingeborg BACHMANN/ Via Bocca di Leone 60/ <u>ROME</u>/ Italie', *Paris, 12 may 1970, from:* 'Gisèle CELAN, 78 rue de Longchamp, Paris 16', *Rome, 13 May 1970; MAN/ANL folder 9, p. 16* (supplement): *hw. account by Jean Pollack.*

4 May [. . .] *into the Seine*: PC threw himself into the Seine (evidently from the Pont Mirabeau, not far from his apartment). His body was found in a grate by Courbevoie, a northern suburb of Paris. The LIB contains the editorial obituary from the *FAZ* of 6 May 1970, 'Die magische Formel. Zum Tode von Paul Celan' [The Magic Formula: On the Death of Paul Celan] (*MAN/ANL folder 12, p. 1*) as well as an interview with Weber conducted by the *NZZ* after the news of PC's death: 'Paul Celan' (10 May 1970, foreign edition; *MAN/ANL folder 12, p. 2*).

230.1
Supplement (Jean Bollack, report)

Paul was buried this morning at nine o'clock at Thiais cemetery, in the presence of around thirty people, Gisèle's family and a few friends. Not counting the municipal police officer from abroad. Under a light spring rain. The mourners bowed in front of the grave before embracing Gisèle and Eric, who, transformed, seemed strangely like his father.

Tuesday 12 May 70

Jean

NOTES

Bollack: GCL sought advice from the Hellenist, a friend of PC who also lived in Paris, concerning the management of PC's works; PC had met him in 1959 through Peter Szondi.

Thiais: The Celans' first son, François (1953) and GCL herself (1991) were also buried in the Parisian cemetery, south of the city border.

a few friends: Including Klaus Demus.

231

Gisèle Celan-Lestrange to Ingeborg Bachmann, Paris, 23 November 1970

78 rue de Longchamp
Paris 16
23 November 1970

My dear Ingeborg,

I cannot tell you how moved I was by the flowers and the little note you sent today. You are truly the only person to give me a sign today. And you know what this 23 November can be this year!

I would always be happy to see you again if you come to Paris. I have been to Rome several times, but I did not have your address, I did not know if you would want to meet with me, I did not dare to give you a sign.

I have often wanted to write to you.

Since those terrible weeks last April, I have thought time and time again about this whole disaster without any answer, without any solution.

Paul chose the most anonymous and lonely death there is. One can only be silent, respect it, but it is very hard, as you know so well. I am sure you know that I had not been living with him anymore for the last two years. I could not help him, only destroy myself with him, and Eric was there too. I think Paul certainly understood at times. But that was very hard. Was this the solution? Was there one? Which one? Was I right? I think a great deal about it. If I had known? How I feared it! I cannot write about all this; I can barely live with it. And I go from one failure to the next. But why am I telling you all this.

Sometimes I have heard news about you, very vague things, that you were not well, and I have often thought about your difficult fate.

Believe me, all my best wishes went out to you. To you, your life, your work.

I try to fight, but sometimes it is too hard for me to go on, and I too have often broken down.

Your flowers are there: roses. You already sent me roses once before. I have not forgotten—the flowers that Paul so loved. They are there, from someone who also suffered on account of Paul and who also loved Paul.

Forgive me that I can only say these words very clumsily, but I am very moved to feel you close to me today—

If I come to Rome—perhaps around Christmas?—could I come to see you?

Eric is fifteen, an age when a father is perhaps most needed. He is a very nice boy, but causes me a great deal of worry.

He is unhappy with himself, does not work well, and is in the middle of adolescence. It is nothing dramatic, but I find it difficult to help him.

I send you my fondest regards and all my affection, and thank you again

Gisèle

Tell me your news. I would like to know that you are well now. Please.

NOTES

MAN/ANL folder 9, p. 18: *hw. letter, envelope missing.*

23 November: PC would have turned 50 in 1970. The LIB contains press items published on this occasion: a collection of small prose texts by PC in *Die Welt*: 'Jüdische Einsamkeit' [Jewish Loneliness] (1969), 'Das grauere Wort' [The Greyer Word] (1958) and 'Doppelzüngigkeit' [Deviousness] (1961) (21 November 1970; *MAN/ANL folder 12, p. 3*), i.e. the speech given to the Hebrew Writers Association and the responses to two questionnaires by the Librairie Flinker, Paris.

the little note: Not found.

to Paris: IB and GCL did not meet in Paris.

the last two years: PC did not return to the family apartment after his compulsory stay at the Psychiatric University Clinic in Paris (January–October 1967).

you were not well: Alongside the completion of *Malina*, IB had to deal with repeated illnesses and small mishaps.

Your flowers [. . .] *sent*: See NOS 214 and 215.

232

Gisèle Celan-Lestrange to Ingeborg Bachmann, Paris, 20 December 1970

78 rue de Longchamp
Paris 16
Sunday

My dear Ingeborg,

the holidays that have long weighed on my mind are now approaching. Eric is going skiing in Austria.

I have had a number of small health problems lately, and I have to get out of Paris and my house, for they are suffocating me. Because I have always been quite bad at making plans, I only decided today that I would attempt to leave. A very kind friend of mine has invited me to Rome. I will try to get hold of a train ticket there right away tomorrow.

I would very much like to see you, if you would not have anything against that, and I will try to call you if I find your number—

If I get a ticket for next Wednesday I will arrive in Rome on Thursday morning. Or the day after, I hope. I will stay for around ten days.

I will be staying with Marianne KRAISKY, via Ludovico di Monreale 12, (interno 16) 580 74 55.

I hope you are well now, and that you are working.

See you soon. Most affectionately

Gisèle.

NOTES

MAN/ANL folder 9, pp. 19–20: hw. letter to: 'Mademoiselle Ingeborg *BACHMANN/Via Bocca di Leone 60/ROME/(Italie)*', Paris, 21 December 970.

holidays: GCL wrote in German on the last page of her pocket calendar: 'End of the year,/finally!' (GCLE).

Rome: GCL left for Rome on 23 December 1970.

see you: GCL met with IB on 27 and 29 December 1970 (GCLE).

KRAISKY: GCL knew PC's Bucharest acquaintance (1945) from her Rome visit in January 1965.

233
Gisèle Celan-Lestrange to Ingeborg Bachmann, Rome, 1 January 1971

1 January 1971

My dear Ingeborg,

our encounter in Rome was a true encounter for me, important and serious like the true things in life. Rare.

I am only worried that I may have exhausted you, stayed too long and kept you from sleeping. I hope everything went well in Frankfurt, and that your return to Rome will also be a new beginning.

Never forget that it is important to me to know you are there, that you are well, that you are working.

I think of you a great deal. Fondest regards

Gisèle

Thank you for welcoming me

NOTES

MAN/ANL folder 9, pp. 21–2: hw. letter to: 'Madame Ingeborg *BACHMANN/Via Bocca di Leone 60/(interno 2)/ROME*', Rome, 2 January 1971.

Frankfurt [. . .] *new beginning*: IB met with Unseld in connection with her change to Suhrkamp as the publisher of *Malina*.

234
Gisèle Celan-Lestrange to Ingeborg Bachmann, Paris, 11–13 February 1971

78, rue de Longchamp
Paris 16
11 February 1971.

My dear Ingeborg,

this evening I am thinking of you a great deal, and perhaps a little egotistically. If Rome were not so far away I would call you and say: let us spend the evening together, I do not have the courage to stay alone! And so I am writing to you.

If you can, send me a few lines from time to time. You know that I worry about you. How are you faring now? I would be happy if your shoulder problem were resolved completely. I would be happy if you were able to tell me that you feel well in Rome, that you are working, that you are reading, that you are writing, that you have kind friends close by when you need them, and that life has finally stopped treating you so badly!

When is your book coming out? You must send it to me, and I hope that it will be also translated into French, and quickly.

When you saw me in Rome I was feeling well, after a very difficult time, and since then I have had ups and downs. Not enough sleep, and sometimes periods of great despair. I am trying to continue the elan of Rome, to make gouaches—and, whenever the task of earning a living permits it, I do some work. But you know, it is very discouraging that the etchings and the gouaches have no real possibility to enter a dialogue. Everything stays in the drawers, and it is very discouraging. Nonetheless, I try to continue this work, which is a way to live in spite of everything. But I am very lonely.

Eric is becoming more and more trying. I understand his problems, his difficulties, his rebellion, his dissatisfaction with school, but sometimes I can hardly bear it. He can—as one can be at that age—be so egotistical, even wicked—and, you know, not being able to help a child to whom one feels so close, and whom one thinks one understands well, is also very hard—

What else is there to say? I go here and there, I kill time, I go to dinner with one group of people, to the cinema with others, only to find myself all the more lonely afterwards, but then I have at least escaped from the house, and from myself, for a few hours—It is terrible to reach such a point, and I generally make mistakes and blunders, and get into awful situations—But I do not want to talk about all that.

(. . . Saturday)

Beda Allemann is still in Paris, he is an associate professor at the Grand Palais (which belongs to the Sorbonne and houses some of the language departments, especially German) for a year. That is where I work, so I often see him.

I think he has started some very serious work on Paul's poems, but it is very difficult for me. When he is being given millions of francs for this work, and considering bringing two of his assistants to Paris for three years, I think to myself— and I cannot do so without a certain bitterness—that it was not so easy to live off Paul's poetry while he was alive, and I also ask myself where the poetry really is in all these index cards, photocopies and references. But that is how it is— Nowadays, one does not hesitate for long before using the most modern methods to publish hastily.

Will you come to Paris some time?

If I am back in Rome, I will let you know.

Sometimes I just want to give everything up and leave behind this work, the friends I have here, this city and this apartment!

I will soon be going, with Eric, about 100 km outside of Paris, where, as I am sure you know, we have a house. Everything is quiet and solitary there. Eric likes it very much, and spends his energy going for moped rides or making things out of wood. I go for long walks without meeting anyone, I generally have time to read and draw, and I sleep quite well there. But all these places are haunted by so many memories, so much presence and absence, that I find it hard, very hard to feel comfortable there too.

But where do I feel comfortable now anyway?

I send you my warmest and fondest regards

Gisèle—

MAN/ANL folder 9, pp. 23–4: hw. letter, envelope missing.

shoulder problem: IB had injured her shoulder through a fall (see NO. 231n).

your book/in French: *Malina* was published in March 1971 (Frankfurt: Suhrkamp, 1971, GCLE). The novel contains many references to PC's life and work. GCL's copy of the French translation by Philippe Jacottet (Paris: Editions du Seuil, 1973; date of purchase '23 July 1973', GCLE) contains numerous reading traces, some of them connected to PC.

gouaches: Three of these are included in the catalogue of the Tübingen exhibition *A l'image du temps—Nach dem Bilde der Zeit. Gisèle Celan-Lestrange und Paul Celan* [In the Image of Time: Gisèle Celan-Lestrange und Paul Celan], Valéry Lawtischka ed. (Eggingen: Edition Klaus Isele, 2001), NOS 25–7.

earning a living: Since 1968, GCL had been secretary to Germanist Claude David, the director of the Institute of French Studies (Paris, Sorbonne) in the Grand Palais.

millions: Funding of the preliminary work for the historico-critical edition of Celan's works, published in Bonn, where Allemann was professor of German Studies, by the Deutsche Forschungsgemeinschaft [German Research Community]. Allemann's assistants Rolf Bücher and Dietlind Meinecke were often in Paris. The first volumes of the edition only appeared from 1990 onwards.

to Paris [. . .] *in Rome*: There is nothing to suggest that IB and GCL saw each other again.

work [. . .] *apartment*: GCL resigned from her position as a secretary in the summer of 1971, but only moved out of the apartment on rue de Longchamp in 1976.

100 km outside of Paris: GCL went to the country house in Moisville (Eure), which the Celans had bought in 1962.

235

Gisèle Celan-Lestrange to Ingeborg Bachmann, 18 March 1971

> 78, rue de Longchamp
> Paris 16
> 18 March 1971

My dear Ingeborg,

how can I thank you for your call? I was very touched, and the signs of friendship came to me from far away today: Tel Aviv, Rome and Vienna—one is more alone at home in Paris!

I passed on your message to Peter Szondi, I hope he will call you as he told me he would. I had not seen him in a very long time, and it was good to meet again.

I have just decided to go to Israel for two weeks at Easter. You know that I always find it very difficult to decide on leaving, but staying in Paris when I am on holiday from my idiotic work at the Grand Palais is always a burden, for I never manage to do any work of my own and, with all my inability, I am afraid of this solitude. It was the very kind telephone call from Tel Aviv, inviting me so warmly, that made me decide. I will go from 3 April to 20 April. But I do not want to miss you when you come to Paris.

If you can, send me a note to tell me when you could come.

The book of Paul's translations published by Mercure de France came out today, it seems, and I will receive it tomorrow for my birthday. This touches me all the more because several of Paul's books came out on the same day, and he was always happy about that publication date. (I have just found this out through a call from André du Bouchet.)

How did you know it was my birthday?

Now your new book is coming out; let me send you once again, and with all my heart, my best wishes for it and for you. I wish you a good stay in Germany. I hope to see you very soon. My fondest regards.

Take care of yourself—

Gisèle.

NOTES

MAN/ANL folder 9, p. 25: hw. letter, envelope missing.

18 March 1971: GCL turned 44 the following day.

Tel Aviv, Rome and Vienna: GCL is referring to the birthday greetings from—among others—Mihal and David Seidmann, a former classmate and friend of PC from Czernowitz living in Tel Aviv, IB and M. Kraisky (Rome), as well as Klaus and Nani Demus (Vienna).

Szondi: The content of the message, presumably passed on in person, is unknown. IB and Szondi had been friends since 1959, and IB met him in Rome in 1968.

Mercure de France [. . .] André du Bouchet: PC himself had selected poems and prose and guided' (according to the volume's editor) their translations by André du Bouchet, Jean-Pierre Burgart and Jean Daive for *Strette. Poèmes suivis du Méridien et d'Entretien dans la montagne* [Stretto: Poems, Followed by The Mediridan and Conversation in the Mountains]. The volume was published on 15 March 1971. At least two books were published around 19 March during PC's lifetime: *Sprachgitter* (see PC's dedication, PC/GCL) and *Schwarzmaut* [Black Toll] (1969, PC/GCL), consciously delivered on 19 March 1969, GCL's 42nd birthday. GCL remained in contact with the French poet du Bouchet, who had been close to PC in his difficult last years; they had also translated each other's works.

new book [. . .] Germany: IB went to Frankfurt for the publication of *Malina*.

236
Gisèle Celan-Lestrange to Ingeborg Bachmann, separate dedication for the group of three etchings entitled Fin d'année 1971, *Paris, late 1971*

With my best wishes for
1972

Gisèle.

NOTES

MAN/ANL folder 9, p. 28: hw. greeting, envelope missing.

Fin d'anée 1971: Only the second of the three etchings was found (owner: Christian Moser); IB owned copy NO. 10 of each [*see Figure 18*].

237
Gisèle Celan-Lestrange to Ingeborg Bachmann, Paris, 2 January 1972

<u>704 39 63</u>
2 January 1972

My dear Ingeborg,

I am still deeply moved by your call last night: I was slightly paralysed by the surprise, the distance, what you represent for me, and I could not find the words I would have wanted to say to you—

I am very touched by the attention you give me; I feel so strongly how important it is to you that I am well and that I find a path for myself, thank you for thinking so warmly of me.

You know, you know . . . the difficulties everyone has with themselves, with life. One tries, one loses one's way, one finds paths that lead nowhere, one takes steps that are not always the right ones and finds oneself at a dead end again . . .

It has been like that for four years. I have been lucky—it was not always like that. I had, as you know—and at what price!—my years of true life, when there was never any doubt that my path was the right and true one. One day I lost everything, I drifted away from this truth, from my truth—Since then, one failure after another, efforts in the wrong directions, and the days of solitude afterwards—I have friends, good friends, a few, and that is very important to me— but . . .

I have a great deal of trouble with the time: with the yesterday from which I am still living, the yesterday that forms a part of my present. What I am today transpires as a result of this yesterday becoming present. But yesterday sometimes paralyses today by imposing itself too strongly. I have tried to keep a distance, undoubtedly in an overly brutal way, and this ever-present yesterday caught up with me. I know very well that I will never disown it, that I neither can nor want to do so. But living with it while keeping the minimum necessary distance is a balancing act that I do not find easy. I try, I try, I take steps, I walk—but not very well.

My work helps me; but you know, with age, watching the generations follow each other so quickly, the pit of solitude becomes deeper every day, and when I am in front of the copper, in my efforts to engrave, I am sometimes very discouraged— I still try to remain faithful to myself in this work.

Ordering Paul's papers, which I am doing with the help of an Austrian friend who lives in Paris and also speaks good French, upsets me every time. It also stimulates me—We are doing it very conscientiously, very slowly and with all the respect it deserves—I think—but sometimes it overwhelms me. So much life, in which I had a small share, written down on the smallest page. Luckily I have confidence in this friend, and his discretion and sensitivity are a great help to me when the burden becomes too great for me.

In the case of Allemann, however, I am slightly troubled. He has too many things to do for his university, his students, his personal work, and he has also had a great deal of trouble with his health for the last year—His work concerning Paul is not coming along very quickly—That would not be so bad if he were at least doing something, but I fear that his assistants might be becoming too important because of his weaknesses, and in this case I do not feel that Paul is being adequately served—

Perhaps I will go to Bonn for a few days. He has not responded to six letters of mine, and they were not without importance—

Everything is discouraging me a little at the moment, and the sleepless nights returned a few weeks ago, which does not improve matters at all. But you said it, you knew it: these periods of false holidays do not help, and I have long found it very difficult to deal with them. I find you courageous in the way you repeatedly find the strength to start again in a different country. After Austria came Germany, Italy, and now Africa. I send all my wishes for the warm welcome I want you to receive there.

I would like to see you more often.

I hardly dare to leave Eric alone at the moment. Not that it would make him unhappy—on the contrary. But his activities and his friendships worry me a little. He sometimes engages in activities that worry me; even though he is not completely taken over by them and it does not last very long, my concern is great nonetheless.

He has trouble with himself, with the world around him, with his age. How could it be otherwise? Sometimes I am upset by how serious he is, while sometimes his light-headedness saddens me. He is searching, searching for himself, and it is difficult to help him at the moment. I try to be there when he wants me to, which does happen, to keep a sort of welcome for him, something that is available. I think I cannot do much more for him than that, and it is very little.

Some time, if you are able, you could write me a few lines. If not, I will still know that we are close, and I will understand and respect your silence.

I think of you, a great deal. It is important to me that you are well, and that you continue to work, to be there courageously in some part of this world. But I would like more. I would like to know that your life is finally surrounded by a little warmth, a little tenderness, a little true life.

I send you my fondest regards. I send you my fondest, most affectionate regards

Gisèle

I had sent you a little sign of my work 'towards 1973'. Did the Italian postal service bring it to you safely?

NOTES

MAN/ANL folder 9, pp. 26–7: hw. letter, envelope missing.

for four years: That is, since the separation from PC.

living with it: The difficulties led to a suicide attempt by GCL later that year.

Austrian friend: The painter and etcher Jörg Ortner, with whom PC had been in contact since 1963.

Allemann/ to Bonn: On account of such problems, GCL managed PC's work herself until her death. GCL reviewed the meetings with Allemann in Bonn between 24 and 27 March 1973 in her diary.

Austria [. . .] *Africa*: After growing up in Austria, IB had lived almost entirely abroad since 1953: in Germany (Munich and Berlin), in Switzerland (Zurich) and in Italy (Naples and Rome). The trip to Africa planned for the spring of 1973 was not undertaken.

'towards 1973': The etching was not found.

'Let us find the words'
The Correspondence between Ingeborg Bachmann and Paul Celan

The respective backgrounds of the lovers who came together in May 1948 in occupied Vienna could not have been more different: she, the philosophy student daughter of an early Austrian member of the NSDAP; he, a stateless German-speaking Jew from Czernowitz who had lost his parents in a concentration camp and was himself a survivor of a Romanian labour camp. It is from this irrecon-cilable difference that Paul Celan developed his role as a Jewish poet writing for German readers and his high standards for poetry in German after the Jewish catastrophe. For Ingeborg Bachmann, who had already confronted the most recent past of Germany and Austria, it became a new impulse—to spend her life fighting the danger to forget, and to champion Celan's work. Both this difference and the striving to resume the dialogue—precisely because of that difference—characterize their letters, from the first gift of a poem in May/June 1948 to the last letter in the autumn of 1967. A great document of two lives, the correspon-dence is as dramatic as it is moving—and yet different from what the years of speculation had led one to expect. With the present edition, our knowledge about the relationship between Bachmann and Celan and its effects on their work has finally been given a secure foundation.

Writing formed the focal point in the lives of both correspondents, often named in the same breath as the leading exponents of post-war German poetry during the 1950s. For both, however, writing—including letter-writing—was no easy matter. The struggle for language and the conflict with the word assume a central role in the correspondence. Time and again, there are references to unsent letters: some of these were failures and hence discarded; some were kept, and appear between the others as documents of doubt. Some other drafts were sent with considerably later letters—sometimes incomplete, as the recipient is not meant to know certain things; the time that has passed has also softened them, so that they can communicate what was previously unspeakable—or, unwritable. For Bachmann in particular has more faith in the spoken word, sometimes even just an account passed on by mediating friends who, she believes, can describe difficulties better. The phrase 'you know' [*Du weisst* or *Du weisst ja*] often stands in for a direct statement, and telegrams or short letters often promise longer letters, which do not always come. And time after time the requests, the begging, for letters—Bachmann reduces her expectations to the plea 'But at least write to me' (NO. 26), while Celan makes it clear in a rather tortuous sentence how difficult he finds such a request: 'Now I am writing to you, just a few lines, to ask you likewise for a few lines' (NO. 195). Sometimes the prolonged silence of one causes the waiting other to reflect on how they might have caused it—'because my flood of words on the telephone made it even more difficult for you' (NO. 116), or: 'Perhaps my letter was not a very wise one' (NO. 34). Sometimes all that remains is to invoke possibilities of dialogue: 'Let us find the words' (NO. 148).

This silence, in some cases a source of torment for one of the two parties and in others maintained by a tacit agreement, is an important element throughout the six phases that can be identified in the correspondence, whose boundaries are closely connected to biographical turning points in both lives. Between the weeks spent together in Vienna and the last of 196 documents—letters, postcards, telegrams, dedications and a page of conversation notes—these events are: Celan's departure from Vienna to travel to Paris in late June 1948; the meeting at the conference of Gruppe 47 in Niendorf (their last for several years); the resumption of the love affair after a conference in Wuppertal in October 1957; Bachmann's encounter with Max Frisch in the summer of 1958; and, finally, the intensification of Celan's mental crisis in late 1961 following the climax of the Goll affair, instigated by Yvan Goll's widow Claire Goll with accusations of plagiarism. This led to the end of Celan's correspondence with Bachmann (though not Celan's letters), as well as with his other friends. These are the points of intersection of a highly varied dialogue of letters characterized by its discontinuity— each of the phases marked by the turning points gains a character of its own through a particular tone, particular themes, particular dynamics, particular forms of silence and thus an asymmetry that must constantly be redefined.

The first phase, the time of the encounter in Vienna, is represented in the correspondence by a central document, Celan's dedicatory poem 'In Ägypten'. It makes a number of important aspects of this friendship clear at the very outset, aspects that remain valid until the end. Using the rhetorical formula of the *Decalogue*, the poem, whose title locates it in a state of exile, reveals a fundamental opposition between three women bearing Jewish names, to whom the 'thou' being addressed belongs on the one hand, and one who is characterized only in terms of her strangeness. In nine 'commandments', an unnamed authority confers upon this 'thou' the duty of upholding, both as a speaker *and* a lover, a mediatory relationship between the two sides—an erotic relationship and, at the same time, a relationship between the poet and the reader that remains mindful of their difference. The connection between the stranger located in the present and the 'thou' is impossible without sorrow for those assigned to the past; but only by turning to the nameless woman, the non-Jew, can there be a remembrance of those lost, those belonging through a shared pain to the 'thou'. Bachmann is not this stranger; almost a decade later, Celan shows with reference to this very poem how different a view he has of the connection between life and poetry which must *constantly be revised* in the process of reading: 'Every time I read it I see you step into this poem: you are the reason for living, not least because you are, and will remain, the justification for my speaking' (NO. 53). This constantly renewed act of stepping into the poem becomes possible because the encounter—even if Celan denies this, referring to a word carefully *crossed out* by Bachmann in an early let-ter—has an 'exemplary' (NOS 18 and 19) quality, and it is precisely this that is already implicit in the dedicatory poem.

Neither of the correspondents is so sure about the significance of their encounter or for their respective poetic articulation in the years directly after. The rather loose sequence of letters between the turn of 1949 and the spring of 1952 is characterized by reflections on what has been, as well as tireless efforts to find some liveable form for the relationship after what are viewed as conclusive sepa-rations. The few weeks in Vienna form the point of reference, though they prove unrepeatable; ultimately, a 'friendship' remains the only possibility. The repeated failure of the relationship is described by Celan in 1957 as an incomprehensible process of 'hound[ing] our hearts to death' over 'trifles' (NO. 63). The reader does not learn of any real reasons for the constant misunderstandings; the mediatory conversations with common friends Nani and Klaus Demus left only scant traces, while the confrontations during Bachmann's two visits to Paris in 1950 and 1951 left practically none. It does become clear, however, that the initiative for new attempts comes primarily from Bachmann, and that she has the larger stake in the written dialogue—not only materially, but also emotionally. Ultimately, she rightly states: 'I put all my eggs in one basket and lost' (NO. 28). Yet the correspondence is centred on Celan to a quite astonishing degree during this time. An important aspect of this is his work, which Bachmann tries to support wherever she can, even—and especially—in times of relative distance. Her letters fluctuate between a fairy-tale-like, 'romantic' tone invoking what was lost on the one hand, and purely factual references to journals, publishers or the route to Niendorf on the other—sometimes even in the same letter. As in early 1958, when the letters deal with obtaining texts for the journal *Botteghe Oscure*, such ruptures are sometimes also reflected in the letters themselves.

The long, meagre period after Niendorf—a mere 11 documents in more than five years—lies entirely in Bachmann's hands, aside from a book dedication by Celan. She at least makes an effort to maintain the friendship suggested by Celan, even if only through signs of life—signatures on postcards from others, as found only once in the rest of the correspondence, in the difficult spring of 1960—or, even more 'mutely', a book sent by her publisher as a gift in her name. In this phase, however, Bachmann's work is present for the first time—not only through a book dedication but also in the shape of four poems, enclosed with a letter, for an Austrian anthology to be compiled by Celan. In a manner one could consider almost rude, he does not comment on them. His decision to short-list one of the poems for the book, however, is revealing: the poetic speech of 'Grosse Landschaft bei Wien' is not only informed by the shared experiences in Vienna but is also one of the poems in which Bachmann quotes from Celan's early poems—that is, poems with which she became acquainted during the time in Vienna. The hiatus that followed the unanswered letters regarding the anthology was barely interrupted for several years; during that time, Bachmann, who went to Paris for a longer stay in 1956, probably without Celan's knowledge, seems to have continued the dialogue outside of the correspondence by these poetic means. Many of the poems in *Anrufung des Grossen Bären*, written in 1953 and later, quote, as had some of those in *Die gestundete Zeit*, from both Celan's early work and his current cycle *Von Schwelle zu Schwelle*, of which she had presumably acquired individual manuscripts through others. Celan was able to observe this referential dialogue through pre-prints (perhaps intended for this purpose) of Bachmann's poems: 'Das Spiel ist aus' or parts of 'Lieder einer Insel' in *Jahresring 54/55*, for example, which also featured poems of his own. But this 'dialogue' also remained one-sided; Bachmann did not even receive such a *poetic* response, either at this time or later. The fact that Bachmann's *work* does not seem to be present in Celan's poems does not, however, mean that she did not continue to provide impulses for important poems as a *person* after 'In Ägypten'. This is clear in the poems written in 1957/58 after the resumption of the love affair. But later texts may equally be connected to conflicts between the two, or belated memories: Celan's initially unpublished poem 'Es kamen Jahre, eh du kamst', probably written in the autumn of 1959, 'Flimmerbaum' from the spring of 1964 or 'Mittags', written after a visit to Rome.

The fact that Celan also continued the *dialogue* shows how fundamentally the character of the correspondence changed after the Wuppertal encounter. The renewed engagement was certainly 'prepared': Celan had bought *Anrufung des Grossen Bären* in Cologne in 1956, and he went to Vienna in summer 1957 for the first time since 1948; he did not meet with Bachmann, who was in Rome, but he wrote the poem 'Sprachgitter' there, in which he attempted to re-envisage the difference formulated in poems such as 'In Ägypten'. The shortest, yet richest, phase of the correspondence after the encounter is now dominated both materially and emotionally by Celan, who writes letters of an intensity that is without parallel in any of his correspondences. Focused on Bachmann as a person once again, he is truly focused on her work perhaps for the first time as well as upon the uniqueness of their relationship. He floods her with letters and poems to such an extent that she finds it impossible to reply. Now she forces him to deal with silence; initially, at least, she seems to force herself to maintain a certain distance in order to protect herself— Celan is married and has a son. Despite the four meetings and the numerous telephone conversations, some of them documented in letters, these few months also constitute a climax in the density of the written dialogue. The new, old love is the focal point: 'when I met you, you were both for me: the sensual and the spiritual. That bond can never be broken, Ingeborg' (NO. 53). It is no coincidence that Celan sends unaccompanied poems in place of letters, especially at the start; along with the book dedications and a wealth of enclosed poems and poem translations, they testify to the poetic dimension of the event. Recollections of the meetings in Vienna and Paris, and of poems written during that time, also contribute to this. And, in the following years, the experiences between October 1957 and May 1958 themselves become a point of reference for recollections.

It is in this context that Bachmann, in the first autumn spent living together with Max Frisch, writes: 'last autumn is forcing its way into this autumn' (NO. 107). The correspondence is now defined by a friendship that is accepted by both and by their respective partners but that is by no means always unproblematic. The supplementary correspondences between Max Frisch and Celan (16 letters) and between Bachmann and Celan's wife Gisèle Celan-Lestrange (25 letters) are also dealt with in the written dialogue—indeed, they form a part of it. Not only do some of these letters become sources of conflict between Bachmann and Celan but also more than a few are written in place of letters that seem difficult, even impossible, to send to their true addressees; in some cases, it is through them that the correspondence is set in motion again. This phase sees an intensified preoccupation with one of the subjects that defines the literary dialogue in the correspondence as a whole, and is connected to the standards upheld by each correspondent for his/her own work. How much compromise can poetry withstand if it is understood as an 'epitaph', as Celan formulates in a moving letter on 'Todesfuge' (NO. 145)? How much compromise can it withstand if earning a living—Bachmann is in a completely different situation from Celan, who is financially secure through his marriage—is always a consideration too? How much support does the work of each need from the other? Bachmann stands by Celan's work wholeheartedly. Celan, on the other hand, who does not seem to agree so unconditionally with her work, presumably thinks that Bachmann's poems, radio plays, stories or translations successful enough and therefore not in need of any particular support. As late as 1961, Celan greatly overestimates, as he already had 10 years earlier, the opportunities open to the non-Jewish Bachmann in the Austrian and German literary scenes in comparison to the resistance he perceives to his own work as that of a Jew. The difference formulated in the early dedicatory poem still forms the defining framework when both correspondents describe their respective stances regarding Martin Heidegger: while Bachmann, who has a profound knowledge of his work from the time of her doctorate, speaks in a differentiated manner about the philosopher and the politically entangled man, Celan characteristically relates his assessment to what he perceives as the *current* token efforts to 'deal with' Germany's past. Hence he does not 'pass judgement' on him once and for all, and does not do so independently of those recent events. The written dialogue with Celan during the years with Max Frisch takes on a new quality, alone through the parity—at least initially—of their respective contributions. In contrast to the years after 1953, during which Claire Goll's accusations of plagiarism begin and he largely remains silent, Celan now confides in his friend about the profound injuries he suffers at the hands of his contemporaries and readers: anti-Semitic attacks in connection with a reading in Bonn in 1958; Günter Blöcker's review of *Sprachgitter*—perceived by Celan as anti-Semitic—in 1959; and the new accusations of plagiarism in 1960. As before, Bachmann is willing to approach Celan after such injuries and help him to the best of her ability. But the parity of the correspondence also becomes apparent in a self-confidence on Bachmann's part rarely in evidence before. For now, at the same time as stepping in for Celan, she demands that he perceive her problems too: the problems in her relationship with Frisch, some of them resulting from Celan's expectations of unconditional solidarity; her banal material worries; and her difficulties with the German literary scene. And she expects Celan to pay as much attention to her work as he wants her to pay to his. This period also sees Bachmann's turn towards fictional prose, by no means received kindly by the press, something already hinted at in the letters written in early 1958—in parallel, incidentally, with a new preoccupation on Celan's part, albeit never as exclusive and ultimately abandoned, with narrative texts. In this light, the small poem enclosed in 1958 with Bachmann's last letter *before* her encounter with Frisch, 'Wohin wir uns wenden im Gewitter der Rosen', which already plays a significant part directly after the renewed encounter in Wuppertal—and, as the only poem supplement with no pragmatic function, constitutes an event in itself—seems to be a farewell, not only from her love for Celan but also from the poem as the centre of her literary work. The same period, with her Ungaretti translations, also sees a turn to a form of literary work previously claimed by Celan entirely for himself. In a draft from the autumn of 1961 (NO. 191), she formulates her requirements for a friendship with Celan on an equal footing, as well as her interpretation of his situation, in an impressively incisive and astute fashion; even if it never reaches its addressee, it reaches a moving conclusion.

In the years after 1961, the correspondence—presenting a mirror image of Bachmann's dominance between 1952 and 1957—is entirely in Celan's hands. But his two letters, as short and far apart as they are, show how much each of the correspondents, despite the absence of any personal contact and Bachmann's silent refusal to start anew, still means to the other. On both occasions, Celan reacts to news about Bachmann found in the press and augmented by information from common acquaintances. In the final letter, this is Bachmann's resolute and angry defence of Celan the translator after her own publisher turns him down for a volume of Akhmatova translations in favour of Hans Baumann, a Nazi poet with a highly tainted past. The letter, as short as it is moving, testifies— like Bachmann's correspondence with Gisèle Celan-Lestrange beyond Celan's death, and not least her novel *Malina*, in which she repeatedly quotes and speaks to Celan—to the indestructibility of a special relationship, for all the instances of destruction one can observe in it, an indestructibility extending beyond the word entrusted to the writing paper.

Barbara Wiedemann and Bertrand Badiou
February 2008

'My life is over, for he drowned in the river during deportation,' says the dream ego of the stranger with the black coat in Ingeborg Bachmann's novel *Malina*: 'he was my life. I loved him more than my life' (IBW 3, 195). In April 1970, Paul Celan had thrown himself into the Seine and died. In the 'Legend of the Princess of Kagran' and in the dream chapter, Bachmann's novel recalls her love for Paul Celan. The word 'deportation' [*Transport*], from the Nazi bureaucracy of extermination, connects his suicide to the catastrophe of the Jewish genocide. The sections inserted into the novel-in-progress after Celan's death—the 'Legend' and the dream scenes in the chapter 'The Third Man'—constitute a memorial text for her former lover, a web of quotations from Celan's poems and biographically significant memories such as the black coat or the songlike voice of the stranger.

'I want to preserve the secrecy of letters. But I also want to leave something behind'

The love affair between Ingeborg Bachmann and Paul Celan constitutes one of the most dramatic chapters of literary history after 1945. The correspondence edited here reveals both the literary and the historical aspects of the relationship between these two important German-language poets. The letters are symptomatic writings whose secret lies in the problem of writing and authorship after Auschwitz. Both authors were aware of the 'exemplary' quality of their relationship and their correspondence (NOS 18 and 19). Indirectly expressed in the first poem, 'In Ägypten', then directly in later letters, this question leads to the central motif of the secrecy of letters in the final chapter of *Malina*. Just as Celan used the topos of literature as a message in a bottle, Bachmann gave the riddle of the private and personal in literature a more fundamental, existential perspective. The letters preserve the unique 'voice' and 'muteness' of each correspondent, even more defenceless and abandoned than in the letter secret in the poems, and more contradictory and dramatic, as *two* mortal 'soul creatures' (GW III 177) search for their way with and against each other, each burdened with their own background and history.

'Behold, I sleep next to her!'

'Splendidly enough,' writes Ingeborg Bachmann to her parents on 20 May 1948, 'the surrealist poet Paul Celan' has fallen in love with her. Her room is 'a poppy field', for he 'inundates' her 'with this flower' (NO. 1n). Three days later, Celan dedicates the poem 'In Ägypten' to her, a love poem that opens the correspondence (see Figure 11).

Bachmann and Celan met in post-war Vienna, where she was studying philosophy and he was living as a 'displaced person' fled from Romania. They would never have been able to find each other if Bachmann had not already started to break out of the world of her father, defined by National Socialism and war, and absented herself from the folkish community of the NS period. Reading and writing became a form of inner emigration. In the middle of the time of 'total war', the 17-year-old girl wrote a historical short story in which she opposed the murderous politics of the NS with the vision of a language transcending boundaries, as well as her utopian idea of the bridge. Working on the terrain of the idyllic regional novel, the schoolgirl Bachmann created that 'other' represented by the books banned by the Nazis. At the end of the war, she wrote in her diary that 'Thomas Mann and Stefan Zweig and Schnitzler and Hofmannsthal' (PNIB) had strengthened her 'belief in the "other"', a belief she resolved never to abandon (NO. 26).

After the liberation by the Allies in the early summer of 1945, she met an officer of the Royal Army, a young Jewish intellectual who had fled to England from Austria and was now returning with the liberating army—and for her, the victory of the Allies could not be anything but a liberation. Her friendship with him made her realize what it meant in Austria, even after the end of Nazi rule, after this 'catastrophe', to 'go with the Jew' (PNIB). He, Jack Hamesh, encouraged her in her desire to study philosophy. As a student, she then came to Vienna via Innsbruck and Graz, not least on account of her own writing. She had already contacted a number of literary institutions in Vienna, and continued her studies in philosophy there. In September 1947, she made the acquaintance of Hans Weigel, the famous writer and literary patron who had returned to Vienna from exile. The two entered a very open relationship that was still continuing when Bachmann began her love affair with Paul Celan in May 1948.

Celan, born to Jewish parents in Czernowitz in 1920, was a decisive six years older than Bachmann. His parents had been murdered in a German concentration camp, and he had survived a Romanian labour camp. After the war, he went to Bucharest, worked—as someone at home in several languages and literary traditions—as a translator, as well as continuing his own literary work. 'Todesfuge' was published in Romanian in 1947. He fled in December 1947, travelling via Hungary to Vienna, where his name had already been mentioned in connection with his poems. In a letter to Otto Basil, editor of *Plan*, Celan's Romanian mentor Alfred Margul-Sperber referred to Celan's poetry as 'the only lyric pendant to Kafka's work' (9 October 1947), an assessment that the 'poetry book'—the later volume *Der Sand aus den Urnen*—indirectly acknowledged as the memory of the Jewish catastrophe.

In the relationship that begins in 1948 between the burgeoning poet and the author who, as the note accompanying the 17 poems printed in the spring issue of *Plan* states, has written 'the most important volume of German poetry in recent decades' (Margul-Sperber), the additional difference that needs to be taken account of alongside their entirely contrasting backgrounds, and the young woman's cultural isolation woman in Carinthia during the NS period, is the age gap. Celan was 27 years old when he wrote the poem 'In Ägypten'; she was 21. Six years later, when she was as old as he had been at their first meeting in Vienna, she was writing the poems for her second—and last—poetry volume *Anrufung des Grossen Bären* (1956).

Authorships

'In Ägypten' (NO. 1) proclaims nine commandments of love and writing after the Shoah. 'You also know,' Celan later writes in a letter with reference to this poem that marked the start of their relationship, 'when I met you, you were both for me: the sensual <u>and</u> the spiritual. The two can never separate, Ingeborg' (NO. 53). 'In Ägypten' speaks of pain over the death of the once and forever beloved Jewish women—'Ruth! Noemi! Miriam!', and it defines the new, ceremonial bond: remembrance of the dead in the love for the 'stranger', thus surpassing every previous love—'Thou shalt adorn the stranger next to thee most beautifully of all./ Thou shalt adorn her with the pain over Ruth, over Miriam and Noemi./Thou shalt say to the stranger:/Behold, I slept next to these!' The poem, a utopian blasphemy in the face of established historical and religious norms, confers upon its male addressee the duty of commemorating the dead. The nine commandments regulate the relationship with the Jewish women, and the 'stranger' is used as a medium of connection to the dead; she is the union of beloved and language. Under the title 'In Ägypten' stands the dedication 'For Ingeborg', and at the end the poem's place and date: 'Vienna, 23 May 1948'.

In the letter to Bachmann written almost 10 years later (NO. 53), Celan returns to this inaugural poem of their relationship. Every time he reads 'In Ägypten' he sees *her* 'step into this poem'. For him, the poem is a threshold between those separated; the 'stranger' as the beloved woman is his 'reason for living'; she is and will remain 'the justification' for his 'speaking'. The young author could observe herself in a similar role to the 'stranger' in Celan's poem in a *roman-à-clef—Unvollendete Symphonie*—written by Weigel, her companion at the time, about a young artist from the Austrian province. She, whom Weigel revealed as 'the young Ingeborg Bachmann' in a new edition of the novel (1992), had proved to the survivor the purpose of his survival and return. In Weigel's novel, she is the one who is described and discussed, even when she speaks as the first person in the novel: 'I knew so much about your dead—[. . .]. I understood what it meant for you thus to bring them to life with me [. . .]. And I saw how the bitterness that *they* are no longer there does not let go of you' (p. 74). Weigel's words—and Bachmann maintained the second major correspondence of her Vienna years with him—already show an insight into a mutual strangeness for which neither protagonist is personally to blame but which separates them 'irretrievably and insurmountably'. It is they, the banished and murdered, who 'were not here': 'That, that is what sets us apart. Our fear is not your fear. Our being saved is not your being saved' (p. 183).

Weigel lets the woman speak with *his* voice; his novel has no place for *her* voice, and the problem of a female authorship does not arise. Hence there is none of what lends the letters and texts of Bachmann and Celan their drama, what causes the far-reaching impairment of communication, speech on the point of suffocation, the concealed and open recriminations, the misunderstandings, the 'sudden silences' (NO. 191) and the whole gamut of symptomatic utterance. 'Heaviness', 'darkness', 'silence' and 'guilt' are central words in the epistolary dialogue which constantly seeks more light, does not want to fall silent; in the process, the thematic words in the history of the correspondence go through the most varied modulations, differentiations and changes. 'I sometimes tell myself that my silence is perhaps more understandable than yours, for the darkness that imposes it upon me is older,' writes Celan on 20 August 1949 (NO. 9).

Celan's 'darkness' was undoubtedly older, but Bachmann too wanted to understand *her* darkness, *her* 'fears', as one of her most chilling poems from 1945 ('Ängste') is entitled, and she insisted on her other utopia, which was not fulfilled by that of the 'stranger' from Celan's 'In Ägypten'. A notion of this other history, a different darkness, a different, female history of authorship and a different utopia would be conveyed by the 'In Ägypten' of her novel *Das Buch Franza* [The Book of Franza]. But this insistence on her difference does not mean that the NS extermination ever ceased to be the centre and culmination of all previous historical and private crimes. From the start of their encounter in Vienna until his death and beyond, she bore witness for Celan, in her own writing and her tireless endeavours on behalf of his poetry, of that extermination. Bachmann's letters document the multifaceted nature of this mission known in the discourse of Shoah remembrance culture as 'secondary testimony' (Lydia Koelle)—as a reader of Celan's poetry, as a strategist in the preparation of his public effect, as a writer referring to his images of the Shoah, as a lecturer on poetics in Frankfurt, and in the prose of *Todesarten* [Ways of Dying]. She believed that she could 'read his poems better than others because she 'encounters' him in them: 'You are always my concern, I ponder a great deal on it and speak to you' (NO. 5). She takes up his ciphers into her own formulations in letters and everyday life, thus keeping his poems alive by making them part of her existence. 'Sometimes I live and breathe only through them,' she writes, and adds, quoting from 'Wasser und Feuer': ' "think that I was what I am" ' (NO. 26).

Orpheus and Eurydice after 1945

The quotations from Celan used by Bachmann have often been noted in examinations of her work; but while 'the dialogical as a poetic and poetological principle in Paul Celan' (Gilda Encarnação) has been explored in advanced studies, the specific poetics of Bachmann's engagement with Celan's poems has not yet been reconstructed in more precise and coherent work-historical terms. The tensions of the symptomatic speech in the correspondence, the misjudgements and misunderstandings, the recriminations or the contradictions manifested through silence make all harmless notions of dialogue and intertextuality seem questionable. It is the correspondents themselves who read the poems as an exemplary representation of their conflicts—or indeed as the experienced happiness of union; both reflect in their letters on the historicity of their relationship, and demand of each other a 'faithful remembering' (NOS 19 and 20) that constitutes the precondition for the connection between them that is often re-established with such great effort.

'Dura legge d'Amor' [O harsh law of love]—with this quotation from Petrarch at the start of 'Lieder auf der Flucht', Bachmann transfers the topos of the lovers' quarrel to post-war literature. The settings of her poems are scenes of a battle of life and death, and it is precisely in the most violent scenes that she refers most directly to Celan's images and the 'harsh law' of writing dictated by them. 'Die Saite des Schweigens/gespannt auf die Welle von Blut,/griff ich dein tönendes Herz./Verwandelt ward deine Locke/ins Schattenhaar der Nacht,/der Finsternis schwarze Flocken/beschneiten dein Antlitz' [The string of silence/stretched upon the wave of blood,/I grasped your resounding heart./Your curl was transformed/into the shadow-hair of the night,/the black flakes of darkness/snowed upon your countenance] (from 'Dunkles zu sagen' [To Speak Dark Things, or Dark Things to Speak]). The words 'Schattenhaar der Nacht' and 'Locke' in Bachmann's poem are Celan's verbal symbols of the Jewish genocide— as in 'Dein aschenes Haar Sulamith' [Your ashen hair Shulamith] (from 'Todesfuge') and 'Judenlocke, wirst nicht grau' [Jew's curl, you'll not turn grey] (from 'Mandorla'). Bachmann's lines 'der Finsternis schwarze Flocken/beschneiten dein Antlitz' refer to Celan's poem 'Schwarze Flocken' [Black Flakes], which speaks most explicitly about the murder of his parents in the country 'where the widest river flows'. It begins with the statement: 'Schnee ist gefallen, lichtlos' [Snow has fallen, lightless].

Bachmann's Orpheus poem depicts the dramatic scene in which the memory of the 'dark river' erupts into the scene of love: 'Vergiss nicht, dass auch du, plötzlich,/an jenem Morgen, als dein Lager/noch nass war von Tau und die Nelke/an deinem Herzen schlief,/den dunklen Fluss sahst,/der an dir vorbeizog' [Do not forget that you too, suddenly,/on that morning when your bed/was still wet with dew and the carnation/slept by your heart,/saw the dark river/that flowed past you]. Her title—'Dunkles zu sagen'—changes the formulation 'wir sagen uns Dunkles' [we speak dark things to each other] from Celan's 'Corona' into an obligation, and Celan's symbols of the Shoah are used to indicate the reason for the lovers' separation. The poem closes with the consolation that art opens its eye when the lover's eye has closed. 'Und ich gehör dir nicht zu./Beide klagen wir nun.//Aber wie Orpheus weiss ich/auf der Seite des Todes das Leben,/und mir blaut/dein für immer geschlossenes Aug' [And I do not belong to you./Now we both lament.//But like Orpheus I know/that life is on death's side,/and your eye, forever closed/turns blue for me]. Bachmann was distrustful of this consolation of the successful poem, which is based on the separation of art and life, from the beginning. The 'I know' at the end of the poem is part of the long line of phrases such as 'I know', 'you know' or 'we know' in the letters. Even much later, in *Malina*, the 'Legend of the Princess of Kagran' still recalls this knowledge when 'the stranger [. . .] silently designed his death and her first.' In 'a frightful silence' he had 'already driven the first thorn into her heart. He did not sing her any parting song.' 'But she smiled and mumbled in her fever: "Oh I know, I know!"'' (IBW 3, 70).

'Over there your beloved sinks in the sand'

Bachmann sent Celan a dedicated copy of her poetry volume *Die gestundete Zeit* in December 1953; no answer from him has survived. At this point, the correspondence had been broken off for more than a year. In the title poem, she followed a trail that probably only Celan would have been able to decipher as the letter secret of the poem. The symptoms of the relationship manifested in the letters, the reproaches, the silence or half-voiced objections now come into view as a 'case' of female authorship. Bachmann's poem depicts the beloved's falling silent as her being silenced, and thus simultaneously constitutes an objection and an accusation. This discrepancy of the female first person's history, as a supplement to the major discrepancy of their different backgrounds, lies at the heart of the unmistakable conflicts waged in both the letters and the poems. 'I am slowly beginning to understand why I resisted you so strongly, and why I may never stop doing so. I love you and I do not want to love you, it is too much and too difficult; but, above all, I love you,' writes Bachmann in a letter that was initially unsent but then enclosed with a later one (NO. 18.3). This passage and other similar ones in the letters suggest that the scene of the beloved's death in 'Die gestundete Zeit' should be read as a view of the other side of authorship after 1945. The relationship between the poetess and the poet revolves around the 'inevitable dark history that accompanies his history, and tries to supplement it, but which he separates and excludes from his clear history', to cite the much later formulation concerning the relationship of the female first person with the male authorial position of *Malina* in Bachmann's novel (IBW 3, 22f.). Referring to Bachmann in the fourth of her Frankfurt lectures on poetics ('Voraussetzungen einer Erzählung: Kassandra' [Preconditions for a Narrative: Cassandra]), Christa Wolf speaks of a 'generation-wide terrain' in which the writing woman is in danger of being lost to the man, to literature as a male institution: 'I maintain that every woman who has dared, in this century and in our cultural sphere, to venture into the institutions shaped by male self-identity—"literature" and "aesthetics" are such institutions— had to become acquainted with the desire for self-destruction.'

In the 'personal' coding of the experience of 'borrowed time' [*gestundete Zeit*], the second part of the poem constitutes a turning point, the shocking development that brings the thematic concerns of *Todesarten* into view as a second, palimpsestic layer of meaning. What is even more shocking is the fact that, in this turn towards the beloved's 'way of dying' [*Todesart*], one can see central verbal images from Celan's poems shining through: 'Drüben versinkt die Geliebte im Sand,/er steigt um ihr wehendes Haar,/er fällt ihr ins Wort,/er befiehlt ihr zu schweigen,/er findet sie sterblich/und willig dem Abschied/nach jeder Umarmung' [Over there your beloved sinks in the sand,/it rises around her blowing hair,/it interrupts her,/it commands her to be silent,/it finds her mortal/and willing to part/after every embrace]. The next stanza begins with the line 'Sieh dich nicht um' [Do not look back], which brings the Orpheus motif into play. It is not the mythological citation but, rather, the seven lines preceding it that constitute both the event in the cycle of poems and an event in the correspondence between Bachmann and Celan, which would not have existed between 1952 and 1957 without the poems as bottle messages: 'Drüben', the first word of these seven lines, refers to the title of the first poem in Celan's volume *Der Sand aus den Urnen*, published in Vienna in September 1948 and in Bachmann's possession. The 'sand' that engulfs the beloved is, in Celan's volume, a cipher for the extermination of the Jews. The 'blowing hair' of the beloved around which the sand rises recalls Annette von Droste-Hülshoff's poem 'Am Thurme' [At the Tower], in which the female first person is forbidden by the gender laws of her social class from letting her hair 'flap' in the wind. In Bachmann's literary bottle message, however, Droste's early feminist evocation of greater freedom—even if it were 'at least' the same as men's—is overlaid with the memory of Celan's poem 'Auf Reisen', written in 1948 immediately after Celan's departure from Vienna. The commemoration of the dead in the world's hour of the Jewish extermination, which 'makes the sand the retinue' of the poem's first person and makes its 'black eye the blackest eye', forbids the hair from flapping during the farewell: 'Your hair would like to flap when you depart, it is forbidden—those who remain and wave do not know it.' 'Todesfuge' had closed with the lines: 'your golden hair Margarete/your ashen hair Shulamith'; in the poem 'In Ägypten', which opens the correspondence, Celan wrote: 'Thou shalt adorn them with the cloud-hair of the stranger.' The history of poetry after the Shoah is implicit in the images of 'hair' and 'curl' in Celan's poems. Bachmann's poem 'Die gestundete Zeit' is aware of this history, yet does not accept the hair of the beloved being buried by the sand and 'her' being silenced. What Bachmann registers in the letters, namely that there was 'always something choking' her, 'not unlike that which had carried' their letters before that (NO. 10.1), and also the moments of falling silent mentioned time after time and the complementary evocations of breathing—all this is condensed in those seven lines from 'Die gestundete Zeit' in a scene of oppressive personal and historical drama.

'I am still guilty. Pick me up'

In its dialogue with Celan, Bachmann's work has 'its centre and its depth' in 'the pain over her love for a poet damaged by the Shoah and its consequences, and in the *resulting* responsibility in her writing and thinking', writes Lydia Koelle in her study on the ' "Temporal Core" of Paul Celan's Poetry'. The letters point even more strongly to this 'temporal core' *and* to the resistance and attempts to break free of the most personal burdens imposed by the consequences of the Shoah. In some of her poems, Bachmann represented this imposition of guilt in the extreme vulnerability of a first person, but also, in the poetics of *Undine geht* or the multi-stanza poem 'Lieder von einer Insel', rebelliously celebrated the irresponsible escape: 'If someone leaves, he must throw his hat/ together with the shells he gathered over the summer/into the sea/and go forth with his hair flapping'—and, repeated with an exclamation mark at the end of the stanza: 'and go forth with his hair flapping!'

In the other multi-stanza song cycle, 'Lieder auf der Flucht', which concludes the second volume of poems, one again encounters the image of the beloved sinking in the sand from the title poem of the first volume, this time transposed into the image of dying in the 'snow'—this, along with 'sand', is another symbol of the Shoah in Celan's work. The second of the 'Songs', which begins with a quotation from Sappho, hence again with the memory of a writing woman, reads: 'Ich aber liege allein/im Eisverhau voller Wunden.//Es hat mir der Schnee/noch nicht die Augen verbunden.//Die Toten, an mich gepresst,/ schweigen in allen Zungen./Niemand liebt mich und hat/für mich eine Lampe geschwungen!' [But I lie alone/in the ice-blockade full of wounds.//The snow has/not yet bound my eyes.//The dead, pressed against me,/are silent in all tongues./No one loves me and/swung a lamp for me!]. After the resumption of her love affair with Celan in the autumn of 1957, Bachmann asks Celan, after he had told her in Cologne that he was 'forever reconciled' with her, 'to read my "Lieder auf der Flucht" again': 'I was at my wits' end during that winter two years ago, and accepted my rejection. I no longer hoped to be acquitted. To what end?' (NO. 52). The 'Songs' deal with a verdict of guilt pushing down the female first person and divides the lovers into the parties of judge and judged: 'Mund, der das Urteil sprach,/Hand, die mich hinrichtete!' [O mouth that uttered the verdict,/O hand that executed me!] begins a scene of nightmarish violence and passionate longing for salvation in the thirteenth stanza: 'Ich bin noch schuldig. Heb mich auf./Ich bin nicht schuldig. Heb mich auf.//Das Eiskorn lös vom zugefrornen Aug,/brich mit den Blicken ein, die blauen Gründe such, schwimm, schau und tauch://Ich bin es nicht./Ich bin's' [I am still guilty. Pick me up./I am not guilty.

Pick me up.//Remove the ice pellet from the eye frozen shut,/crack with the glances, seek the blue grounds, swim, look and dive://It is not I./It's me] (IBW 1, 146). In the poem, the symptomatic speech of the letters takes the form of a self-destructive struggle with the question of guilt in which rescue from paralysis and muteness is ultimately transferred to the medium of language. The icy paralysis is transformed into singing water, and the 'ice pellet' is removed 'from the eye', as one could note regarding this transferral, which is distantly reminiscent of the medium as which the eye of the 'stranger' in Celan's 'In Ägypten' is supposed to act: the water, in which the dead remain alive. The female first person in Bachmann's poem is lost in this transformation; what remains is the 'silence' from which the poem draws its own conclusions at the expense of the living—with an allusion to Rilke's *Sonnets to Orpheus*: 'doch das Lied überm Staub danach/wird uns übersteigen' [yet the song above the dust afterwards/will exceed us].

'the two/heart-grey puddles'

Celan knew 'Lieder auf der Flucht', the final poem of the volume *Anrufung des Grossen Bären*, which he had owned since 1956, probably before Bachmann requested him to read it in a letter while he was writing 'Sprachgitter' in Vienna during the summer of 1957. The parenthesized stanza in 'Sprachgitter'—'Wär ich wie du. Wärst du wie ich. (Standen wir nicht unter *einem* Passat?/Wir sind Fremde.)' [If I were like you. If you were like me./Did we not stand under *one* trade wind?/We are strangers.]—could refer to his kinship with the 'stranger' in Vienna at the time, as 'eye' and 'water' also refer to 'In Ägypten'. The final stanza of 'Sprachgitter' begins with a word that points to the innermost region of the Jewish extermination: 'Die Fliesen. Darauf,/icht beieinander, die beiden/herz-grauen Lachen:/zwei/Mundvoll Schweigen' [The tiles. Upon them,/close together, the two/heart-grey puddles:/two/mouthfuls of silence]. The real letter secret of these five lines, each of which reveals a new aspect of meaning in the fragmentation of sense, lies in the emphatic proximity of these 'two', of a coexistence in the middle of a semantic space which pinpoints that extermination. And that is precisely where the 'two' authorships are assigned a place in Celan's poem on equal footing, 'close together' and on the 'tiles'. Written on 14 June 1957 in the Rennweg in Vienna, close to the 'Hungarian alley land' of the third district, it makes one understand how, after meeting with Bachmann again, Celan experiences the ecstatic joy—not evident anywhere else in the correspondence—of a new togetherness and mutual support; how the world unlocked itself for him in a new legibility, and everything found a way of coming together. Reading and writing, letter and poem, even muteness and silence are now experienced as togetherness—'But that alone, my speaking, is not even the point; I wanted to be silent with you too' (NO. 53)—and Bachmann's poems are met with their first response in Celan's letters, because he reads them—'And know, finally, what your poems are like' (NO. 72). Two months later he asks her for a copy of her radio play *Der gute Gott von Manhattan*, explaining his request with the words 'You know, Ingeborg, you know' (NO. 90).

'*Read, Ingeborg, read*'

Now it is he who requests poems from her and sends his own as love letters, even reading his earlier poems as a validation of their current experiences—'Think of "In Ägypten"' (NO. 53)—appending 'f. y.' (for you) to several of his poems as a dedication, and now also incorporating Bachmann's reservations about Celan's family situation into his current poems. He passes his own wonder at the beauty of his poem 'Köln, Am Hof'—beginning with the word 'Herzzeit'—on to her and sees the reason for the poem's creation in her reference to 'the dreamt ones' (NO. 53). And now it is she, the one who had so often reminded him in her early letters of 'the dreams we once dreamt' (NO. 11), who insists on a clarification: 'The addition, you say, must be "Into life". That is true for the dreamt ones. But are we only the dreamt ones?' (NO. 52).

Celan's letters from mid-October 1957 contain an effusive evocation of reading that opens the world and includes the beloved. The boundaries of art and life have become permeable, and the act of reading, as in Bachmann's essay 'Das Gedicht an den Leser' (undated [The Poem to the Reader]), takes on utopian aspects. It is important to him that her eyes 'rest' for 'a few moments' on the translations he wishes to send her (NO. 56); in the train compartment on the way from

Munich to Frankfurt he finds a woman reading Bachmann's poems; he sees that 'her eyes were reading, again and again. Again and again. I was so grateful' (NO. 69). In Frankfurt, where he is staying with a friend, he sees both their books standing 'side by side' on the shelf (NO. 69). In 'Köln, Am Hof' he refers to this new experience of convergence as 'heart-time', and she calls the poems from *Sprachgitter* 'poems from our time again' (NO. 117)—during these years, everything becomes part of their time together, the separate spaces and times lead into one another and into a world full of correspondences. Rummaging through old papers, Celan stumbles on 'a pocket calendar from 1950' (NO. 56) and finds, under 14 October, the entry 'Ingeborg': 'It was the day you came to Paris. On 14 October 1957 we were in Cologne, Ingeborg./You clocks deep in us.' The line 'You clocks deep in us' is the one that concludes the poem 'Köln, Am Hof'. In her volume of poems *Die gestundete Zeit*, reissued in 1957 by Piper, Bachmann writes the dedication: 'Munich, Am Hof' (NO. 68), and over a year later he was to send her an old 'correspondence card' found at a bouqinist's stall in Paris with a photo and the message 'Greetings from Vienna. 1st district, Am Hof' (NO. 118). He bought the card at 'almost the same spot where the poem occurred to me over a year ago' (NO. 120). And indeed, under 'Köln, Am Hof', sent to Bachmann on 20 October 1957, he had written: 'Paris, Quai Bourbon,/Sunday 20 October 1957,/ 2:30 p.m.—' (NO. 47).

For both poets, it is precisely during these years that such 'correspondences' are increasingly accompanied by theoretical reflections on their own time and their own locations as writers and readers, whether in Celan's Bremen speech (1958) or the 'Meridian' poetics of his Büchner Prize acceptance speech (1960)— or in Bachmann's 'Das Gedicht an den Leser' in Musik und Dichtung (1959), the speech given before the war-blind, 'Die Wahrheit ist dem Menschen zumutbar' [People Can Be Expected to Deal with the Truth] or the Frankfurt lectures on poetics. In his Bremen speech, Celan connected the question of writing and reading to the 'question of the clock hand's direction' and associated the poem, as 'a manifestation of language, and thus dialogical by nature', with the notion of a 'message in a bottle' that is heading towards something, for 'something standing open, something occupiable, perhaps towards an addressable Thou, towards an addressable reality (GW III, 186). In her sketch 'Das Gedicht an den Leser', on the other hand, which resolutely opposes the biblical myth of petrifaction, Bachmann invoked the relationship with the reader as a utopia, and, with an allusion to 'Corona', also thought of Celan as her co-reader: 'I want to walk after you when you are dead, turn around, even under threat of petrifaction, I want to sound, [. . .] and make the stone blossom' (IBW 4, 308).

'who am I for you, after so many years?
A phantom [. . .]'

The 'Goll affair' and the anti-Semitic undertones of Günter Blöcker's *Sprachgitter* review cast Celan into an existentially threatening crisis. His letters to Ingeborg Bachmann and Max Frisch, with whom she lived from November 1958, became 'cries for help' (NO. 146, 17 November 1959). Her inability to react adequately to her friend's 'cry for help' is one example of the misunderstandings and failures to reach each other that can be observed in this symptomatic correspondence. In a letter to Frisch, Celan described this complex of impaired communication in the continuing aftermath of Auschwitz as the 'objectively demonic' element—'without really doing justice to it with this formulation': he spoke of a 'something' that was ' "interfering" here, interfering—in one way or another—with all of us'. ' "Coincidence" would perhaps be another auxiliary term for it, in the sense that it coincides and has coincided with us' (NO. 206). It was part of this 'objectively demonic' element that Bachmann did not write her long, self-assured letter of 27 September 1961 at the right time, and indeed knew that it was 'once again not the right time'—but there is no right time, otherwise I would have had to bring myself to do it before' (NO. 191). Bachmann's letter, her most major text in this correspondence alone for its length, was written to clarify their relationship. Looking back critically on the history of her relationship with Celan, she speaks of the 'sudden silences', the history of misjudgements and misunderstandings, and asks whether she is a 'reality' alongside him or if she is condemned to a ghostly non-existence. 'I want to be the person I am, today,' she writes. After the re-encounter in Wuppertal she had 'believed in this "today" ': 'I affirmed you and you affirmed me in a new life.' She accuses him of wanting 'to be the victim' and sanctioning the attacks on him. But she refuses to join him on this path: 'then that is your affair, and it will not be mine if you let it overwhelm you' (NO. 191).

She left the letter unfinished and did not send it, planning to bring it to Paris, 'fill it out in conversation' and also let Celan 'fill it out'—'to make something clearer that concerns no one but you and me' (NO. 192). In the end, she did not go to Paris. Her last letter—aside the formal Christmas greetings from her and Max Frisch (NO. 194)—testifies to her meanwhile pathological inability to write letters: 'it has long been like an illness; I cannot write, I am already crippled when I write the date or put the paper in the typewriter' (NO. 193). After a long silence, a letter from Celan reaches her on 21 September 1963; he has heard that she has 'only just returned from hospital'. He too has 'a few less than pleasant years' behind him, 'as they say'. He writes that in his volume *Die Niemandsrose*, which was soon to be published, he has 'taken a rather "inartistic" path [. . .] The document of a crisis, if you like—but what would poetry be if it were not that too, and radically so?/So please, write me a few lines' (NO. 195). No written response by Bachmann has survived. As an author, however, she likewise took *her own* '"inartistic" path', her writing perhaps more in agreement with him now than ever before.

'*the sick whom one can count on*'

Bachmann's *Todesarten* cycle is precisely that radical work that takes the path through sickness. 'So it is the sick whom one can count on, and who have not yet lost their sense of what is unjust and monstrous' (TA I, 174), she writers in preparation of her Büchner Prize acceptance speech, a first crossing of the zones of an inner and outer illness. In the foreword she refers to the word 'coincidences' [*Zufälle*] (IBW 4, 278), which Büchner uses to describe Lenz's illness; she uses it in the sense invoked by Celan in a letter to Max Frisch (NO. 206) in order to render visible the word's implicit dialectic between the outer and inner situations of a first person.

Bachmann views the title character's journey to Egypt in *Der Fall Franza* (TA II: *Das Buch Franza*) as a 'journey through an illness' (IBW 3, 341). The scene in which the woman is buried in the desert sand as part of the game, such that she cannot cry out and is unable to move in any way, is still connected to the Shoah in the sense of an ultimate conclusion to the story, which reaches far back, of the woman who is repeatedly silenced and 'exterminated'. A further central motif, present from the letters and early poems on and continuing to the late *Todesarten* novels, including the *Franza* fragment, is the question of the identity and history of the daughter/wife/sister who emancipates herself from her father's authority: 'who am I, where do I come from, what is my situation' (IBW 3, 446). The revolt in victimhood, both here and now and in the past, is one of the motifs that extend far back into her past. *Requiem für Fanny Goldmann*, another novel fragment from *Todesarten*, could—in a continuation of the questions raised in the correspondence with Celan, be read as Bachmann's most biographically radical fictional engagement with her own background, both in the title figure's critical view of her youth and the attention to the different self-conceptions of Jewish identity with which she, the Viennese Fanny Wischnewski, finds herself confronted in the changes characterizng her Jewish husband's life history.

In *Malina*, the only published novel from *Todesarten*, the authorial first person is split into a male and a female double in order to narrate the inward drama of the question of authorship. It is precisely in this construction that the questions arising in the relationship with Celan can be depicted in a more analytical, yet also more vivid fashion than Bachmann achieves in her last story, 'Drei Wege zum See' [Three Paths to the Lake] (*Simultan* [Simultaneously], 1972), where her love for Celan is mirrored directly in the recounted relationship between Elisabeth Matrei and Franz Joseph Trotta. It was her 'great love', but also the 'hardest to grasp, and the most difficult, burdened by misunderstandings, quarrels, failed communication and distrust'. He 'made her aware of many things because of his background, and he, a truly exiled and lost man', transformed her, 'an adventurer who was expecting all manner of things from the world in life, into an exile because, only after his death, he slowly dragged her down with him to her ruin' (IBW 2, 415f.).

In *Malina*, the experience of violence in the drama of the female authorial first person, which could be followed in the letter and poem scenes, becomes the subject of a new, 'intellectual' mode of narration that has 'something philosophical' about it, and struck Bachmann as 'the most important thing' (GuI 104): a philosophical novel, understood by the author as an 'imaginary autobiography', in which a first person sick from love speaks as *l'homme revolté*. Once again we encounter the thematic scenery of the beloved sinking in the sand, now transformed into the image of the 'wall' into which the female first person is driven; she falls silent, while Malina, the male part of the first person and the work's advocate, remains: 'It is a very old, a very strong wall; no one can fall out of it, no one can break it open, and no sound can ever issue from it.//It was murder' (IBW 3, 337). The central dream chapter in *Malina* explains the historical preconditions for this murder with the combination of paternal violence and the history of extermination, and this history extends into the very process of writing. In the series of dreams with the father as the embodiment of violence in an eternal war whose centre is the Nazi extermination enterprise, the death of the stranger is interpreted as an after-effect of those events. But here, in the space of the Shoah, he appears like a magical sacrifice 'in his blacker-than-black sidereal coat', freed from all contradictions, as part of a counter-history that manifests itself in gestures of affection towards each other, in the caution and solidarity of the persecuted, in mutual understanding: 'I see him pointing to his head; I know what they did to his head' (IBW 3, 194f.).

'a leaf that met us drifts after us on the waves'

In the autumn of 1957, Celan found Bachmann's poem 'Im Gewitter der Rosen' in the *Frankfurter Zeitung*; there he was able to read the new stanza she had added to the poem, which had already been published in *Die gestundete Zeit*, for Hans Werner Henze's musical setting in *Nachtstücke und Arien*. When she sent Celan the volume *Die gestundete Zeit* at Christmas in 1953, directly after its publication, she had appended the earlier version of this poem on a strip of paper (NO. 42n). The stanza newly added to 'Im Gewitter der Rosen' read as follows:

> Wo immer gelöscht wird, was die Rosen entzünden,
> schwemmt Regen uns in den Fluss. O fernere Nacht!

Doch ein Blatt, das uns traf, treibt auf den Wellen
bis zur Mündung uns nach.

[Wherever the fire lit by the roses is put out,
rain washes us into the river. O more distant night!
But a leaf that met us drifts after us on the waves
up to the river's mouth.]

In the 1957 stanza he perhaps saw the return of the 'leaf' he had given her during the time in Vienna. He believed it 'lost' (NO. 3), because she no longer had it in her 'medallion'. 'Let me end by telling you—the leaf that you placed in my medallion is not lost, even if it has long ceased to be inside it; I think of you, and I am still listening to you' (NO. 4). More than 20 years later, the Celan passages in the dream chapter of *Malina* return to the memories of the city park in Vienna mentioned—only by Bachmann—in the early letters. Now, in the literary dream, it is the male 'beloved' who says: 'Be calm, think of the city park, think of the leaf, think of the garden in Vienna, of our tree, the Paulownias are in bloom.' After that, a stranger in the dream asks after 'the Princess of Kagran' in order to bring her the news of his death. He identifies himself with 'a dried leaf, and then I knew that he had spoken truthfully. My life is over, for he drowned in the river during deportation; he was my life. I loved him more than my life' (IBW 3, 195).

Hans Höller and Andrea Stoll
April 2008

NOTE

1   The original word *Briefgeheimnis* has a certain ambivalence; on the one hand, it is a legal term—'secrecy of letters' or 'privacy of correspondence', referring to the right to confidentiality—while on the other hand its literal meaning is 'letter secret', implying a letter as a secret source (here of the poems); as the legal term is not one of the most well-known, the latter would probably suggest itself first to the reader. Consistency of translation has therefore been sacrificed here for the sake of reflecting the tone of each use—sometimes the implication of confidentiality, sometimes that of epistolary origin. [Trans.]

23 November 1920
Paul Celan born in
Czernowitz, Bukovina, into
a German-speaking Jewish
family.

25 June 1926
Ingeborg Bachmann born
in Klagenfurt; siblings:
Isolde (1928) and Heinz
(1939).

1932
Her father joins the NSDAP.

12 March 1938
Hitler's troops march into
Klagenfurt.

September 1939
Her father drafted for
military service.

June 1942
Deportation of his parents
Friederike and Leo Antschel

(died in winter 1942/43 in Nazi death camp in Mikhaylovka, Ukraine).

May/June 1945
Encounter with Jack Hamesh, a British-Jewish occupation soldier from Vienna.

October 1946
Continues studies in philosophy begun in Innsbruck and Graz in Vienna; address: Vienna III, Beatrixgasse 26.

17 December 1947
Arrives in Vienna after fleeing from Bucharest via Budapest.

16 May 1948
First encounter between Ingeborg Bachmann and Paul Celan.

20 May 1948
Start of the love affair

Late June 1948
Departs from Vienna to Paris via Innsbruck (5–8 July 1948).

13 July 1948
Arrives in Paris, address from August (?): 31, rue des Ecoles (V).

August (?) 1948
'Edgar Jené. Der Traum vom Traume'.

September 1948
Der Sand aus den Urnen.

June 1949
Moves to Vienna III, Gottfried-Keller-Gasse 13.

23 March 1950
Completes of Ph.D. (thesis: 'Die kritische Aufnahme der Existentialphilosophie Martin Heideggers).

14 October–mid-December 1950
Bachmann stays in Paris.

Late December 1950–February 1951
Travels to London from Paris.

23 February–7 March 1951
Bachmann stays in Paris, then returns to Vienna.

April–August 1951
Works for the American Occupation Authority.

September 1951– late July 1953 Works for the radio station Rot-Weiss-Rot as scriptwriter, later editor.		
		Early November (?) 1951 First encounter with Gisèle de Lestrange.
28 February 1952 First broadcast of *Ein Geschäft mit Träumen*.		
		21 May–6 June 1952 Trip to Germany, participates in conference of Gruppe 47 in Niendorf.
	23–27 May 1952 Meetings in Niendorf and Hamburg.	
1 November 1952 First encounter with Hans Werner Henze, with whom she lives on and off from 1953.		
		23 December 1952 Marries Gisèle de Lestrange
		December 1952/ January 1953 *Mohn und Gedächtnis*
May 1953 Awarded prize by Gruppe 47 (Mainz).		
		July 1953 Moves to 5, rue de Lota (XVI).

August–October 1953
Stays with Henze in Ischia.
Further extended stays with
Henze in winter 1954/55,
February to August 1955.

October 1953
Moves to Rome: Piazza della
Quercia 1.

December 1953
Die gestundete Zeit.

25 March 1955
First broadcast of *Die Zikaden*
with music by Henze.

May 1955
Literature prize of the
Cultural Area in the Federal
Association of German
Industry.

August 1953
First accusations of plagiarism sent by Claire Goll to
critics, radio staff and
publishers in Germany.

7/8 October 1953
Birth and death of first son
François.

6 June 1955
Birth of son Eric.

June 1955
Von Schwelle zu Schwelle, with
printed dedication 'FOR
GISÈLE'.

July 1955
Moves to 29, rue de
Montevideo (XVI). Becomes
a naturalized French citizen.

July/August 1955 Participates in International Seminar of Harvard University, trip to New York.		
October 1956 *Anrufung des Grossen Bären.*		
November/ December 1956 Stays in Paris, Hôtel de la Paix, Rue Blainville 6, without Celan's knowledge.		
January 1957 Rome, Via Vecchiarelli 38.		
26 January 1957 Literature Prize of the Free Hanseatic City of Bremen.		
April 1957 *Die gestundete Zeit*, second edition.		
September 1957–May 1958 Dramatic adviser at Bavarian Television in Munich. First apartment: Biedersteinerstr. 21a.		**September 1957** Literature Prize of the Cultural Area in the Federal Association of German Industry.
	11–13 October 1957 Bachmann and Celan meet again at the conference 'Literaturkritik—kritisch betrachtet' held by the Wuppertaler Bund.	

14 October 1957
Meeting in Cologne after the conference. Resumption of the love affair (until May 1958).
Afterwards, shared editorship of the German section in of the multilingual journal Botteghe Oscure, 21 (1958).

November 1957
Moves to 78, rue de Longchamp (XVI).

7–9 December 1957
Celan visits Bachmann in Munich.

2–11 December 1957
Travels to Germany

Mid-December 1957
Moves to Franz-Joseph-Str. 9a.

28–30 January 1958
Celan visits Bachmann in Munich; discreet handwritten dedications of individual poems in *Mohn und Gedächtnis* (second edition; 1955).

23–30 January 1958
Travels to Germany, including to Bremen (for the Bremen Literature Prize, 26 January 1958).

April 1958
Participates in protest against nuclear weapons in the army.

7/8 May 1958
Celan visits Bachmann in Munich, end of love affair.

4–8 May 1958
Travels to Germany.

29 May 1958
First broadcast of *Der gute Gott von Manhattan.*

23 June–early July 1958
Bachmann in Paris, meetings with Celan on 25 and 30 June and 2 July. First encounter between Bachmann and Gisèle Celan-Lestrange.

3 July 1958
Meets Max Frisch in Paris.

November 1958
Der gute Gott von Manhattan.

September 1958
Arthur Rimbaud, *Das trunkene Schiff* (translation). Alexander Block, *Die Zwölf* (translation).

November 1958– autumn 1962
Lives with Max Frisch; first Zurich, Feldeggstr. 21, from March 1959 Uetikon am See, from June 1959 extended stays in Rome, some together with Frisch.

Early December 1958
The doctoral student Jean Firges defends an anti-Semitic caricature made by acquaintances after a reading by Celan in Bonn (17 November 1958).

3 December 1958 In Paris with Frisch without informing Celan.	**End of 1958** Gramophone record *Lyrik der Zeit* with recordings of Bachmann and Celan reading.	
17 March 1959 Radio Play Prize of the War-Blind, acceptance speech: 'Die Wahrheit ist dem Menschen zumutbar'.		**March 1959** *Sprachgitter*.
	19 and 22 July 1959 First personal encounters between Celan and Frisch in Sils.	
October 1959 Working apartment in Zurich, Kirchgasse 33.		**From October 1959** German Assistant at the École normale supérieure, Rue d'Ulm.
		11 October 1959 Review of *Sprachgitter* by Günter Blöcker, viewed by Celan as anti-Semitic, in *Der Tagesspiegel* (Berlin).
25 November 1959– **24 February 1960** Lectureship in poetics in Frankfurt.		**November 1959** Ossip Mandelstamm *Gedichte* (translation).
	Mid-January 1960 Third of Bachmann's 'Frankfurter Vorlesungen' (13th?); Celan reads from *Die junge Parze* (16th) in Frankfurt. No meeting.	

March 1960
Participation in a poetry symposium in Leipzig.

22 May 1960
Premiere of Henze's *Der Prinz von Homburg* with Bachmann's libretto.

25–28 May 1960
Celan travels to Zurich to present the Droste Prize to Nelly Sachs; several meetings with Bachmann, some including Gisèle Celan-Lestrange and Max Frisch.

30 October 1960
Meeting at Hôtel du Louvre; Frisch and Siegfried Unseld also present.

March 1960
Paul Valéry, *Die junge Parze* (translation).

April/May 1960
Accusations of plagiarism published by Claire Goll in the Munich journal *Baubudenpoet*. In May, consults with members of S. Fischer Verlag and Klaus Demus in Frankfurt: plans to publish a response in *Die Neue Rundschau*.

August 1960
'Gespräch im Gebirg' published in *Die Neue Rundschau*.

22 October 1960
Receives the Georg Büchner Prize in Darmstadt.

Around 20 November 1960
The 'Response' [*Entgegnung*]
to the plagiarism charges is
printed in *Die Neue Rundschau*
with the signatures of
Bachmann, Klaus Demus
and Marie Luise Kaschnitz.

25–27 November 1960
Celan in Zurich: daily
conversations about the
plagiarism charges in the
national press. These are
their last meetings.

January 1961
Büchner Prize speech 'Der
Meridian'.

March 1961
Sergei Yesenin, *Gedichte*
(translation).

June 1961
Das dreissigste Jahr.
In Rome with Frisch: Via de
Notaris 1 F.

Summer 1961
Giuseppe Ungaretti, *Gedichte*
(translation).

Late 1961
Last letter from Bachmann,
a Christmas greeting from
her and Max Frisch to Celan
and Gisèle Celan-Lestrange.

Autumn 1962
Separation from Frisch, followed by severe mental problems and suicide attempt.

Late 1962/early 1963
Hospital stay in Zurich.

Late 1962/early 1963
First in-patient treatment at a psychiatric clinic.

Spring 1963–late 1965
Lives in Berlin, first at Akademie der Künste, then from June 1963 in Berlin-Grunewald, Königsallee 35.

July/August 1963
Hospital stay in Berlin.

Late October 1963
Die Niemandsrose.

1964
Begins work on *Todesarten*; changes in concept, terminates it, restarts until her death.

16 April 1964
Celan and Frisch meet in Rome.

17 October 1964
Receives the Georg Büchner Prize in Darmstadt.

12 December 1964
Meets Anna Akhmatova in Rome.

1965
Büchner Prize speech *Ein Ort für Zufälle* with drawings by Günter Grass.

7 April 1965
Premiere of Henze's *Der junge Lord* with Bachmann's libretto.

February/March 1965, November 1965, May and late summer 1966, February 1967
Hospital stays in Baden-Baden, several weeks each.

Autumn 1966–late 1971
Rome, Via Bocca di Leone 60.

18 March 1967
Leaves Piper Verlag after Hans Baumann, an author with a Nazi past, is chosen over Celan to translate Akhmatova; changes to Suhrkamp.

24 November 1965
Attempts to kill Gisèle Celan-Lestrange, subsequently compulsory admission to various psychiatric clinics (until 11 June 1966).

June 1966
Leaves S. Fischer Verlag, which he feels did not give him sufficient support in the Goll affair; changes to Suhrkamp.

30 January 1967
Attempts to kill Gisèle Celan-Lestrange and himself; emergency operation on Celan and compulsory admission to a psychiatric clinic (until 17 October 1967). In April, Gisèle Celan-Lestrange requests separation.

30 July 1967
Last letter from Celan to Bachmann.

September 1967
Atemwende.

19 September 1967
Presumably final meeting between Celan and Frisch in Zurich.

September 1968
Fadensonnen [Thread Suns].

21 November 1968
Grand Austrian State Prize

November 1968–February 1969
Final compulsory admission to a psychiatric clinic.

Around 20 April 1970
Suicide in the Seine.

June 1970
Lichtzwang [Force of Light].

Summer 1970
The chapter 'Die Geheimnisse der Prinzessin von Kagran', written after Celan's death, is added to the completed fair copy of *Malina*.

27 and 29 December 1970
Gisèle Celan-Lestrange and Ingeborg Bachmann meet in Rome.

March 1971
Malina.

September 1971
Simultan.

From early 1972
Apartment at Via Giulia 66,
Palazzo Sacchetti.

2 May 1972
Anton Wildgans Prize of
Austrian Industry.

2 January 1973
Last surviving letter from
Gisèle Celan-Lestrange to
Ingeborg Bachmann.

14 March 1973
Death of her father.

May 1973
Reading trip across Poland.
Visits Auschwitz death
camp.

Summer 1973
French translation of *Malina*
by Philippe Jaccottet.

25/26 September 1973
Severe fire accident during
the night.

17 October 1973
Dies in a Rome clinic.

4 April 1991
Death of Max Frisch
(b. 1911) in Zurich.

9 December 1991
Death of Gisèle Celan-
Lestrange (b. 1927) in Paris.

BIBLIOGRAPHY OF BIOGRAPHICAL SOURCES

Letters and Primary Sources

BACHMANN, Ingeborg. *Wir müssen wahre Sätze finden. Gespräche und Interviews* (Christine Koschel and Inge von Weidenbaum eds). Munich and Zurich: Piper, 1983.

——. *Die kritische Aufnahme der Existentialphilosophie Martin Heideggers* (dissertation, Vienna, 1949) (Robert Pichl ed., with an afterword by Fritz Wallner. Munich and Zurich: Piper, 1985.

——. *'Todesarten'-Projekt* (Monika Albrecht and Dirk Göttsche eds). Munich and Zurich: Piper, 1995.

——. *Kritische Schriften* (Monika Albrecht and Dirk Göttsche eds). Munich and Zurich: Piper, 2005.

—— and Hans Werner Henze. *Briefe einer Freundschaft* (Hans Höller ed., with a preface by Hans Werner Henze). Munich and Zurich: Piper, 2006; second edition.

BARNERT, Arno. 'Paul Celan und die Heidelberger Zeitschrift *Die Wandlung*. Erstveröffentlichung der Korrespondenz' [with letters by Marie Luise Kaschnitz], *Textkritische Beiträge*, 6 (2000): 111–20.

——. 'Eine "herzgraue" Freundschaft. Der Briefwechsel zwischen Paul Celan und Günter Grass', *Textkritische Beiträge*, 9 (2004): 65–127.

—— and Wilhelm Hemecker. 'Paul Celan und Frank Zwillinger', *Sichtungen* (2000): 56–70.

BONN OFFICE FOR THE CELAN EDITION. *Catalogue of Paul Celan's library*. Paris and Moisville; compiled in 1972–74 (Paris) and 1987 (Moisville) by Dietlind Meinecke,

Bibliography

Stefan Reichert and others. Transcribed with corrections, additions and critical notes on the current locations of the books by Bertrand Badiou (unpublished).

BÖTTIGER, Helmut (in collaboration with Lutz Dittrich). '"Mich freuen solche Bitterkeiten und Härten". Die Beziehung zu Paul Celan', in *Elefantenrunde. Walter Höllerer und die Erfindung des Literaturbetriebs* (Berlin: Literaturhaus, 2005), pp. 43–51.

CELAN, Paul. *La Bibliothèque philosophique—Die philosophische Bibliothek* (catalogue based on annotations by Alexandra Richter, Patrik Alac, Bertrand Badiou, with a preface by Jean-Pierre Lefebvre). Paris: Éditions Rue d' Ulm, 2004.

—— '*Mikrolithen sinds, Steinchen*'. *Die Prosa aus dem Nachlass* (Barbara Wiedemann and Bertrand Badiou eds). Frankfurt: Suhrkamp, 2005.

—— and Gisèle Celan-Lestrange. *Briefwechsel* (with a selection of letters from Paul Celan to his son Eric; Eugen Helmlé and Barbara Wiedemann trans. and Bertrand Badiou ed., in collaboration with Eric Celan). Frankfurt: Suhrkamp, 2001.

—— and Klaus and Nani Demus: *Briefwechsel* (with a selection of letters from Gisèle Celan-Lestrange to Klaus and Nani Demus, Joachim Seng ed.). Frankfurt: Suhrkamp, 2009.

—— and Hanne and Hermann Lenz. *Briefwechsel* (Barbara Wiedemann ed., in cooperation with Hanne Lenz). Frankfurt: Suhrkamp, 2001.

—— and Nelly Sachs. *Briefwechsel* (Barbara Wiedemann ed.). Frankfurt: Suhrkamp, 1993.

—— and Peter Szondi. *Briefwechsel* (with letters from Gisèle Celan-Lestrange to Peter Szondi and excerpts from the correspondence between Peter Szondi and Jean and Mayotte Bollack; Christoph König ed.). Frankfurt: Suhrkamp, 2005.

—— and Franz Wurm. *Briefwechsel* (Barbara Wiedemann ed., in cooperation with Franz Wurm). Frankfurt: Suhrkamp, 1995.

ECKARDT, Uwe: 'Paul Celan (1920–1970) und der Wuppertaler "Bund"' [letters to Jürgen Leep], in *Geschichte in Wuppertal 1995*. Neustadt an der Aisch: P. C. W. Schmidt, 1995.

BERMANN FISCHER, Gottfried and Brigitte Bermann Fische. *Briefwechsel mit Autoren* (Reiner Stach ed., in collaboration with Karin Schlapp; Bernhard Zeller introd.). Frankfurt: Fischer, 1990.

FRISCH, Max. *Jetzt ist Sehenszeit. Briefe, Notate, Dokumente 1943–1963* (Julian Schütt ed. and afterword). Frankfurt: Suhrkamp, 1998.

HILDESHEIMER, Wolfgang. *Briefe* (Silvia Hildesheimer and Dietmar Pleyer eds). Frankfurt: Suhrkamp, 1999.

HUCHEL, Peter. *Wie soll man Gedichte schreiben. Briefe 1925–1977* (Hub Nijsse ed.). Frankfurt: Suhrkamp, 2000.

MAYER, Hans. *Briefe 1948–1963* (Mark Lehmstedt ed.). (Leipzig: Lehmstedt, 2006).

PICHL, Robert (ed.). *Registratur des literarischen Nachlasses von Ingeborg Bachmann* (Christine Koschel and Inge von Weidenbaum comp.) Vienna, 1981.

——. *Ingeborg Bachmann als Leserin. Ihre Privatbibliothek als Ort einer literarischen Spurensuche* (Vienna: Löcker, forthcoming).

PIZZINGRILLI, Massimo. '"Votre aide qui est / m'est si précieuse". Paul Celan's Mitarbeit an der Zeitschrift *Botteghe Oscure* und sein Briefwechsel mit Margherite Caetani', in *Celan-Jahrbuch 9 (2003–2005)* [with letters from and to Eugene Walter and excerpts from letters by K. L. Schneider, H. M. Enzensberger, H. Heissenbüttel and W. Höllerer], pp. 7–26.

RICHTER, Hans Werner. *Briefe* (Sabine Cofalla ed.). Munich: Hanser, 1997.

Wiedemann, Barbara. *Die Goll-Affäre. Dokumente zu einer 'Infamie'.* Frankfurt: Suhrkamp, 2000.

Recollections

DODERER, Heimito von. *Commentarii 1951 bis 1956. Tagebücher aus dem Nachlass.* Munich: Biederstein, 1976.

DOR, Milo. *Auf dem falschen Dampfer. Fragmente einer Autobiographie.* Vienna and Darmstadt: Zsolnay, 1988.

FRIED, Erich. *Ich grenz noch an ein Wort und an ein andres Land. Über Ingeborg Bachmann— Erinnerung, einige Anmerkungen zu ihrem Gedicht 'Böhmen liegt am Meer' und ein Nachruf.* Berlin: Friedenauer Presse, 1983.

KASCHNITZ, Marie Luise. *Orte. Aufzeichnungen.* Frankfurt: Insel, 1973.

——. *Tagebücher 1936–1966* (Christian Büttrich, Marianne Büttrich and Iris Schnebel Kaschnitz eds, Arnold Stadler afterword). Frankfurt: Insel, 2000.

SCHWERIN, Christoph Graf von. *Als sei nichts gewesen.* Berlin: Das Neue, 1997.

SPIEL, Hilde. *Kleine Schritte. Berichte und Geschichten.* Munich: Ellermann Heinrich, 1976.

Bibliography

Other Literature

ALBRECHT, Monika. *'Die andere Seite'. Zur Bedeutung von Werk und Person Max Frisch in Ingeborg Bachmanns 'Todesarten'*. Würzburg: Königshausen & Neumann, 1989.

—— and Dirk Göttsche (eds). *Bachmann–Handbuch*. Stuttgart and Weimar: Metzler, 2002.

BEICKEN, Peter. *Ingeborg Bachmann*. Stuttgart: C. H. Beck, 2001.

BRIEGLEB, Klaus. 'Ingeborg Bachmann, Paul Celan—Ihr (Nicht-) Ort in der Gruppe 47 (1952–1964/65. Eine Skizze', in Bernhard Böschenstein and Sigrid Weigel (eds), *Ingeborg Bachmann und Paul Celan. Poetische Korrespondenzen. Vierzehn Beiträge*. Frankfurt: Suhrkamp, 1997, pp. 29–81.

EMMERICH, Wolfgang. *Paul Celan*. Reinbek: Rowohlt, 1999.

ENCARNAÇÃO, Gilda. *'Fremde Nähe'. Das Dialogische als poetisches und poetologisches Prinzip bei Paul Celan* (Würzburg: Königshausen & Neumann, 2007).

Fremde Nähe. Celan als Übersetzer. Eine Ausstellung des Deutschen Literaturarchivs. Rxhibition and catalogue by Axel Gellaus, Rolf Bücher, Sabria Filali, Peter Gossens, Ute Harbusch, Thomas Heck, Christine Ivanović, Andreas Lohr and Barbara Wiedemann in collaboration with Petra Plättner. Marbach am Neckar: Deutsche Schillergesellschaft, 1997.

GEHLE, Holger. *NS-Zeit und literarische Gegenwart bei Ingeborg Bachmann*. Wiesbaden: Deutscher Universitätsverlag, 1995.

GERSDORFF, Dagmar von. *Kaschnitz. Eine Biographie*. Frankfurt: Insel, 1992.

GOSSENS, Peter and Marcus G. Patka (eds). *'Displaced'. Paul Celan in Wien 1947–1948*. Frankfurt: Suhrkamp, 2001.

HAPKEMEYER, Andreas. *Ingeborg Bachmann. Entwicklungslinien in Werk und Leben*. Vienna: Verlag der österreichischen Akademie der Wissenschaften, 1990.

HOELL, Joachim. *Ingeborg Bachmann*. Munich: dtv, 2001.

HÖLLER, Hans. *Ingeborg Bachmann* (Reinbek: Rowohlt, 1999.

IVANOVIĆ, Christine. *Das Gedicht im Geheimnis der Begegnung. Dichtung und Poetik Celans im Kontext seiner russischen Lektüren.* Tübingen: Niemeyer, 1996.

KOELLE, Lydia. '". . . hier leb dich querdurch, ohne Uhr". Der "Zeitkern" von Paul Celans Dichtung', in *'Im Geheimnis der Begegnung'. Ingeborg Bachmann und Paul Celan*. Iserlohn: Institut für Kirche und Gesellschaft, 2003, pp. 45–68.

SCHARDT, Michael Matthias (in collaboration with Heike Kretschmer). *Über Ingeborg Bachmann. Rezensionen—Porträts—Würdigungen (1952–1992). Rezeptionsdokumente aus vier Jahrzehnten.* Paderborn: Igel, 1994.

STOLL, Andrea (ed.). *Ingeborg Bachmann's 'Malina'.* Frankfurt: Suhrkamp, 1992.

WEIGEL, Sigrid. *Hinterlassenschaften unter Wahrung des Briefgeheimnisses.* Munich: dtv, 1999.

WIEDEMANN, Barbara. 'Paul Celan und Ingeborg Bachmann: Ein Dialog? In Liebesgedichten?', in *'Im Geheimnis der Begegnung'. Ingeborg Bachmann und Paul Celan*, pp. 21–43.

———. '"Sprachgitter". Paul Celan und das Sprechgitter des Pfullinger Klosters', *Spuren* 80. Marbach: Deutsches Literaturarchiv, 2007.

WOLF, Christa. *Voraussetzungen einer Erzählung: Kassandra. Frankfurt Poetik-Vorlesungen* Darmstadt and Neuwied: Luchterhand, 1983.

INDEX

WORKS BY INGEBORG BACHMANN

TRANSLATED WORKS BY INGEBORG BACHMANN

WORKS BY PAUL CELAN

TRANSLATED WORKS BY PAUL CELAN

INDEX OF PERSONALITIES